BULLDOG

A Mike Romano Novel
Fourth in a Series

By

Joe DeCicco

Copyright 2014© Joe DeCicco, All rights reserved. No part of this book may be used or represented in any manner whatsoever without written permission except in the case of a brief quotation embodied in critical articles or reviews. For information, contact the author at JNJ Associates Inc. PO Box 237, Hampstead, and N.C. 28443
You may use e-mail at: romanonovels@yahoo.com

Originally Published: July 31, 2014

ISBN-10:0-9897227-3-2
ISBN-13: 978-0-9897227-3-5

Printed in the United States of America
Charleston, South Carolina for

Associates Publishing Co
Hampstead, North Carolina

Joe DeCicco

Other Mike Romano novels in the series

Angel with a Gun (2006)
Worms in the Apple (2010)
Dirty Baggs (2011)

Additional Mike Romano Novels will follow

Joe has been a featured guest on
Americas Heroes Talk Radio
San Dimas, California
and
Blueline Radio
Wilmington, North Carolina

Dedication

Thank you to the many modern centurions who have walked the "Thin Blue Line" along with me. It is through interaction with them, that I am here, able to put words to paper.

In particular; Kurt Bottoms, who I first met as my training officer. After one set of tours, we partnered for my entire stay in my first command. The early years we spent together were invaluable. Many thanks, Kurt.

A special thought goes to the memory of Richard Gordon who taught me how to be a better detective. Richie is no longer with us. He is in a better place; where there is no need for Detectives.

As always, I am especially grateful to my loving wife, Judy, who has made me complete. I still love her as much as the day we married over 22 years ago.

A special thank you is in order to author James Kaufman, for being my friend and mentor. His guidance has been invaluable in guiding me to hone my craft.

Prologue

For some time now, Mike Romano had been working as a uniformed officer in Tottenville, Staten Island. True to his moral code and tenacity, he had been instrumental in the investigation and arrest of a corrupt cop.

It began one rainy afternoon as Mike drove to work totally lost in thought. The sound of his car's tires hissing on the roadway almost hypnotized him.

Suddenly, the unmistakable sound of gunshots jolted him back into the physical world.

Mike instinctively stopped his vehicle and slid low in his seat and drawing his own weapon. He rose slowly, cautiously looking in the direction of the sound and saw a truck shoot off into the woods. Seeing no other activity, he left his car and checked the area.

After finding an apparently lifeless and bloody figure lying prone alongside the road, Mike knew that he just witnessed a murder.

As a result of that chance encounter, Romano spent many hours interacting with the detectives assigned to the case and contributed some valuable information. Because of his efforts, the hunt for the murderer began to bear fruit.

As a reward for his diligence, department brass temporarily reassigned Mike to work with the squad until the case was cleared.

During his tenure with those detectives, Police Officer Romano made a decision. Deciding that the work was much more stimulating than his regular duties he set his next career goal; he would earn a "Gold Shield" and the rank of Detective. Mike silently vowed that he would eventually work in a Detective Squad office until the day he retired.

During the weeks spent with the squad detectives, Romano learned that the fastest avenue to the coveted "Shield" was to spend time in the Narcotics Division and quickly filed an official request for an interview.

Romano felt that the rigors of that particular type of assignment would be just what he needed to forget the trauma of his recent divorce. Most importantly, it would release him from the nether world of being a White Shield Investigator among Gold Shield Detectives and help him to obtain his 'Golden Fleece.'

Mike Romano had no way of knowing that several months in his future, Divine Providence, would create a chance encounter that would once again restructure his personal life.

CHAPTER ONE

After the dramatic arrest of part time mobster, Police Officer Henry Capelli; Michael Romano spent several more days with the One Two Oh Squad until the courtroom drama regarding that highly unusual case was completed. It was during those last few days with the squad that Mike was summoned to the City's other island, Manhattan. He was to report for an interview in the thirteenth floor offices of the Organized Crime Control Bureau (OCCB), Narcotics Division, at One Police Plaza

***

The squad's commander, Sergeant Andrew Flynn, had called Mike into his office. Before he delivered the official notification he began with, "Michael, we've been notified that Capelli's sentencing date is two days from now."

"I heard Boss."

"In addition, it is my pleasure to notify you that you have been ordered to respond down to "The Puzzle Palace" (mocking nickname used by cops for One PP) exactly three days from today. Be there at 1000 hours for an investigative interview."

Mike, surprised, only said, "Really!"

Flynn continued, "Mike, I want you to know that I expect a successful conclusion and your subsequent transfer to a narcotics assignment. You deserve the chance and you'll be on the fast track to your shield. Let me know when you receive the coveted bauble. If I'm given the opportunity, I'll be more than willing to bring you back into my squad, permanently. I imagine that the timing of the interview is sort of a celebratory gift. It's the 'Job's way of saying, 'thank you for your work', just one day after Capelli goes away on his State sanctioned vacation."

The entire squad was present when Capelli was sentenced to life in prison without parole on Wednesday, May16th.

As the squad left the courtroom, Sergeant Flynn spoke to Mike, "Michael, I heard that little exchange between you and Capelli as he was led out of the courtroom. Just Wha...?"

Mike knew what Flynn was getting at and interrupted him. "What statement Sarge? Was it about something I said during testimony? "

"I heard you call him Baggs and I heard him responded with something like, 'how could you now?' You smiled and answered, 'Because I can.' What was that all about?"

Mike wasn't about to inform Flynn about his friendly relationship with Rocco Banducci, a 'made man' in the Costello Family. He didn't know the sergeant well enough. Yet, he didn't want to lose the friendship that he developed, nor the chance to possibly work under his command in the future. He attempted to answer the question without being definitive.

"Sarge, he was a bag man for the Mob, you know a collector of ill-gotten gains, bad money, a bag man. I was referring to that and made a joke."

"Don't bullshit me Romano. There was more to it than that. I saw the look of complete surprise on his face. What gives? "

Romano was enjoying Flynn's peaked interest and decided to have some fun. "Maybe I'm psychic Sarge, I don't know. But I'll make you a deal. After I get my shield and get assigned to your squad, I promise to answer your question and share all my secrets with you and only you."

Flynn answered, "What secrets? You seem like the most upfront guy I ever met. What the hell are you talking about? "

Mike answered in the friendliest tone of voice he could muster, "Sarge, you know that my goal is to become a permanent member of your squad. Make it happen and I'll surprise you. So much so, that you won't believe what I tell you. Is that a deal?"

Flynn chuckled as he asked, "You're not going to answer me, are you? Well, I guess I'll have to wait."

"Sorry Sarge."

"You sure are one interesting cop Romano and you'll make one hell of a detective." Flynn led the way to the office door and said, "Come on, I'll buy you a beer."

***

The following day, Mike first was required to report to Lefrak City for a medical screening. After filling out a medical questionnaire, he was called into a lavatory, as were, in turn, all the other applicants. He had to give a urine sample for a Dole Test, the required narcotics drug screening. Now in a normal situation, that would pose no problem, but he was dealing with a paranoid and cynical police department; the examiner insisted on watching!

To a veteran like Mike, it presented no problem but there were lots of young, unsophisticated officers there too. Some of them had never been in the military or even urinated in the same room with another person. They were shy and consequently, having someone watch them deliver the goods presented an enormous difficulty.

The supervisors, having previously experienced that problematic circumstance, kept plenty of iced water on hand to help stimulate the bladders of that those individuals. One particular young man was having that particular difficulty.

The candidate stood six-foot-four and was built like the mythical Hercules. Looking at the kid, one would think that nothing would ever bother him however; he made several trips to the lavatory accompanied by the supervisor, producing negative results. Some forty five minutes later, while all the other applicants were finished and were busy completing other processes, the candidate triumphantly walked back into the room holding a small tagged sample bottle. Everyone cheered, he blushed. The incident lightened everyone's mood and broke the tension.

***

May, 17th, Mike responded to his final interview. Before going the ferry, Mike signed in at the squad office. Sergeant Flynn had told him to call for a possible pick up after the interview and he would send someone if a man was available.

By 8:57 a.m. the "Captain Freemen" docked at the Ferry Terminal in Manhattan. Mike hustled, arriving at One PP at 9:30 a.m. After flashing his identification, he went directly to the elevator bank. If all went well, Mike was about to join an elite group of cops in the Narcotics Division of the New York Police Department.

Excitedly, Romano began to shuffle his feet as the number 13 glowed on the panel above the elevator doors, signaling the forthcoming stop. Excitedly, he stepped out before the doors were fully opened and moving quickly, found the double glass doors emblazoned in blue and gold, "OCCB Narcotics Division".

Mike stood, almost at attention, before the closed glass doors and after anxiously taking a deep breath, pulled open the door on the right and slowly entered, stopping just short of the gated barrier that stood before him like a silent sentinel, boldly displaying the crimson words "Restricted Area."

At that moment in time, he was scheduled to have a dreaded face to face interview before a panel of ranking officers, a tricky Q and A session. This was the last hurdle to clear before receiving the much desired transfer.

It was obvious to Mike that his pervious psychological interview and the results of the Dole test for any controlled substances in his system cleared him for the coveted assignment or he wouldn't be there. Romano was confident that he would "pass" the interview, yet he was still apprehensive about it. On the off chance that he wasn't approved, he would be sent back to patrol in the Two Oh on the Island.

To ease his tension, he said to himself, *well, at least this place isn't painted that ugly pea soup green.*

After making sure his ID card was properly attached and visible, he walked up to the reception officer and announced, "Officer Michael Romano reporting as ordered for an interview."

The young female officer looked up at him, smiled and referred to a printed sheet of paper containing several names. Apparently finding his name, she looked up, smiled again and answered, "Officer Michael Romano, One Two Three precinct, scheduled to be interviewed for assignment at 1000 hrs. Please step through the gate and make the first right you come to. Go down the corridor to the end and then left to room 1347A. They're waiting for you."

With butterflies in his stomach, Mike could only respond with, "Thank you."

As he entered the restricted area, she said, "Good luck and don't be so nervous, you'll do fine. Hope to see you soon."

Romano squared his shoulders and advanced into the canyons of the elite. He walked about thirty feet along a corridor constructed of pale gray metal partitions behind which he could hear the muffled sounds of a busy office before he came upon an opening on his left.

He continued as instructed and saw another forced left about twenty feet before him. Continuing, he passed several doorways on each side and on the far end, a large window announcing the obvious outer wall of the building. Mike slowly walked until he saw the door marked 1347A, it was the last door on the right and finding it closed, he knocked.

From inside, an unknown voice said, "Please come in."

Mike opened the door, entered the room and gently closed it again.

"Michael Romano One Two Three Precinct reporting as ordered," he stated as he looked at the four men seated around the rectangle shaped.

The room wasn't very large, maybe 10' x 15' and besides the table itself, contained a total of eight chairs, two file cabinets and a telephone. What caught Mike's eye, was the tape recorder sitting in front of the man who sat at "the head" of the table, he wore captains bars and had a very commanding presence. To his right sat a man in civilian clothes. On the Captain's left were a Sergeant and another man in civilian clothes.

The Captain spoke first, "Officer Romano, please take a seat, this will not take long. First allow me to introduce myself to you; I am Captain Swanson, OCCB." He waved his hand to the right in an indication for the others to introduce themselves.

"Good morning Michael, I'm Doctor Rosen, from Physiological Services," as he reached out to shake hands. Mike accepted.

In turn the other two men announced, "Michael, I'm Sergeant Folger, Intel, pleased to meet you."

The last man finally spoke. "Guess I'm next, Lieutenant Borg, Internal Affairs Bureau. I'm happy that you could be here Officer." Mike was still standing, Borg added, "Please sit down and try to relax."

Mike responded with, "Sir," pulled a chair out and sat down, nervously placing his hands on the table.

Captain Swanson reached to start the tape recorder and said, "Officer Romano, don't let the fact that this interview is being recorded bother you. It's for later reference in the event that the people in this room do not come to a unanimous decision regarding the outcome of your interview. It also eliminates note taking for us all. Do you prefer that we turn this off before we proceed?"

That was the first sneaky physiological question. They don't waste time do they? He answered, "Not at all Sir, I prefer that you record this session. I really want the assignment and if you can't agree, the tape will give me a second chance. Thanks."

Borg continued, "Michael, first let me say that we have reviewed your personnel file and are reasonably impressed. You've been a busy cop and are an asset to the Department. Please know that there is no pass or fail regarding this interview, if you were not accepted to join OCCB, you would not be here. This interview is to assure us that we made the proper decision before awarding the assignment. Do you have any questions so far?"

Fairy tale number two. This is gonna be fun. Mike loved head games; he referred to it as human chess. His nervousness was almost gone. "No Captain, not yet," he responded with a smile.

The doctor shot out with, "Michael did you ever try drugs or use them now?"

Slowly and deliberately Mike responded with, "Yes, before I was married, I'm divorced now, but you know that already. Anyway, I was attending college and went to a party where there were a lot of loose women and various drugs. I refused the hard stuff but tried marijuana a few times. It made me hungry and with drinking a few beers, I don't like to lose control of myself, so I never did it again. Before you ask, I'm a scotch man."

Mike was now enjoying the interview.

Borg was next with, "Tell us Michael, according to your jacket, you've made a few bribery arrests. That's a bit unusual, isn't it?"

"No Sir, I don't think so. I believe that if someone tries to bribe a cop, they should be arrested, plain and simple. I don't think it usual at all."

Swanson jumped in and asked, "Officer Romano, if you get this assignment, you will have access to money and drugs on a daily basis. If it was rumored that your partner was suspected of taking money or sampling drugs during the course of your work, would you report him or her?"

Mike was silent for a few seconds, *another trick question.* "Well, I don't know if this is the correct answer, but, I would be working in a potentially explosive environment and I would have to trust and rely on my partner on a daily basis. That person would not be my partner if I didn't feel that way about him or her, so I would not react on a rumor or suspicion. What I would do is to tell my partner what I heard and act accordingly after that."

Borg raised an eyebrow and asked, "And just what is 'act accordingly after that?' What would you do? Report your observations to your supervisor or IAB?"

"No, because I know that things like that take too long and could get messed up. It would really upset me, but I would make an arrest on the spot."

Rosen remarked, "Wow, what an unusual response."

Swanson asked, "Why take such action yourself Romano?"

"Because during the course of my career, I've learned that sometimes reports get lost. If I observed a cop engaging in the type behavior you described, I would not want to chance relying on a lost report, Sir!"

Borg spoke again, "Officer Romano, I saw in your file that you were instrumental in the apprehension of a cop killer during your rookie days and even more recently in the apprehension of a killer cop. You didn't make those arrests yourself; they were the results of reports, how do you explain that Officer Romano?"

"Because the reports were handled by good cops and they didn't get lost, Sir."

Borg's face took on a very quizzical expression as he asked, "Officer Romano, is there anything that you want to tell us that's outside the scope of this interview? You seem to be hinting at something. What is it?"

Mike quickly answered, "No, nothing at all. Maybe someday if something comes along that I thought that you should know, I would tell you, but there's nothing now."

Swanson took his turn again, "Officer Romano, Mike, you seem to have been very happy and productive working in uniform. You even made a city wide top ten list for latent print identification results. There are many glowing letters from civilians praising you in your folder. Please try to tell us why you want to work in a narcotics office and be constantly chasing bad guys for potentially long and stressful hours."

Mike quickly responded with, "That's and easy one to answer Captain. As you know, for the last several weeks I have been temporally assigned to work with the One Two Oh detectives under Sergeant Flynn on the Capelli case. I had the pleasure of working with a great boss and terrific guys."

"He had many nice things to say about you too."

Mike continued, "Besides learning new things and getting a bad guy, I enjoyed the work. It was like getting paid for doing what I wanted to do anyway. I asked if it was possible to be transferred to the squad permanently. It was explained to me it wasn't because on Staten Island Borough policy that, those squads could only be manned with cops having the rank of Detective; unlike the rest of the City where guys can work with the White Shield as investigators and become eligible for the Gold after eighteen months in investigative assignment. I was also told that the fastest route to a Gold Shield was thru Narcotics, so here I am, Sir."

"Swanson grinned as he spoke, "An honest and interesting answer Romano. Do you realize that if you ever obtain the rank of Detective, there is no guarantee that you will be assigned back with Sergeant Flynn on Staten Island"

"Yes. I understand, but there's always a way Sir."

Swanson smiled and looked around at the others.

"Are there any other questions for this Officer?"

There was no response. Swanson reached for the tape recorder and turned it off, and then stood and extended his right hand to Mike, "Officer Romano that was what I would call refreshing. You have given us one of our most interesting interviews to date. We'll let you know soon. Good luck."

As Mike shook Swanson's hand, the other men only smiled , then looked away, their actions reaffirming that the interview was over and that he was now dismissed. Mike gently closed the door as he left the room.

The corridor didn't look as foreboding as it did before the interview. He felt good. Passing the girl at the gate, Mike said, "Hope to see you soon. I think it went well."

Mike then walked out of the office and rang for the elevator. It seemed like he waited for several hours.

When the elevator arrive, he entered to a cab that was almost filled to capacity. When the occupants shuffled around to make room for him, Mike thought, *They know that I'm part of OCCB and are showing respect.* He was elated and anxious to leave the building so he could breathe again.

***

Outside, Romano was still filled with residual stimulation over his probable eminent transfer to Narcotics and chose not to call Flynn for a ride back. Instead he decided to burn off some energy by walking back down to the South Ferry Terminal. It a fine sunny day and it had been awhile since he had walked through the streets of Manhattan and enjoy the ambiance. He didn't get the chance earlier as he raced to his interview and decided to take a more leisurely walk back downtown. Mike headed west over to Broadway after leaving Headquarters and spent an hour walking south, enjoying a cigar as he strolled. Just before entering the terminal, he sat in the park and enjoyed a coffee.

Once inside the Terminal, he checked the posted schedules, then found a pay phone and called Andy Flynn.

"Persons Squad, Sergeant Flynn speaking. How can I help you? " the now familiar voice asked Mike.

"Sarge, Mike Romano, on this end. I just left the Narcotics interview a little while ago. I'm at the ferry terminal and should be back by 1300 hours."

"Fine, Michael. How did it go? "

"Well Sarge, I think that I answered all their questions in a proper way to get the assignment."

"Did anyone give an indication of how you did?" Flynn asked.

"Not really. Every man at the table was carefully non-committal and only Captain Swanson; the lead interviewer shook my hand when it was over. I don't know if he liked me or was only being polite, I'll have to wait and see. Thanks for asking and I'll see you soon."

Flynn responded with, "Don't eat anything, the boys and I are treating you to a restaurant lunch and get this, it was your buddy Jim Jim's idea. I guess he's happy that you're leaving. Bye."

The ferry crossing was uneventful and gave Mike a chance to relax after his interview. By 12:40 p.m. he was walking up the ramp from the terminal and towards Richmond Terrace and the office.

CHAPTER TWO

To Mike's surprise, Detective Jim James, aka; Jim Jim, the man who irritatingly punctuated Mike's temporary assignment to the squad by jealously mocking his expertise with snide remarks, was the first man to offer a word of encouragement to Mike as he walked into the squad room.

"Well, Romano, things are looking good for you now. You just completed the final step to your new assignment. No more patrol work for you. Someone with your talents deserves a permanent investigative position."

"Thanks Jim," was Mike's response. He thought that James had finally mellowed towards him. But, Jim once again showed Romano what a jealous jerk he really was.

"Well, the squad room will have to order more lighting fixtures; we're losing our shining star."

Mike answered, "Up yours Jim Jim,"

Flynn stepped into the fray. "Children, let's knock that crap off and celebrate Romano's advancement by going to lunch. Mount up boys. Mike, get a portable, and ride with me, will you?"

Mike passed Joe Johnson's desk, Joe, Mike's close friend in addition to squad Sergeant Flynn, said, "Go get 'em Mike. Get your shield and come back, I'll partner up with you anytime. Sorry to see you go."

Once outside, Flynn announced, "We're heading for the Roadhouse on Victory and Clove. They're expecting us. Johnson, you ride with me and Mike. See you guys there."

The men climbed into their two non-descript Chevys and headed for the intersection of Clove and Victory.

Sergeant Flynn took the opportunity to say, "Mike, you and Johnson seem to have developed strong working relationship. I just want to say that you two guys make a great investigative team and I would be proud to have you return to my command as soon as you get your shield."

"Thank you. I'd be proud to be here."

"If you need anything while you're in Manhattan, don't hesitate to call and if I'm not here speak to Joe. He'll get your request to me personally. I'm actually sorry to see you leave the borough, but you gotta do what you gotta do."

Mike turned towards Johnson and said, "Yeah, Sarge, we did develop a good working relationship. Joe's a great detective and a stand-up person. I hope that someday we can work together again. What do you think Joe, could you stand it?"

Johnson answered, "Anytime. Mike. Working with you has been a pleasure."

The drive to the restaurant took less than a quarter hour. Flynn had just parked his vehicle as the car driven by Bill Statler bounced into the parking lot. The detectives all walked into the Roadhouse together and were shown to their table in far corner of the dining room.

As the host waved his hand for them to sit, he spoke to Flynn, who he knew, "Andy, we put you and your guys here, so you can take off your jackets and not alarm the public. You know, six men with guns, they might think that we cater to the mob."

He chuckled at his own joke. A waiter arrived with two pitchers of beer and put them down as they shuffled into their chosen chairs. Mike sat to Flynn's left with Johnson sitting next to him. The rest of the men scattered around the circular table while the waiter filled the glasses.

Detective James, sitting directly across from Romano spoke first, "Mike Romano, a good cop and investigator," he knocked on the table for attention. When everyone was quiet, he paused, looked at Mike, lifted a glass, held it up and continued, "I saluted you. When you first walked into the squad room, I thought that you were just another smart ass wanna be detective patrol cop." With a chuckle he continued, "Well, I was almost right. You are a wanna be detective and you are smart, but you are not an ass. I salute you."

The other men at the table quickly filled their own glasses, raised them and concurred with the accolade.

Mike was somewhat embarrassed as he raised his own glass and said, "Thank you all. It was a true learning experience. Sergeant Flynn is a terrific boss. Joe Johnson, who I usually partnered up with, taught me a lot and Jim Jim here, kept me stimulated by constantly busting my gonads with his remarks. Thanks Jim. Let's order. I'm hungry."

***

The men had just finished off their third extra-large pizza, one loaded with homemade Italian sausage, and waved for more beer to wash it down. Mike almost choked as he peered over his glass when he brought it to his lips for another mouthful of the amber liquid.

Walking toward him, casually dressed, his face flushed and pumpkin-like as he remember him, was the huge bulk of Deputy Inspector Dennis Bryan.

Mike froze and his mind instantly flashed back to key incidents regarding the man. His thoughts raced. *Dennis protected his brother-in-law, a pedophile, when I was first on the job and living in Jackson Heights and married to that whore. Dennis was a also graft taking* cop and took $8,000 as explained by my family friend, Rocco Banducci, for pushing to void a lawful arrest that I made while working in Midtown South......

Mike remembered his parting conversation with The Great Pumpkin as he left his command for the last time. Mike has hosted a going away party in the basement lounge of the command. It was a time honored custom 'back in the day.' *What a sight, I thought as he walked closer to me and I carefully chose my words. "Well, Deputy Inspector Bryan, all I can say is that it has been a true experience serving in your command."*

Bryan smiled, took a swallow of beer and answered, "Glad to see there's no hard feelings Romano. You're a good cop. A little crazy, but a good cop. By the way, hope you like your new command. Where is it?"

Mike *remembered thinking before answering, either he's playing me or he's drunk and can't remember where I'm going. I answered, "It's the One-Two-Three Precinct, Tottenville, on Staten Island. Sleepy town, not very busy."* Romano remembered the big man asking what he thought Bryan should have known the answer to, *"How did you manage that? Got a hook?"*

Mike remembered that he paused, before craftily responding with, *"Well, Boss, you've seen my jacket. It's got bribery collars and killing a pedophile. I saw you at his funeral, don't you remember? Anyway, Staten Island is slower than Manhattan and you know that I like being active. I've usually had steady tours and haven't worked the clock more than a total of three years in my entire career. In Tottenville there are no steady tours. I'll have to work the clock. The midnights will be boring. I like to fish though. I'll probably carry a fishing pole in my trunk on the midnight tours and sneak some fishing in. Do you like fish?"*

"Sure do Mike. Are you going to come for a visit and bring me some?"

Romano smiled inwardly as he recalled Bryan's face frowning and twisting at the same time during the confrontation as he answered, *"No."*

"How will I get the fish then?"

Mike remembered that his response was just loud enough for most of the men to hear, *"I'll send the heads to you by way of Department Mail. Enjoy."*

Inwardly, Mike Romano chuckled as he recalled the response, *Dennis's eyes got wide and his ruddy complexion paled, as he dropped the open can of beer soiling his pants and shirt. The six pack of beer balancing on his ample belly thumped to the floor.*

"Just what the hell are you trying to say Romano?"

Mike wanted to shout as he remembered smiling at the ruddy faced gourd as he answered, *"What I'm saying is that you and your bigotry can kiss my fuzzy Italian ass!"* With his eyes still focused on Bryan, Mike quickly put his glass down on the table.

The Great Pumpkin moved closer to Flynn, held out his right hand and asked, "Sergeant Flynn, One Two Oh squad, I believe?"

Andy Flynn hesitated for a split second before reaching out and grasping the big man's hand, "Inspector Bryan, am I correct? Are you still the CO of the Academy? "

Bryan was pleased to see that Romano was paying close attention to the exchange. His ruddy face emulated the magical Cheshire cat from Lewis Carol's Alice in Wonderland as he answered, "No, I managed to work my way into the South Manhattan Borough Office as XO, second in command."

Andy put his left hand on Mike's shoulder and commented, "Nice place to be."

Bryan remained silent.

Flynn continued, "We're here celebrating the transfer of Officer Romano to Manhattan Narcotics; he's a sharp patrol officer on his way to a gold shield."

Receiving no response, with his hand still on Romano's shoulder, continued, "Mike was temporally assigned to our squad to work with us on a homicide case and it turned out that the shooter was a dirty cop. You probably heard about it, the guy was a bag man and part time enforcer for the mob. Without Mike, I don't know if we would have ever solved the case. His instincts are sometimes uncanny."

Dennis quickly answered, "Yeah, I heard about it. Officer Romano and I know each other from some time ago."

Turning his attention to Mike, Dennis continued, "Romano, it seems you've always had a knack for doing the unexpected. It worked out for you again, didn't it?" Bryan's tone had a menacing edge to it.

Mike realized that the conversation was quickly becoming personal, as it usually did when he was still under Bryan's command in Midtown South. He wasn't going to risk the friendship of Sergeant Flynn and the men around him by playing into The Pumpkin's hands and he took his time before answering. First he picked up another slice of pizza and sprinkled a generous amount of crushed red pepper on it, examining it carefully before, slowly put it down into the plate in front of him, as his body tensed.

Sergeant Flynn had no idea what they were talking about, but his hand was still resting on Mike's shoulder and feeling the cop's muscles tighten, he gently squeezed the shoulder in a silent plea for Mike to control himself.

Feeling Flynn's cautionary signal, Mike turned and spoke, "We're fine Sarge. The Inspector and I are just reminiscing, that's all. Aren't we Inspector?"

There was no response. Mike's scrappy personality couldn't resist getting a little dig in, "Oh, by the way, eat any good fish lately?"

Bryan's face began to glow a deep crimson at the pointed question. From past experience, Dennis knew that Michael would not back off and began to dread, what foul secret the ballsy Italian cop would drop if the conversation continued as it was going?

The inspector remained quiet and awkwardly, once again reached for Flynn's hand, while nodding at the other men and mumbled, "Nice to see all of you."

Conjuring up a menacing and malevolent stare, Ryan looked Romano, and icily added, "I Hope that someday you get that promotion, if you can stay out of trouble."

Mike couldn't help himself, "Probably make the rank of Detective before you make full Inspector. Have a nice day."

Bryan's face flushed as he opened his mouth to respond, but apparently had second thoughts, turned and slowly walked away, while shaking his head and mumbling aloud to himself.

His mind was spinning, remembering full well the past problems, both real and imagined that he had attributed to Mike.

The job was loaded with people who were afraid of him, Mike Romano, not only was not one of them, but he would come back at him when pushed with an unnerving confidence that suggested that the young cop would always be a step ahead of him. Bryan's guts churned as he tried in vain to understand why Romano was so comfortable doing it. As he left the restaurant, Bryan only thought about Romano and when they would again cross swords. While the Bryan-Romano exchange was happening, the men at the table sat dumbstruck while Mike sparred with the high ranking superior officer.

Andy Flynn now faced Romano and broke the sound of silence with, "Mike, I know that you're a quick witted cop, but I never got the idea that you were suicidal. Why would you go nose to nose with a Deputy Inspector?"

Mike remained silent and picked up his pizza.

Flynn continued, "I take it that you're not a fan of his. What happened while you were under his command? Can you talk about it?"

The men of the Two Oh squad shuffled and began to whisper among themselves. They all leaned forward, sitting on the edge of their chairs, waiting to hear the background of the quick, pointed exchange that they had just witnessed.

Mike put the slice down and took a swallow of beer before he answered, "Well, first let me say that generally, I'm not in the habit of challenging a superior officer, but, when warranted, I have made exceptions. Without going into details, I'll say that Dennis Bryan and I have disagreed on a moral issue."

Sergeant Flynn spoke as Romano paused to gather his thoughts, "Mike, just before we had our coordination meeting with Inspector Rothwell from One PP and the Boro Commander, on the Capelli case, I got to look at your folder, what problem could you have had with Bryan?"

All eyes and ears were on Mike as he answered, "I had no moral problem; he did, and it wasn't prudent to announce it during that meeting."

There was low inaudible wave of comments from around the table. Ignoring them, Mike continued, "Oh, and before you ask, no, I'm not in the rat squad. Dennis just offends me and knows better than to pull any shit with me, that's all."

There were several rhetorically stated expletive comments around the table regarding the loaded answer.

BULLDOG

Ignoring them all, Mike quickly changed the subject, "Let's get back to my going away party," he quipped, as he again picked up the pizza slice in front of him and chomped down, taking a large bite.

Detective James took the opportunity to remark, "Romano, after seeing that little joust, I'm happy that we're parting on good terms. Something tells me that if really pissed off, you could be a handful."

There was subdued laughter all around. Half an hour later the men were headed back to the Two Oh. As Flynn, Johnson and Romano rode back to the station house, Flynn's portable radio announced, "Two Oh Squad Sergeant, your location, K?"

Andy grabbed the radio and answered, Two Oh Squad Sergeant is on the air and in route to the Two Oh, K."

The dispatcher added, "Oh Sergeant, the desk officer requests that you stop there when you arrive. Acknowledge."

"Two Oh Sergeant, will respond as directed, K." Putting the radio down on the seat next to him, Flynn remarked to no one in particular, "Wonder what's so important?"

Back at the station house, Andy turned to his passengers, "You two go upstairs with the rest of the guys, while I stop at the desk. See you in a few minutes."

Less than ten minutes later, Flynn entered the squad room and headed directly to his office cubicle. Passing his men, he requested, spoke, "Romano, please, come into my office, I have to speak to you."

Mike had been sitting with Joe Johnson, fielding questions about Bryan. He welcomed the interruption, and quickly responded, "On the way Sarge."

Romano found Andy busy making an entry into the telephone message book as he entered. He waited.

Flynn heard him and spoke without looking up, "Mike Romano, you must have had some interview this morning. Captain Swanson just telephoned our Desk Officer and your old command."

Mike asked, "Old command?"

Flynn happily continued, "Yes, Michael, as of 1500 hours today you are officially assigned to OCCB Narcotics Division. The directive left you working with us for tomorrow. You swing out Saturday and Sunday for your RDOs.

"You're kidding Boss, aren't you?"

"Be quiet and listen. You're directed to report in civilian clothes on Monday at 0800 hours to the second floor auditorium in the Police Academy on 20th Street for orientation and narcotics training. Congratulations son. You're going to be a narco ranger."

Mike could only say, "You're kidding me. I never thought they would work so fast."

Flynn smiled broadly as he answered, "Michael, you impressed me the minute we met at the homicide scene on that rainy highway. It's obvious to me that you also impressed the review board this morning. You'll be a terrific asset to the unit. The official typed orders will probably arrive with the Department Mail run tomorrow morning. You're welcome to spend the rest of today's tour here with us or go home to celebrate and I'll sign you out myself at end of tour. See you tomorrow morning either way."

Mike elected to spend the balance of the tour making small talk with Joe Johnson. The Ryan questions were replaced with sage advice from his friend. At end of tour he signed out and went directly home.

It was 7:30 a.m. the next morning, when in a celebratory mood, Mike walked into the office carrying two boxes of mixed doughnuts and a crumb cake in an effort to gather some laughs. Even though the only person with any narcotics experience was Sergeant Flynn, the men of the squad offered guidance and quips about working narcotics. Mike took the day's conversations and jibes in good spirit.

At the end of the tour, he shook the hand of each man in the room, again expressing how fortunate he felt for the experience of working with each one of them and how much he would miss the entire squad. When Mike shook hands with Sergeant Flynn, he was handed a copy of the written orders regarding his transfer and a slap on the back.

Finally, as he left the squad room for the last time before his two day swing, followed by the Academy indoctrination for his new assignment, Mike recognized the voice of Jim James shouting, "Thank you God for finally getting that crazy Italian out of here." Guffaws could be heard over Mike's own laughter.

CHAPTER THREE

After leaving the squad, Mike had two free days before reporting to the Police Academy to begin narcotics training. During his swing, he had made several attempts to contact his kids with negative results. Mike surmised that his ex-wife had spirited them away again. Even though he loved his children; he was beginning to lose interest in chasing them down and especially tired of having any contact at all with his immoral ex-wife, Betty

To ease the tension generated by the loss of contact with his kids and his new assignment, Mike spent the balance of his free time in the confines of his old command, fishing along the beach where Sharrot's Road touched the Atlantic Ocean.

Recalling his intense dislike of Dennis Bryan, Mike thought, *Boy would I love to land a big one and send it to Bryan,* but he caught nothing.

Monday finally arrived. Romano was up and about by 5:30 a.m. In slightly less than half an hour after springing out of bed, Mike had shaved, showered and conjured himself up a hardy breakfast of eggs, sausage, hash browns and toast, washing it all down with two cups of strong black coffee, and he felt energized.

By 6:30 a.m., he was pulling into the parking lot of the New York Fire Department's Marine Company 9 near the ferry terminal and pulled into an empty space along the chain link fence bordered the actual terminal. Several months before, while still working with the squad on the Capelli case, Mike had met the Battalion Commander, becoming somewhat friendly with him.

After placing his "120 Precinct" identification placard on his dashboard, he walked to the firehouse.

Entering with his police shield in his hand Mike he announced his name to a uniformed fire officer who was sitting inside a cubicle that doubled as a reception area, and asked for the officer in charge.

"I'm Fireman Tim Blakely, at your service. The Chief isn't on duty at this time. He's in his bunk. Can I help you? If you're here officially, I'll have someone wake him."

"No, this is a personal request. I met Chief Brennan some time ago and we hit it off. I'm starting a new assignment today and I'll be taking training at the Police Academy. I'd like to park here for a few days while at the Academy. My police ID is on the dashboard of the grey Chevy. It's the last car parked along terminal side of the fence. Do you think he would mind? If you think it's a problem, I'll leave."

Tim answered quickly, "No problem. We get special requests like this from time to time and the Chief doesn't mind. I'll give him your name and let him know it's only a temporary thing. Stop in when you return and check to see if he left you a message. Good luck."

Mike thanked him, and left for the ferry terminal. He was anxious and wanted to have plenty of time to reach 20th Street and 2nd Avenue well before 8:00 o'clock.

In Manhattan by 7:08, Mike hailed a taxi for a quick ride uptown. The heavy morning traffic rush wasn't at full throttle yet. Fifteen minutes later, Romano entered the Academy building and identified himself to the security officer on duty. His heart was almost jumping out of his chest in excitement.

***

As Mike entered the Auditorium, he saw that there were other early arrivals. Scattered in the first few rows of seats, were about a dozen or so other people, most of them sitting alone. In front of the room, just below the stage area, was a cop in civilian clothes, holding a long lead attached to the collar of a beautiful Golden Labrador who was sitting quietly, watching the people entering the room, with an occasional glance back at its master.

Close to the duo were two long tables laden with several large opaque plastic containers and that looked like a knotted rag.

The dog handler smiled, nodded sporadically and softly announced, "Welcome", as more people filtered in. Looking around before he actually sat, Mike examined two men dressed in business suits in the rear of the room. They occupied two aisle seats in the last row on the right. He noticed them when he first entered and now was curious as to who they might be. He too had chosen an aisle seat near the front and tried to relax.

After what seemed like hours, those very two men stood and strode to the stage apron. As they passed him Mike recognized Captain Swanson. The two men positioned themselves dead center, stopped and examined the crowd before them. Mike looked at his watch; it was exactly 8:00 a.m.

The Captain began, "First, good morning to you all and congratulations. I'm Captain Swanson, some of you may remember me from your pre-appointment interview and I'm the 'XO' of the Manhattan Narcotics. With me is Lieutenant Stabler from Special Projects. The man with the dog is Detective John Greer and the dog is Walter." As Walter heard his name, he stood, wagged his tail and gave a short bark of acknowledgement to the delight of all present.

Swanson continued, "If   everyone would please move up and kind of bunch together into the first couple of rows of the center section, we can then begin."

Everyone moved quickly. The Captain waited for everyone to settle down again before continuing. "From here it looks like all thirty two of our new people are present and we're happy to have you with us. You are all special. You folks have earned the right to be here and should be proud of the fact that you   passed a rigorous round robin." (complete and in depth investigation)

Lieutenant Stabler handed a clip board to the trainee sitting closest to him and said, "Please sign in and add your tax I D number. Failure to do so will return you to your old command." There was complete silence.

Then with a big grim, he added, "Like that's going to happen." With a chuckle he added, "Signing twice will only confuse us, especially the dog."

There was some low mumbles emanating from the crowd at the mild humor that was tactfully designed to relieve some of the tension the new comers might be feeling.

After a short pause, the Captain waved his hand indicating those he had just introduced, "They will be giving all of you some interesting bits of information. They will also show you some of the special equipment that is available to you, should you need it in the future. Detective Greer will also give a demonstration of what Walter and other dogs like him can do."

Pausing for effect, Swanson continued, "Then, you'll take a noon meal hour. When you return, report directly to room 233 for further instruction. Be prompt, as there is much cover. Thank you. I must leave now. Detective Greer and Lieutenant Stabler will remain." He then waved his right arm and said, "Lieutenant, your show," as he walked away.

Stabler moved to one side of the stage and spoke directly to Greer, "John, I'm sure that everyone would like to see Walter in action, you have the floor."

John stepped forward with Walter eagerly following close behind. After positioning himself, he began, "Now you all have heard about narcotics search dogs through various media reports and other cops. Walter here is one of the best." Again the dog gave a quick, "Woof", at the sound of his name.

"He likes compliments." Greer continued, "Of all a dog's senses, its sense of smell is the most highly developed. Dogs have about 25 times more olfactory receptors than humans do. These receptors occur in special sniffing cells deep within a dog's snout, they are what allow dogs to 'out-smell' humans."

Some muffled comments like, "dogs sure do out smell humans, they down right stink" and the like were heard.

Greer waited, and then continued, "Dogs can sense odors at concentrations nearly 100 million times lower than humans can. They can detect one drop of blood in five quarts of water!"

There were murmurs of astonishment within his audience.

"In the wild, canines rely on smell for hunting and also use smell to decode scent messages left by other animals, friend or foe, predator or prey. A wild canine's sense of smell is especially important in habitats where seeing prey is difficult, such as the thick underbrush of a forest."

Walter was becoming slightly agitated and John had to rest his hand on the animal's head to calm him down.

When the dog was calm, John continued, "A dog can sniff out all sorts of odors that a human nose will miss. They're capable of detecting a wide variety of specific scents, such as drugs, explosives or the scent of other animals, mankind included. Because of that keen

sense of smell, we can train them for jobs such as tracking, rescue, or drug and bomb detection."

From somewhere within the crowd, a male voice said, "I don't need a dog to smell you, do I?" resulting in more muted laughter.

Greer was used to comments and after another pause he continued, "Dogs that make a living by sniffing are trained to alert their handlers to the presence of these things by pawing, barking, or in the case of something dangerous, sitting quietly. Walter and dogs like him are not especially fond of narcotics. There's no place for narcotics in psyche of a dog. They're trained by the promise of a favorite toy or play time each time they successfully sniff out the target scent."

The audience was completely silent.

"Some handlers reward their charges with a ball; I prefer to use a toy that doesn't bounce away. That way, the toy or the dog doesn't interfere with other working officers. You may have noticed the knotted rag on the nearby table; it's Walter's reward for good work."

Greer walked over to the table and picked up the dog toy, holding it behind him and tucking it into his waistband at the small of his back. Walter saw the move and quickly was on the alert.

John remained still and spoke, "You'll now see just what Walter can do. Before you all got here, the Lieutenant and I hid various small amounts of narcotics around the room. We entered the room separately, each not knowing where the other person hid his substance targets. We each hid two packages. Walter wasn't even in the building at the time, yet he should find all four of our little packages when asked."

It was as if the dog understood every word. He got up on his hind legs licking John's face. John gently pushed him down, held his lead and said, "Seek, Walter, seek," as they began moving about the room.

Greer guided the dog towards the table and swung his arm above the objects on the tabletop. Walter sniffed along and after a few seconds put his paws on the tabletop next to one of the large bins and pawed it. John then reached in and removed a plastic bag of marijuana. He gave his dog a few neck rubs and kind words. Next, John guided the dog along the lower apron of stage area with negative results.

There was a murmuring of disappointment heard among his audience.

Greer then brought his animal up on to the stage and worked the entire perimeter of the large raised platform. Walter stopped dead at the base of the backdrop curtains and pawed at the bottom of the heavy material. From behind it, John removed a small package that he claimed was marked as heroin.

Returning to the sitting area he stopped announce, "I will now move about among you, please do not pet the dog or distract him in any way while he's working in and around you people. Thank you"

He moved his dog among the attentive spectators much to their delight.

In the middle of the first row of unoccupied seats directly behind the trainees, Walter sat and pawed an upturned seat. John flipped it down and removed what he said was heroin.

At that point he stated, "Now, we have one more stash to find, this may take some time. I only know that it's somewhere towards the rear of the room. Let's go Walter," he said as he led the dog to the rear of the auditorium. As John guided the dog, he kept encouraging him to "Seek".

Finally, after what seemed like an eternity, the dog sat next to one of the seats that were previously occupied by the bosses when the session first began.

Apparently, Captain Swanson had previously tapped a package to his seat as he rose to and returned the seat to its upright position, blocking it from view.

There was mild applause as John said, "Good boy Walter, you scored four out of four." He then pulled the knotted rag from the small of his back and offered it to Walter as he unhooked the lead. The dog grabbed his toy with great gusto and ran several circles around the detective.

John reached for the dog's toy, taking it from him and flung it towards the stage. Walter took off as if he was shot from a cannon. Quickly retrieving the rag, he dropped down under one of the tables and began to happily play with his reward, vigorously shaking it, then dropping it and rolling over on top of it. There was mild applause and comments from the group of onlookers. Walter, was in doggie heaven, completely ignored the accolades.

***

After the demonstration of what a "drug sniffing dog" could do, Detective Greer and Lieutenant Stabler took turns demonstrating the equipment that was stored in the containers. Stabler explained the use of special pagers designed for undercover cops. They were actually pagers and pulled double duty as remote transmitters, sending conversations to a backup man or team that could be secreted close by. The entire transmission was heard and usually recorded.

The new Narco cops were especially interested in several military type night scopes. Lieutenant Stabler added that they could be obtained only on a special needs basis and were exclusively controlled by his office. All requests must be in writing and signed off by an investigator's supervisor.

The auditorium lights were turned off leaving the room in total darkness except for the minimal light cast by the exit signs. Looking through the scopes, even into the darker corners of the room, one could see almost as well as if in full daylight except that the images had an eerie, other worldly green cast to them. Stabler added that a camera could also be attached to the scopes and night photos taken.

Both instructors then demonstrated the use of field testing kits, describing their uses and how to properly use them. Lieutenant Stabler added that everyone, as part of in service training would eventually be formally instructed and certified in their use. Time flew by. It was 11:45 a.m. when the lieutenant finally asked, "Any questions?"

The group had been attentive, and receiving no response, Stabler waved his hand towards Greer, who bent down and took the rag toy from a now sleepy dog, signaling the end of the session. Walter barely noticed.

Stabler dismissed all with, "Okay, you're all on meal. Return to room 233 promptly in one hour. Do not be late!"

Mike hooked up with two of the male cops that had been sitting near him during the lecture. After proper introductions, all three walked down the block to a diner type eatery on the corner of Second Avenue for a quick meal. While they ate, the men exchanged a few words and anecdotes about their prior commands; also touching on what they had observed and learned in the last few hours.

Romano never spoke about his time spent with the Two Oh squad and how he got to narcotics; instead, he explained to his new friends, Charlie and Tom, that it was Lieutenant Stonner of the Staten Island Latent Print Unit who suggested that he apply to Narcotics as a possible fast track to earning the "Gold Shield."

Glancing down at his wristwatch Mike noted that they had only ten minutes to get back to the second floor classroom as instructed and interrupted their conversation with, "Sorry to break up a nice bullshit session guys, but we have ten minutes to get back," and slid his chair backwards to rise.

Charlie and Tom mumbled something inaudible as they also stood after leaving a tip on the table for the waitress. Mike almost to the cashier by that time. They rushed up behind him and together paid their bills and hustled out the door.

CHAPTER FOUR

By 1300 hours (1:00 p.m.)Mike entered room 233, looked around and saw that it resembled a small lecture hall, the seats sloping slightly downward to the front of the room.

When everyone in the group was seated, Lieutenant Stabler introduced a new person, "Ladies and other beings, this is Detective Fontana. He splits his time between Special Operations in Flushing Meadows and here at the Police Academy. The detective will show you samples of the drugs you will probably encounter while working in your new assignment and give some interesting facts on the history of narcotics." After waving his hand toward the instructor, Stabler left the room.

"Hello to you all and welcome to the world of narcotics and please call me Bill because that's my name."

"No wonder he's got the gold, he's a genius," and other comments were heard for within the crowd.

Bill countered with, "Sorry, my humor's not up to par yet. Wait until we do the drugs," then he laughed and seemed to be waiting for applause. Not hearing any, he continued, "Sorry to disappoint some of you, but these are educational samples and not the real thing. We might as well begin. Any questions?"

There were several sighs of alleged disappointment heard from his captive audience, but no questions.

Bill began, "As you all know, there is nothing new about the use of drugs, only the form that they come in. Since ancient times, people have smoked opium and such. The Native American has used peyote, mescaline, mushrooms and marijuana since before the white man ever set his feet on American soil."

Laughter and "Oh, yeah", could be heard.

Bill continued. "As some of you may know, during the settling of our American West, the Chinese were the largest ethnic group of imported laborers used to build our expanding railroads. They brought with them, from their homeland, the habit of smoking opium as a way to unwind and relax. Some of our 'Cowboy' movies have even depicted the 'Opium Dens' of the Old West."

One of the females, seated near the rear of the room sweetly asked, "Can you tell us the difference between opium and heroin and where do they both come from?"

"Before I answer that, allow me to give a little history. Use of the opium poppy predates written history. Drawings of opium poppies were found in ancient Sumerian archeological sites dating as far back as 4000 BC."

"That's a long lasting high!" someone quipped.

"The making and use of opium was known to a group of ancient Greeks called Minoans, who were the inhabitants of the island of Crete, off the coast of modern day Greece. They called the sap of the poppy, *opinon,* and that name eventually evolved into the word opium as we know it today." The room was silent as he continued, "Back in the day Opium was used for treating asthma, stomach illnesses, bad eyesight and insomnia. In the past it was not thought of as evil as it is today."

Someone shouted, "Ahhhhhh, the good old days."

Bill continued, "Some nineteenth and twentieth century writers have commented on it, sometimes subtly incorporating those very characteristics in their works. For example, Frank Baum wrote *The World of Oz* in the 1800's. You may remember that while on their way to the Emerald City, Dorothy, the Scarecrow, the Tin Man, and the Cowardly Lion walked through a field of poppies, and both Dorothy and the Lion mysteriously fell asleep."

From an unknown source came the comment, "Sampling, I'll bet."

Bill continued, "The Scarecrow and the Tin Man, not being made of flesh and blood, were not unaffected."

After a pause to let it sink in, he continued, "Then, there's Aldous Huxley, one of my y favorite authors. He was a rather prophetic author who wrote about his vision of the future. Among his numerous works, he wrote two novels in which society was driven by drugs, *Brave New World* and *Brave New World Revisited*. He was born in
1894 and died in 1963."

"In correspondence Huxley once wrote, ... *'If we could sniff or swallow something that would, for five or six hours each day, abolish our solitude as individuals, atone us with our fellows in a glowing exaltation of affection and make life in all its aspects seem not only worth living, but divinely beautiful and significant, and if this heavenly, world-transfiguring drug were of such a kind that we could wake up next morning with a clear head and an undamaged constitution - then, it seems to me, all our problems (and not merely the one small problem of discovering a novel pleasure) would be wholly solved and earth would become paradise'.* "

There were a few "Wows," heard around the room.

Bill summed up with, "I like to quote Huxley's writing as an example of where our world might be going. His writings kind of explain exactly why we're all here. Maybe the man was a user, nobody knows."

Bill's group of trainees remained silent. From the rear a male voice asked, "Did Sherlock Holmes or his creator, Arthur Cannon Doyle use cocaine?"

Fontana answered, " It's an almost universal belief that the fictional detective did and as far as I know, his creator, Mr. Doyle, did not."

From the group could be heard, "Sure, sure and fish don't swim."

Bill continued, "Your question brings us to cocaine and some background about it is in order." Pausing for a second, he continued, "Doyle wrote those novels in the 1880's and at that time, cocaine was a newly discovered drug and thought to be perfectly harmless."

An anonymous, "Harmless my ass", was heard.

Quickly Bill quipped, "We'll discuss your sexual preferences in private later." Laughter was abundant.

Without missing a beat, Fontana continued, "It was commonly used as a local anesthetic and as a nerve tonic. Cocaine is derived from Coca leaves and is a natural substance contained in the leaf of the plant. The natives of South America have been chewing Coca leaves for ages as a stimulus when performing hard manual labor."

Pausing in anticipation of another comment, Bill continued, "As they chew the leaves, the chemical that is released increases their rate of breathing, causing more oxygen intake while they work, it's necessary in the thin air of their usually mountainous work environment. By chemically processing the coca leaves, the white crystalline powder we have come to know as cocaine was created.

"Magic ain't it," was heard.

In the past, cocaine or its derivatives were used in throat lozenges, gargles, and many elixirs. It was also in various wines such as Sherries and Ports. Dentists would inject a cocaine solution into patients for its numbing effect during pre-Novocain days. Some people even injected it into their veins as an aid to losing weight."

The room was silent as Fontana continued, "Sigmund Freud was touted cocaine as a cure for depression and sexual impotence. Thomas Edison thought that cocaine laced elixirs had miraculous properties for its stimulating effects.

From the rear of the room was heard, "It's no wonder he invented the light bulb, he was always lit."

Undaunted, Fontana continued, "The man who invented one of our national icons, Coca-Cola; actually only the syrup, was an Atlanta pharmacist named John Pemberton. He wanted to make a medicine that would cure a number of diseases and also taste good. With Cocaine as a main ingredient in his drink, when first introduced, he advertised it as euphoric and energizing. The infusion of the stimulating drug greatly added to its early popularity as a soft drink."

Snickers were heard.

Bill himself quipped, "No wonder it became our 'national drink'," before continuing.

"Again, because of its numbing effect, Cocaine was also used in toothache drops, for persons of all ages."

From the rear, someone yelled, "It numbs and can prolong sex."

Bill stopped to wet his throat with a drink from a can of Coke on his desk, much to the audible delight of the students, before he continued.

"The film stars of era time openly used the drug in public and praised its benefits in newspaper testimonials. The general public, always wanting to emulate famous people of their era, quickly became addicted without realizing it. Slowly, the American public became aware of the dangers of cocaine use; in particular, the extreme depression as one came down from the induced euphoric state and pressured the manufacturer of Coca-Cola to remove the drug from its soda drink in 1903."

Fontana again paused before injecting a private remark, "Personally, I have my doubts about the date because my parents and grandparents speak of going to the soda fountain at the local drug store for "Coke Syrup" as a treatment for the common cold and sore throats and that was in the 40's. My older brother swears he was given the syrup as a treatment for a sore throat and that was post World War Two. The family was living in Brooklyn New York at the time."

After a short thoughtful pause, Bill continued, "Formally, by 1920, cocaine was included in the 'Dangerous Drug act of 1920' along with heroin and other opiates, but the damage had already been done. Cocaine was now imbedded in our society and to still it continues to be the most problematic drug that's available today. Are there any questions up to this point?"

From the rear came, "What about crack? Isn't that pure cocaine?"

"Crack is the solid form of the old "free base" method of using cocaine. The hydrochloride is removed from cocaine hydrochloride, resulting in what we know as cocaine. Crack is popular because users don't have to be exposed to the dangers of freebasing, like catching fire or blowing themselves up. It's called crack because it cracks as it dries during the manufacturing process and crackles when heated or smoked. Crack as we know it today is relatively new but has actually been around for roughly 125 years. Cocaine, especially crack, is the most dangerous of all the drugs that you will have to deal with while working in this unit, because it is the most available.

The students' silence attested that Bill was a fine instructor and knew the value of a well-placed pause.

He began again, this time emphasizing, "Cocaine is also the only drug for which there is no antidote. When someone overdoses, the only recourse is to wait it out.

Medical science can do nothing for them, they either survive or die!"

In response to Bill's last sentence, muffled comments could be heard from various parts of the room.

"Alright people, let's take a ten minute break from all this interesting but morbid stuff and when you return

I'll have some handout material for you. See you in ten."

***

Mike joined up with his new friends, Charlie and Tom outside in the corridor. They all began speaking at once.

Charley said, "Holy crap guys, now I know why the world is all screwed up, no wonder they need more narcotics cops."

Mike answered with, "It seems like narcotics have been around forever. Now most of them are illegal, giving us job security."

Tom chimed in with, "I could use a smoke. Do you think we can get outside on the muster roof?"

Because the other two men didn't move, Tom answered his own question, "Guess not. Okay, I'll suffer a little while longer. At least we're not bored to death."

Ten minutes passed quickly as the three trio chatted in the hallway, occasionally nodding to other cops from the classroom.

Once all the newly assigned Narcs were seated, Detective Fontana got right back to the business at hand. "Okay people. We covered the drugs most of you are most familiar with, now please, each of you take one bundle of the handouts that I'm about to distribute. Included are pictures of other drugs, mostly in pill or tablet form. All the photos are in full glorious color for your enjoyment." After a slight giggle at his own joke, he added, "Sorry, they're two dimensional only. Avoid any temptation, caution; the use of any recovered product will be cause for dismissal and possible criminal charges and jail. We all know what happens to cops in jail."

The handouts illustrated to the newly trained investigators what they would most likely encounter on the street and were printed in color and actual size. There were various pills and capsules along with their resulting effects when ingested. Bill continued to speak as the material was passed along, "This represents most of, but not all of the various 'pills' that you may encounter. Please note the photos of a non-pill, Angel Dust. It usually looks like marijuana that has been removed from the stems and without the seeds but is very dark. Dust also has a pungent odor, not the pleasant odor that dormant marijuana has. Dust has a kind of odor a person might call acrid. It always makes my nose twitch.'

"I'll bet," someone said.

"Be extra careful when handling it. Try not to touch it directly and keep it away from your face because actual inhalation can cause problems."

He waited until everyone had a copy and then continued, "You will all notice that there are also several highlighted cautions about handling powdered narcotics. I cannot emphasize enough the value of extreme caution when handling any drug that is unwrapped or loose. Always use rubber gloves whenever possible! If none are available, and you come in contact with anything other than a pill or capsule, wash or at least rinse your hands as soon as possible. Some of that street stuff can be deadly, remember, the street dealer is only interested in money, and he or she is not a pillar of society."

Charley asked, "How can we be expected to wear gloves on the street?"

The response was quick, "You can't, but you should always have them available, especially when vouchering seizures in your respective offices or arrest processing areas. Most narcotics officers carry several pairs with them every day. You'll develop your own way of keeping gloves available. That brings another caution to mind, always conduct a thorough post arrest search including a strip search whenever possible."

Lots of whistles and catcalls erupted around the room at that statement including; "Now you're talking."

"Okay, okay. We're all adults here and should always act professionally. Naturally, those searches should be conducted by officers that are the same sex as the subject. I'm sure nobody here wants to lose their job, especially over something that's stupid and uncalled for."

As the room quieted, Bill continued, "Most of you in this room will be investigators; a few of you will be assigned as undercover officers when sent to an office and a team. Remember, you are never to take any drug unless there are dire circumstances; for example putting yourself in danger if your cover might be being blown and never, never inject anything! Should the taking of drugs be unavoidable to maintain your safety, you are to report the incident to your supervisor at once and you will receive appropriate medical treatment. Do you all understand?"

Bill waited a few seconds before continuing, "Ok group, we're about done for today. Go home and digest what you learned. Look at the handouts and try to remember it all. Tomorrow we go over paperwork, warrants and stuff. There will also be a movie. I'm sure you will all find it very interesting. If any of you have any questions, please see me before you leave. You are all free to go. See you here promptly at 9:00 a. m. tomorrow."

As the room emptied, Mike, Charley and Tom chatted just outside the doorway, taking note of the females as they left. It was Tom that remarked, "Wow, guys, some of those girls are really fine looking. Wonder if one of us will get lucky."

Mike responded, "Hope it's one of you guys, I'm getting over a bad marriage and not ready for a new woman. This new job assignment can be my mistress for a while. See you guys tomorrow and don't forget to bring the popcorn."

When Mike got home, the first thing he did was to put the day's handout on the table next to his lounge chair.

His next action was pulling his chilled bottle of Dewars from the fridge and pouring three fingers into a glass over a tower of ice and taking a sip before moving to his lounge   chair. After taking a second swallow of his golden elixir, the fledgling narcotics cop slowly unwrapped a cigar while he agonized about not being able to talk to his children.

Mike lit his Havana knock off and blew smoke rings towards the ceiling. In the center of each ring he could see pictures of previous happy times. Realizing that he was wallowing in self-pity, he finished his drink, stubbed out his cigar.

After reaffirming the fact that he had to move on, he began to devour everything in the handout, determined to memorize every bit of information that he could.

CHAPTER FIVE

It was 8:30 a.m. when Mike arrived at the Academy, going directly to room 233. Detective Fontana smiled as he walked in, "Well Mr. Romano, you're the first to arrive. Please sign. The sheet is next to the movie projector."

Mike responded, "Good morning Detective," and picked up the clip board. Elated to be there, he proudly scrawled his signature in a manner reminiscent of John Hancock's famous signatory statement on the Declaration of Independence and took a few seconds looking around to see if anyone who noticed his childish delight in being the first person to sign in. With the exception of the instructor, the room was empty. He took a seat in the center of the room.

Bill engaged Mike and the other arrivals in small talk as the room slowly filled. Using hand gestures as he spoke, he indicated that they were required to sign an attendance sheet.

When everyone was seated, Fontana cautioned, "If you neglected to sign in, do so now. Thank you." There were a few people who had neglected to sign in.

The fledgling Narc tried to be funny, "Sorry Bill, I thought you were Italian for a minute, waving your hands while you spoke to the room." There were a few chuckles.

Fontana waited until he was sure everyone had signed in, then continued, "Later, after our meal break, you folks will watch a little film."

There were ignored comments as usual.

"It was recorded as it happened and is the genuine article. You should all find it very interesting. Remember it. Burn it into your memories; but that's later."

Bill then began his instruction about warrants by noting that the videoed operation they would view later required a warrant. For the most part, warrants were granted after an undercover, a UC, made a buy from a premises. The buy was recorded, the material vouchered and the lead investigator would then apply for the warrant through the Special Narcotics Court Unit within the DA's office. Bill then informed his students about the agenda for the next day with, "Tomorrow you'll learn about warrants and meet the person who prepares them, Sophie Kiminski."

After listening to some expected remarks about the next day's guest, Bill continued, "Detective Kiminski used to work in Queens as an undercover; tough girl, she's no slouch. Allow me to give you the basics today. Once a warrant is granted, the supervising Lieutenant or Sergeant would coordinate another buy at the location stated in the warrant. When it's determined that the UC is safe, the warrant would be executed. Again, I must stress, as always the safety of all officers is always paramount in our work."

He then handed folders to members of the group, "Everyone, please review the information contained inside these as they reach you and then pass it along after getting another. These folders contain sample case files, use of vouchers and such."

As the material was passed along, Fontana explained the accepted system of creating those folders; reassuring the students that once assigned to a unit, creating case folders would become second nature to each and every one of them. The morning's lecture went quickly and smoothly. It covered the handling of contraband, the need for warrants, use of Department vehicles, narco street slang and such. Lastly, Bill explained the term "ghost", used often in the written material they were looking at.

He explained, "A 'ghost' is a non-participating narcotics cop tailing the UC to and from the "set" or buy location. The 'ghost' also carries a radio and transmits the when and if a buy was completed along with a description of the seller or hand to hand to the apprehension teams. Sometimes there might be two descriptions, a hand to hand and a steerer or middle man. The 'ghost' is, as the name implies, to remain invisible, never to get involved except in dire emergencies that risk the UC's safety or another officer on the set."

At that point, Bill announced, "Okay people, let's break for meal and continue on the issue of safety when you return. One hour only, please return on time. Thank you."

Once again, Mike, Tom and Charley went down the block for a quick meal. The men discussed some lecture items then. Finding that boring, they turned their thoughts to what might be the content of the afternoon movie. Tom even joked about looking for someplace to buy some popcorn. Eating lunch rather quickly, the men hurried back to the afternoon portion of the lecture, so fast that they forgot the popcorn.

As soon as all were seated, Fontana darkened the room, pulled down a screen that hung over a blackboard in the front of the room.

There was an almost tangible feeling of expectation in the room as he announced, "Now folks, you are about to view several buys and the culmination of an investigation from several years ago. The case on the video lasted some time, approximately six months. It included wiretaps; a warrant was required for each individual tap."

"Why each one and not by the case?"

"Because each phone line is considered as a separate location and naturally each location has its own warrant."

"Thanks."

"In this film, you will observe, several high dollar buys. Most importantly, you will also witness the final confirmation buy, just seconds before the final warrant was to be executed and the principal subjects arrested. The action takes place in a motel room, rented by the UC, for the purpose of meeting dealers and buying narcotics."

Waiting for comments and hearing none, Fontana continued, "That particular room was carefully chosen because it had a connecting doorway to the adjoining room where recording equipment was set up and a backup team was always present. The video equipment used here was setup several weeks before, when the room was first rented. The connecting door was always locked when the UC was on the set. During the final buy, in addition to the backup and apprehension team next door, there were also cops stationed outside the motel. This video was to be used to aid in prosecution and conviction of the dealers."

Bill reached for the projector and said, "Enjoy."

The screen came to life as Bill commented about what they were watching; "The sound is not always good, but good enough to hear some conversation as you watch several buys go down. The film is in black and white because high speed film was used to negate the need for additional light sources."

Fontana took a breath and added, "Our UC is the man in the white shirt and wearing the cashier's visor, his trademark. His UC name was 'The Cashier'. About three minutes into the film you will see and hear something out of the ordinary, a rare and potentially deadly occurrence."

Quiet murmurs could be heard around the room as the video continued. As the three minute mark approached, quick as a heartbeat, the action on the screen exploded. Yelling in Spanish could be heard and the word "Policia" shouted over the din of voices. The mixture of languages jelled together like the biblical Tower of Babble.

The six men present in the room jumped around as if the floor was on fire. Kilos of narcotics and cash flew around in every direction as a coffee table was overturned. Weapons were pulled and fired.

" Ohsss", "Ahsss" and "holy shits", could be heard from the audience as the film rolled on.

Everything was happening at once. From the upper right side of the screen, the connecting door exploded into the room in several pieces.

At the same time, the Cashier emptied his weapon at two men in front of him and then appeared to throw himself down on the deck in one motion. The blast and loud report from a shotgun was seen and heard. For several heart beats, the scene on the screen was nothing more than smoke, noise and movement for a few seconds. It was all a blur.

"Holy shit! What the fuck? How's the cop?" was heard from the darkened classroom.

The action was over as quickly as it started. As the smoke cleared, from the opening where the door used to be, three men wearing vests and carrying body shields had erupted into the room, and quickly handcuffed every non- team member the room including UC and those who were prone on the floor and not moving. At that point, Bill stopped the projector turned on the lights. The occupant of nearly every seat in the room continued to burst forth with expletives and questions. The din sounded similar to the inside the losing team's locker room.

Fontana held up his hand and asked, "Some show, wasn't it!? Before you ask, the UC was wounded in his left hand, two dealers met their maker and three are currently serving life sentences under the 1973 Rockefeller Drug Laws."

As Bill paused to take a breath, comments like, "How's the cop now? What's he doing now? Good riddance and I hope they die in jail," were heard.

Mike didn't even hear the beginning of the open discussion that followed. He was lost in reliving the gun battle on the rooftop during the infamous New York City Blackout where he caught up with the child molester and the violent basement shootout among the bean sprout growing trays during his temporary assignment in Chinatown. During those incidents, cover was available. The UC in the video was out in the open, exposed to a rain of bullets. Romano tried in vain to imagine how the UC in the video must have felt.

Mike's thoughts snapped back when Bill called his name, "Romano, you've been in a couple of shootouts, tell us what it's like."

Mike, not wanting to relive his own encounters, quickly answered, "I would be shitless and can't even imagine how the Cashier even functioned. There was no cover of any kind. He was exposed and out in the open."

Fontana, being an astute individual, caught Mike's intention and continued, "You all will be pleased to hear that that the UC is fine and was not actually struck by gunfire. His wound was the result of flying debris caused by the rounds hitting objects during the gunfire."

"Several , "Thank God's", were heard.

"The video you have just witnessed is the first of its kind, the recording of an actual shootout during an UC buy and hopefully it will remain, one of a kind."

Once again Fontana let his words sink in before continuing, "We show that film to every narcotics recruit in an effort to drive home just how dangerous our work is. If anyone has second thoughts and wants out, you will not be penalized. Just sign out and return to your previous command."

Various comments could be heard like, similar to "No, I'm okay with this,". Not a single person moved from their seat.

"Remember", Bill announced, "All the surviving bad guys are serving life sentences and we didn't lose anyone."

There was some soft applause of appreciation.

Pausing for effect, the detective continued, " Post arrest investigation revealed that the lead dealer believed that one of his own men was an informant. As the final buy continued, he saw his own man begin to twitch and felt that his suspicions were being confirmed. In an effort to shoot and kill his own man, he drew his weapon while yelling

'Policia'."

"Yeah, I think heard that," someone shouted

" Of course he never knew that a small army of backup cops were ready to take them all down. If any of you catch a case that works its way up to heavy weight and meet with a supplier where you are in a locked room with a bunch of bad guys, never forget this little video. Yes, we all want to do a good job and lock up the bad guys, but your first priority is to go home every day after work!"

Looking at Mike he added, "Some of you know that first hand."

Bill let that sink in a few seconds then added, "The Cashier now works in Intel and consults on heavy cases."

Questions began at that point. The first was, "Where was the ghost? Was he in the room?"

"After a long investigation and there's video set up there's is usually no ghost even though teams are ready to make arrests. There's no need for a confirmation from a ghost. It's all witnessed as it happens because of the cameras. The roll of ghost is almost always UC safety, to confirm street buys and give descriptions. The ghost is used because the street or set, is wide open and fluid. There's lots of people around and plenty of movement, making it hard for the apprehension team to quickly grab the seller and avoid a chase or a fight.

"Was there two cops in that room?"

"No. In a closed area, everyone already knows who the bad guy is and a ghost is not usually necessary; however sometimes two UC's are used as a team for their own safety. In the case you just saw, the UC previously reported that all the subjects were comfortable with each other and he was accepted. That late in a case, ready to make a final pre-arrest buy, it would not have been prudent to introduce another player."

"How are the undercover officers chosen?"

"In this particular group, you all have chosen to be narcotics investigators."

"What if I want to do UC work?

"If you want to act as a UC instead, once you get to your assigned offices, see your Lieutenant to make the request and arraignments will be made at that time."

One of the young female cops asked, "Does every investigator have a UC assigned to them?"

Bill smiled as he answered, "No. Each narcotics office is made up of a commanding officer who has a desk in the Borough Office or One Police Plaza. Below him are two Lieutenants who share the responsibly of running the field teams. They each command a module or group consisting of several teams each led by a Sergeant."

"Each Sergeant is in charge of three undercover officers and half dozen investigators. The investigators catch cases or 'Kites', they're pink copies of police complaint reports. The investigators are responsible, as the name implies; to investigate the kite and inform their respective Sergeants whether or not there is narcotics activity at the specified location and if undercover officers are necessary."

"The investigator picks any UC to use?"

"Usually the UC's are shared between teams as activity varies. It also prevents them from working the same area too much and limits their risk of exposure. Each module fine tunes their operating methods as necessary based on changing circumstances and the preferences of that particular supervising Lieutenant. Most sergeants, even within the same module, operate slightly different from each other, but they must always remain within Department guidelines. The investigators are also the arresting officers. An undercover never risks exposure by making an arrest."

"Cool," someone remarked.

Bill added, "Lastly, each field office is also an Integrity Control Officer, usually having the rank of Lieutenant."

"Thank you for the explanation. I guess we'll learn more once assigned to a unit."

"There should be very little change from what we just discussed. Are there any other questions?"

Mike asked, "What about cars? What do we drive?"

"Fontana responded, "Good question. Romano. Well, at this time each command has at least two vehicles assigned to it as a UC car. That means, the plates and everything about it cannot be traced and all information concerning the vehicle is false to thwart any sophisticated inquiry."

"Anyone ever find out who's who?"

"We know because there is so much money in drugs and with enough of it people can buy information, so we hide everything. The UC autos have real New York State registrations but the owners and locations are false. Each office also has several team cars. Currently the city has an open account with a discount rental agency; the fact that they are cars rentals helps to avoid 'being made' and traced. To my knowledge, I never heard of any perps breaking that veil."

"That's great because a guy could get hurt," was heard from somewhere.

Bill continued, "The cars are assigned a Department number and a log is kept as if they were City owned vehicles. Each office is also responsible for routine maintenance of their cars. You will sign for any auto you use, just like your patrol days. Oh yes, of course there are no police radios in these cars, that means your only means of communication is with portable radios. Make sure that each person in the team carries their own."

Detective Fontana then slowly walked to the front of the room and announced, "Okay people, we're finished for today. Please return here tomorrow for instruction on warrants and procedures. We start promptly at 10:00 a.m. Thank you."

CHAPTER SIX

Wednesday morning, the third and final day of Mike's narcotics orientation finally arrived. He took a seat in the last row at exactly 9:30 a.m. while holding a cup of steaming black coffee. Romano had been awake most of the night, unable to sleep because in his mind, he kept reliving the night he caught his wife with another man, his ultimate divorce, adding to the fact that he was anxious to begin his new assignment and put that part of his life behind him.

Being sleep deprived, he hardly noticed the tough looking, yet attractive blonde woman standing dead center, in front of the room. After a second look, he assumed that she was a cop even though she wore no uniform. He could care less. He was lost in thought.

The woman, in a loud clear and confident voice, began, "Good morning to all. I'm Detective Sophia Kaminski, and I, along with my supervisor, Sergeant John Jealous, and an assistant, formulate every warrant that is requested by every narcotics unit in the New York Police Department."

As there were no comments, she continued, "Most of you will most probably visit our office in Special Narcotics Court from time to time. It's located on the 5th floor of 25 Worth Street, also known as The Motor Vehicle Building. Today you'll learn, among other things, just what is required by my office to get a warrant. Let's begin."

Several minutes into her lecture, she noticed that Mike appeared to nod off. In a commanding voice, mixed with mild humor she said, "If that obviously Italian, semi good looking guy in the last row finds this information unimportant or boring, perhaps I could sing and dance a little to make it more interesting. If that's not enough, perhaps he should leave. What do 'ya say? "

Mike Romano was slightly embarrassed but never backed down from a challenge in his entire life. He was quick to retort.

"The floor show isn't necessary. I was up all night and so far I haven't heard anything that I didn't already know," he answered without any hint of an apology.

Sophia, at first tried acting pissed off and replied, "Thank you for your input officer." Ending with the hint of a smile she quickly added, " I'll try harder."

Mike could hear muffled conversations and caught a word or two that sounded like, "She's a hard ass', 'has a big hook', 'they claim she has more pull then most captains', and 'I heard about her, he's in deep shit."

Romano enjoyed instantly liked Sophie and enjoyed her spunk. Unsure as to why, he felt that, eventually, they would most likely, develop a long friendship. He smiled back at her.

By 1300, Sophia was announcing the end of her lecture and the approaching meal hour, when Captain Swanson walked to the front of the room. "Thank you Detective Kaminski, excellent instruction as always."

She responded with a short, "Thank you, Boss. If there's nothing else you need me for, I have to get over to my office."

Sawnson replied, "Nothing thank you. You can go."

Sophia headed towards the door and turned back to look at the class, "Good luck to you all and have fun."

Being closer to Romano at that point then she had been during their quick exchange, she looked him in the eye, touched her forehead in mock salute and said, "Bye, till next time."

At the front of the room, the Captain opened a folder that he was holding.

"Ladies and gentlemen; I have the distinct pleasure to announce your new assignments. Pausing for effect, he began, "Hope everyone gets what they want, here goes."

Swanson then recited a litany of names and their respective commands. Mike was the only cop from the group assigned to Manhattan South. Both of his new friends were assigned to Manhattan North Narcotics. The balance of the class members were dispersed all over the map; North Bronx, South Bronx, Brooklyn North, Brooklyn South and a few to Staten Island.

At first Romano was disappointed that he didn't draw Staten Island, but after a few seconds, realized that given the nature of his new assignment, it would be easier and safer to work where he was completely unknown.

Swanson concluded with, "Tomorrow, everyone is to report to your new commands at 0930 hours. Good luck to you all. You're dismissed."

After exchanging goodbyes with Tom, Charley and a few others, Mike Romano, Narcotics Investigator, left the building and headed for home.

During his trip home, Mike had all but forgotten his past life with his family. He didn't even give a thought about
what might have developed with Leona from the Annadale Luncheonette.

The only conscious thought he wasted on his past was, *what a loss. It's probably for the best. Now I gotta move ahead with my life and my new assignment. That gold shield is within my reach, now I have to do is to go get it. God and Saint Michael will help get me through.*

Thoughts of beginning his new assignment began to consume him.

*

CHAPTER SEVEN

According to the Police Department's Directory, Manhattan South Narcotics is housed inside the building that is home to the 4th Precinct and located on the Lower Eastside of Manhattan, south of Delancey Street, just outside an area known by cops as "Alphabet City."

The area earned the nickname because the names of the avenues were letters of the alphabet; Avenues A, B, etc. It's still located on the northern border of an ever increasing Asian population that was stretching the boundaries of an area known as China Town, since the turn of the twentieth century. The languages spoken in the area represent every continent on the planet.

Some blocks west, also on the south side of Delancey were several square blocks that were tagged by New Yorkers as "Delancey Street." The area was first settled by European by a polyglot of immigrants. Some of their descendants still remained. English and Yiddish were the most popular language spoken in the shops, with a mixture of Spanish that reflected a change the trend of immigration. It's an eclectic neighborhood to say the least, one of the original melting pot areas of old New York.

Mike was determined to arrive early and left his residence at 8:00 a.m. for the drive to Manhattan; arriving at Pitt and Broome Streets at 8:45 a.m. The building, a neat two story affair, was covered with red glazed brickwork as was the adjoining Fire Station. The two buildings shared a parking lot reserved for their bosses.

Mike, feeling giddy at the prospect of finally arriving, mumbled aloud to himself and chuckled, "Holy shit, there have been a sale on bricks. This place can survive a direct hit from a bomb."

After parking his car, and placing his old Staten Island police placard on the dashboard, Mike walked around the block. He spent some time looking over the cars that were parked near the building. Mike took special note of the numerous dark, non-descript four door Chevrolet Lumina sedans scattered about and thought; *now I know what kind of cars we use.* From under his shirt, he withdrew his shield that hung on a heavy stainless steel beaded chain as he entered the building.

The first floor of "The Fourth" looked similar to the majority other newer police station houses in the City.

The place was utilitarian, having nothing that could pass for old fashioned early Twentieth Century ambiance. It had not wood trimmed doorways or windows and no huge oak Station House desk. However, he did see that, as usual, everything, even the walls were painted that drab pea soup green, so prevalent in the other commands and most municipal buildings. The security officer on duty nodded and spoke first, "Officer, what can we do for you?"

Mike cordially responded with, "Morning. I'm looking for the Narcotics Offices. I'm newly assigned here."

The cop pointed as he spoke, "Far side of 'The Desk,' then take the first stairway up to the second floor. You'll find it; they have the entire floor on that side of the building."

Excitedly, Mike ascended to the second floor. The first thing he noticed was that the corridor walls were constructed of concrete blocks and not painted pea soup green, instead they were covered with a clean, glazed off white coat of paint. *Guess Narcotics has its privileges,* he thought as he entered the first opened door to his left.

Just inside, butted against the left side of the door jam, at a right angle, was a desk occupied by a young guy sporting a short beard, feather earrings and a colorful tee shirt.

On the desk sat a large telephone with several extension buttons and a second phone that had a note taped to it that read, "Secure calls only." On the wall adjacent to the doorway was a clipboard that was tagged, 'In–Out Sheet.'

Romano glanced around the room. It looked like any other clerical office in a field command. The walls adorned with clipboards containing Department orders and bulletins and the like. What impressed him was the lack of anything identifying the members of the unit. There were no pigeon holes with bosses' names on them, nothing with a cop's name either. It was like the place was manned by Mr. Anonymous and his entire family.

Opposite the doorway, on the far wall, were several heavy steel cabinets secured with steel bars and padlocks.

Mike smiled inwardly and thought, *so that's where the good stuff is. Wonder if my file is in there already or the ICO's office.* On one wall there were also several large cabinets that may have been used for equipment.

The beard looked up and in a friendly manner, asked, "What can I do for you? By the glazed look in your eyes, you must be new. Your name?"

"Romano, Michael, and I just completed the Police Academy orientation and introduction to the wonderful and interesting world of narcotics."

The Beard looked down to his right, opened a drawer and withdrew a clipboard with several sheets of paper on it. After skimming through them, he looked u p and smiled. " Welcome aboard Mike. You're assigned to Sergeant Landers' team and your Lieutenant is Lou Tazzara. Our other lieutenant is Aloe; they run the office, although we do have an Integrity Officer, Lieutenant Cassidy. We have only two modules here but six sergeants and six teams of at least eight members each and few floating UC's."

Mike answered; "Thanks, what's next?"

The Beard picked up the ringing telephone, punched an extension and began speaking into it.

Scant seconds later, he put the phone down, held his hand out and said, "Sorry about the interruption, I'm Bill Rogers, part of a team located upstairs, enjoy. But first follow the corridor around to the last office on the left and meet your Lieutenant."

The men shook hands and Mike pulled down the appropriate clipboard, signed in and replaced it before leaving the room to find his lieutenant.

Opposite the sign in room, he observed another room that was occupied by several plainclothes cops of mixed genders. Without stopping, he turned and began walking, passing two rooms on his left, one obviously unoccupied, and the sound of muted voices emanating from behind the closed door of the second. At the end of the corridor he passed a stairway that lead both up and down and was forced to go left.

In that section of the hallway, on the right side, there were two rooms; the first door was opened and revealed two unattended desks, the second door was closed. Voices could be heard from within that room also.

As Mike continued, two men, engaged in deep conversation. They only nodded as they walked past him, appearing unconcerned about the stranger among them.

Romano thought, *Guess they figure, if I'm up here, I belong,* as he turned to watch them enter the stairway that he just passed. They never even glanced back at him.

On his left was another open doorway. Inside the room were two desks, both occupied by a single male figure. Mike assumed they were Sergeants and went in to ask if they knew where Lieutenant Tazzara could be found. As he approached, one of the men turned to face him, stood up and bellowed, "Mike Romano, I knew that I recognized that name on the orders," Lou Tazzara said in a friendly voice. Louis Tazzara was smiling as he extended his right hand. Mike instantly recognized him from his days back in the Three Two; his new lieutenant had been a cop in the Anti-Crime team when Mike served there. They were never close, but occasionally interacted.

"Louie, excuse me, Lieutenant. It's nice to see you again. So you're my new boss?" Mike asked as he took the offered hand.

"Mike, just call me Loo, it's my rank and my name." Still gripping Romano's hand, he continued to pull him closer.

Turning Romano to face his office mate, he announced, "Al, I'd like you to meet, a new member of my team, Mike Romano. He's a cop from my old command uptown. He was always very active and has done some good work recently. Mike, meet Lieutenant Albert Aloe. Mike, Al, Al, Mike."

Aloe looked like the old Esquire Magazine mascot, the dapper white haired guy with the big white mustache. He smiled, rose up from his seated position slightly and took Mike's extended hand.

"Nice to meet you Michael. You can call me or Loo Lieutenant, but never Al!" he added in a slightly menacing tone.

Mike remained silent, and thought, *Wow! Excuse me.* Turning toward Lou again, he took notice of the physical stature of his new boss.

Louie Tazzara was shorter than Mike but built like a circus strongman. The man's physique reminded Mike of 'Tasmanian Devil' of cartoon fame; big body, short legs, his torso looked like it was constructed of sculptured concrete and gave the appearance that bullets would bounce off.

"This has been a welcome surprise Sir and I consider myself double lucky being assigned to this office and having you for my boss."

"No need to call me Sir, Loo or Lieutenant is good.

I read your personnel folder Mike and I consider myself the lucky one to get such a good man. You seem to have been busy the last few years. Come let's meet your immediate supervisor, Sergeant Landers, you just passed his office."

Tazzara led Romano back to the room where Mike previously heard the muffled conversation. Lou opened the door without knocking, pulling Mike in with him.

Inside were three desks; two side by side, on the wall adjacent to the corridor and one at midpoint of the room against the opposite wall. It was at the single desk, that Sergeant Landers sat, flipping through his team's share of several pink 'kites' that cited real or imagined narcotics violations and had been sent to the after being reviewed in The Puzzle Palace.

"Marvin, meet your new man, assigned to the office as an investigator, Mike Romano. Mike just transferred in from Staten Island."

Landers spun his chair around and looked at Mike a few seconds before speaking.

Responding with a slight icy tone, "Staten Island cop huh? Think you can cut it in big city narcotics? Where else did you serve?"

Landers tone instantly brought up memories of the Capelli case and the Two Oh Squad. Mike vividly recalled the strain between himself and the sometimes arrogant Jim James, aka, Jim Jim. Just as he did with James, Mike decided to either get Marvin Landers to respect him or they would go to war.

Romano took his time before answering. He first looked the man up and down as if dissecting a bug in High School biology class. Landers began to get up out of his chair but remained seated.

Enjoying what Mike referred to as human chess, he answered in his genetically wired direct style, "Well Sarge, I served over five years in the three two and caught a cop killer in between making some bribery arrests. After that, I moved to Midtown South. There I worked the entire command in plainclothes and made more bribery arrests."

Landers' mouth began to open, but he remained silent as Mike continued.

"Having a house on Staten Island, I requested to be transferred there. While working on the Island, I managed to make a city wide best ten list in '82 for latent print recoveries."

Mike paused and quickly looked at his lieutenant who was smiling.

He continued with, "Oh yeah, I also worked on a case that resulted in the arrest of a killer cop who was working for the mob. That's how I got here."

Then with more than slight hint of sarcasm, asked, "Do you think I can handle this assignment?"

The look on Marvin's face caused Lou Tazzara to chuckle. "That's the Mike Romano I remember from the Three Two. What do say Marvin, did I take care of you or not? "

Sergeant Landers was reserved in his response, "Sure he sounds great. Narcotics work is different. Only time will tell"

Mike held his tongue and thought; *wonder how you got here Marvin, with a hook? You're another Jim Jim and you will learn to respect me, you shithead.*

"No problem Sarge. I'm looking forward to working with you. What's next? "

Marvin's face continued to reveal his emotion. He was obviously uncomfortable at his lieutenant's last remark and wanted to change the mood.

First he pointed to the other two men in the room, and said, "Gentlemen, meet the newest member of our family. This is Mike Romano from Staten Island and he's assigned as an investigator to my team. Mike, meet Sergeants Bill Matthews and Jim Billings."

Billings was a huge black man with a ready smile. Mathews, appeared to be of mixed racial origins.

Big Jim rose from his chair and cordially welcomed Mike, wishing him a happy and long assignment in the office. Mathews looked up from his desk, only long enough to exchange a limp handshake with the new man and quickly returned to whatever he was doing.

Landers then thanked the lieutenant for bringing Mike in and said, "Okay Mike let's go across the hall and have you get acquainted with some of our team members."

Marvin rose from his chair and led Mike back to the room he had seen earlier that was located across from the sign in room. This time, Romano took time to digest what he observed.

Running down the center of the workspace were three 8' x3' tan laminate topped tables butted together to form a center work island. Scattered around, seated at various intervals were several cops obviously doing paper work.

Along each of the side walls were three desks with an IBM Selectric typewriter on each one. Separating each desk were three, four drawer metal file cabinets. The drawers were tagged with first names only or what were obviously nicknames; 'Skinny' or 'B-B Eyes' and the like. On the first desk on each side of the room was a telephone.

There were cops and papers all over the place combined with a din of voices. Mike gave the room a second viewing and noticed something that he thought was rather odd. Scattered about the room the tables or desktops next to each seated cop was a bright red book labeled, ' Diary'. Mike thought, *If one had to describe the scene it would be one of 'organized chaos.'*

Everyone stopped whatever they were doing when Marvin spoke, "People, we have a new member of our team, Mike Romano from Staten Island."

All those present varied their response to Marvin's announcement, some grunted a verbal acknowledgement while others were totally indifferent.

Landers waited a few seconds before continuing, "Ralph, you've been in this office the longest, sit with Romano and explain how we work our case folders."

Marvin the turned to Mike, "Mike meet Detective Ralph Thomas. Ralph will explain the basics of our job here. Ralph is on loan from one of Aloe's teams for the last two months. You are his replacement. Later you'll ride with him when we go out." As Marvin, turned to leave he added, "See everyone at 1300 hours."

Ralph waved for Mike to join him at the far end of the center work area. He had a friendly round face capped with sandy blonde hair and had a slightly heavy yet athletic build.

Several weeks later Mike learned that Ralph had played 'Triple A' baseball before joining the force and was known as RT outside the office.

Quietly Ralph said, "Welcome aboard Mike. Let me tell you who's who around here," pointing to and identifying every person in the room, eleven in all, including labeling who was a UC when appropriate.

Mike made a mental note that the three females present were all UC's.

Detective Thomas went on to explain that most of those present were Landers' men and there were two other teams that shared the room. Some of them would be in about noon.

"When all three teams are here, it's like being in a subway car during rush hour", Ralph joked. "The sergeants try to coordinate our working tours in an effort to avoid that kind of congestion. Sometimes it works."

Mike commented, "Yeah it sure is crowded."

Ralph continued, "In addition to the limited space, we do not have unlimited cars. All the cars must be shared, especially our two UC cars. You're gonna love them, one's a dark blue Cadillac Seville, four door sedan with blackout windows and the other is a maroon Olds 442 muscle car."

"A hot rod, huh?"

"The Caddy is for the teams on this floor and the Olds belongs to Aloe's guys on the third floor. Naturally, sometimes there's an overlap or sharing. The plates on both cars are registered to a phony construction company in Queens and the address is an empty lot. The Caddy even has light blue leather seats. I think it was a pimp's car."

Mike asked, "Do the investigators ever get to use the Caddy too? I'd like to use it sometime, it would be interesting."

"Yes, we do and it's a blast. Sometimes you get lucky and can watch a deal through the front window. The dealers never 'make' the car. We keep both cars out of sight in the garage under the building unless they're in use and never park them on the street anywhere near the station house. The safety of our UCs are important."

Mike spent the next three hours with Ralph who patiently showed him several case folders and how the investigators were expected to assemble and keep them updated.

He was also lucky enough to find an unclaimed cabinet drawer. After removing some old trash and assorted debris, he quickly claimed it as his own by borrowing a broad tipped felt marker and tagging it with 'Mikey R' in bold letters.

Mike asked, "Just what do we do with the kites?"

"Each investigator takes their own kites and visits the location described in them . The results are recorded on the back of the kite and in his daily log. We use those thick red diaries you see around; not memo books like on patrol. Usually there's some in the supply cabinet. If not, sometimes we buy our own. They're a common item; just make sure its red." Mike listened intently as Ralph continued, "In addition, we also fill out daily activity reports or DARs, as they're known. The job supplies them and they must be turned in to your supervising sergeant weekly, along with any request for overtime slips."

He cautioned," Mike, never forget to turn in your DARs every week; it could lead to dismissal from the unit."

"They're pretty important then?"

"Your activity log is an abridged version of your daily working diary. You put details into your red diary. I've been here three years and the supervisors have never asked to see mine, however, once in a while though, an ADA will ask."

"Do you give them your book?"

"Never put your book in their hands, only give them a photo copy of the appropriate page and never let your diary out of your sight. Always try to make the copies yourself. They'll never ask for the DARs because they know we turn them in."

"Wow, its serious stuff. Not to worry, I'll probably record too much information," was Mike's response.

Ralph continued, explaining that the 'kites' are sent over from One PP via Department mail every day.

"They're given to the two Lieutenants, who in turn, split them among their sergeants; who then assign them to investigators. It seems that the assignments are random but after a while you'll see a pattern. Once an investigator makes some collars in a given area, he's assigned kites from a different area. That action is twofold; it keeps him fresh and gets him and his partner out of an area for a while."

"So, correct me if I'm wrong Ralph, but we kind of do our own thing on a daily basis. What happens when we locate a dealer and we want to send UC's out and do buy-n-bust?"

"That's easy, you tell your supervisor. In your case, Marvin, what you have and he chooses a time and day for the operation. Just before you go out, he hands you buy money for the UC. You personally record all the serial numbers by putting all the bills on the Xerox machine. They're aligned to show only denomination and serial numbers. I'll show you how we place them later. The Sarge will take one copy to the field and one copy goes into your case folder. You give the money to the UC to use. Count it twice."

"Bet on it."

"When a collar is made and the recovered money matches, it's an easy conviction. We can also recycle the money because of the photocopies. The copies get vouchered into evidence, not the actual cash. The day's cash is returned to your sergeant. The DA's office says that they don't need the actual money to prosecute. Of course sometimes the dealer, the hand to hand person, gets away with the money, but that's rare."

Mike's response was, "I always wondered how the money was 'marked'. I's not really marked, its photo copied. So, do we ever voucher the recovered money as evidence?"

"No, Mike, I can never remember vouchering buy money, only the photo copies. Of course any other recovered money besides ours is vouchered as ill-gotten gains.

"Nice," commented Mike.

Ralph continued, "Usually, if we have two UC's that are free we try to use both; one to buy and one to ghost. Otherwise we use an investigator as the ghost."

Mike asked, "That exposes the investigator so he's useless for another ghost assignment, right? If dealers spot him again, they won't deal."

"You'd be surprised how often they never spot our investigators because we all try to alter our appearance on a daily basis just for that reason. To my knowledge, the problem has never come up."

Ralph continued, "The sergeants try to hit at least two "sets" when we do go out as a team. If something develops into a big operation or we get a direct order from downtown, two teams will hook up and we all work our asses off. For instance, the Puzzle Palace might direct us to cover a particular area. On those occasions we usually bring in at least six to ten prisoners per team and rack up lots of overtime. You'll have fun."

Mike was intrigued. "What about search warrants. How do they work?"

"When we feel that activity at a specific location is either inside or narcotics are passed from an inside a location, it makes a warrant necessary."

"First, we send the UC's to make two buys on different days at that specific location. The buys are recorded and vouchered. There are no collars because we want bigger fish or the stash. Our next step is to fill out a formal 'request for warrant' form and give it to our supervisor."

Mike listened intently, then asked, "But the warrant has to be signed by a judge, who sends it down?"

"The team sergeant usually discusses the particulars with the investigating officer and if satisfied, he authorizes the warrant request. The request is forwarded down to Special Narcotics Court's warrant office."

"How?"

"Usually the officer making the request will bring it; in case there are questions, then it's written up and submitted to a judge for approval. The turnaround is usually two days after it's written and signed by a judge before a warrant is ever returned to our office."

"What happens once it gets back here?"

"After the warrant is here, the investigator makes an execution plan, drawings and all, and then presents it to his sergeant; in your case Marvin. The Sarge either approves the plan or modifies it if necessary before a lieutenant signs off on it and a date to execute it is set."

"Does the whole office go out?"

"No. Just your team. Just before we all go out, the entire team as a tactical meeting and the bosses assign positions and duties. Lieutenant Tazzara usually goes with this teams. If he's not available Aloe might go. Just between us, I prefer going out with the Taz, even though I work for Aloe."

Mike interjected, "Yeah, I can see why, I already met him."

Ralph snorted in approval and continued," Once at the location, the UC attempts to make another buy, confirming that a location is still hot, then leaves the set. If a buy goes down and it's verified by the UC and ghost by radio, we're ready to move in. Usually, if a location is a busy one, we wait until we know our UC is long gone and watch for another deal to go down so we don't burn our UC.

"I can understand that."

"When we rush in it's the best fun you can legally have. It's always gives me a rush,

I would never miss a warrant. Damn, it's almost invigorating as having sex."

During Ralph's explanation, Mike's attention never wavered but he was thinking and finally asked, "Ralph, are our warrants no knock? "

"That's part of the fun; all our warrants are no knock warrants. We get to use lots of toys, like rams and pry bars to beat doors in, then rush inside. Everybody is handcuffed and then search the entire location; everywhere and everything, unless the warrant is specific. The best part is these people are drug dealers and we don't have to be neat or courteous. It's a great stress reliever, if you know what I mean."

Romano felt a twinge at the last remark. He had always tried to be righteous and not abuse people or their property. Of course, he was only human and if provoked or struck, then the avenging angel syndrome usually took over and all bets were off.

He responded with, "Sounds like a good time, I can't wait. Are we going out so you can show me the ropes today?"

"Sure Mike. You heard Marvin, he wants a team meeting at 1300 hours, which means we're going out, but let's get some food first. There's a deli up the block that makes great sandwiches. Care to take a walk? We can bring some food back" Romano was hungry and almost shouted, "Let's go."

When they returned, Mike and Ralph sat at the long center table and ate their lunch. Just as they finished, Sergeant Landers walked in.

"Okay, I see that some members of the other teams are here also. Everybody simmer down please."

He looked around, then continued, "My guys; tomorrow we go out for a buy and bust operation. Use the rest of this tour to double check your kites and get back to me before of tour with any 'sets' that you want to hit. We'll be doing a seven to three tomorrow because there's an early morning set that I want to personally check out. Don't be late. We'll hit the street before 0730 hours. I'll be in my office the rest of the day. Go do what you're paid for."

As Marvin, hit the doorway he said, "Oh yeah, Ralph, take Romano and show him how kites are handled. Thanks." Ralph answered, "Already on it Boss."

CHAPTER EIGHT

After signing out two portable radios and putting one of them into a large grungy looking canvas carry bag, Ralph turned and handed the second one to Mike with.

"We always take our own radios, sometimes it gets hairy."

They then went to the sign in room where a tall, bearded guy was waiting.

"Mike Romano, meet Alex Veranos, aka, Al Summers; he'll be your partner when I go back to my own team."

Alex smiled and extended his hand.

Mike returned the man's smile and extended his hand, "Alex, pleased to meet you and happy to be here. Ralph filled me in on the basics."

"It's my pleasure. Welcome to our little family. Ralph, I have car keys, let's go."

Mike thought, *quick smile and cheery too. Has a nice easy way about him and speaks softly for a big guy. I'm definitely going to get along well with him.*

Each auto key ring was tagged with the last three characters of the corresponding car's license plate. Alex led the way out to the street. The trio found their car parked half a block away. Al had the keys, and assumed the drivers role. Ralph climbed in next to him, with Mike in the rear. He positioned himself in the center.

Alex spoke first as he put the car into gear, "Mike, we cover the entire south end of Manhattan below Central Park, but our work is usually confined below 42nd street. Ralph, you're calling the first set. What do you have?"

Ralph had been shuffling through a stack of pink 'kites', selecting a black and white photo copy of one.

"Al, take us to the intersection of East Houston and Avenue A, I have to check the bodega again. If it's live, we'll hit it again tomorrow with a UC. I already have one buy inside. If we can get another one or two, I can set it up for a warrant."

Within minutes, Alex had their car parked on E. Houston, directly opposite the location. It was a wide six lane roadway with no cover of any kind.

In an effort to mask their real intentions from any interested parties, Alex jumped out and slapped the hood, as if there was a vehicle problem and raised it as if he was looking for the source of the trouble. After recording the time, Ralph then pulled a pair of 7x50 binoculars from his bag, slid down low in the seat and raised them to view the bodega.

Mike commented, "Slick move, to anybody inside the store, we look like a car that broke down. What's going on Ralph? I can see lots of people milling around the far end of the counter."

"Hold on Mike, I'm still adjusting the focus and scoot down will you?"

"Sorry."

Scant seconds later RT spoke again, "Tall, heavy male accompanied by a short female just made a buy. The guy wasn't too worried because he put the goodies right down on the counter as he counted their money. Sure wish I could hear them." He then knocked on the dashboard to alert Alex to come back into the car.

Once inside, Alex turned in his seat and began a conversation with Mike, allowing Ralph some more time to observe the inside of the bodega. "So Mike, what brings you to our office?"

Mike was impressed, "You guys are pretty smooth." He then answered Al's question, "The quest for gold Al. I want a gold shield like Ralph's. You have one?"

"Nah, I'm just a white shield guy like you. Someday, I guess. he job claims that after one year in an investigative capacity, you get one. I've been here five months now."

Ralph interrupted their exchange with, "Got 'em guys. We can go now."

In an effort to be humorous, he added, "Hey Summers, I hope you fixed the car. Let's go and please stop somewhere along the drive for a few minutes. I want to make some notes."

Alex pulled to a stop near the old New York Hospital building. Ralph asked, "Mike, you visited your first set, any questions?"

Mike Romano had several. "How come you had a copy of the kite and not the original?"

Ralph sounded impatient as he answered, "Well, I already have one inside buy, which means that there's already a case folder. Case folders can't be brought to the street. If we need anything from a case folder, we make copies. We can remove a case folder for court appearances only. Oh, by the way, they deal heroin and the glassines are stamped 'Green Dreams'."

Alex turned to Mike in the rear seat and handed him several pink kites. "Here you go Mikey, the next stop will be one to check one of my kites. You pick a fresh one that looks interesting. Might as well get your feet wet Buddy."

"Thanks for the confidence. I'll let you know in a minute. Hope I pick a good one."

"Not to worry, if it doesn't look good, one of us will let you know. You'll do fine."

Mike was silent for a few minutes as Al and Ralph chatted about what they hoped to find after executing a warrant at the location that they had just left. Ralph mentioned that he planned to come back for a second UC buy as soon as possible.

Finally, Mike spoke, "Okay Al, I found one that I think might work out. This 61 (pink copy of a complaint report,) reports drug sales alongside the public school on Lewis and Delancey. It's, just a few blocks from here. Maybe it's a possible location for some buy and bust."

Ralph answered, "Good pick Mike, but call it a kite. Anything near a school is always hot with Downtown. We'll park a couple of blocks away. You and Alex walk the area and get a look see. Use a private channel, tact 2, so you can relay your observations to me back in the car. I'll write 'em down on the back of the kite. No collars, just observations. Understand?"

Mike was now getting pumped up but agreed, "Sure, no collars, I'm ready." Alex already had the car in gear. The team parked two blocks away from the school. Ralph remained behind as Alex and Mike began their slow walk towards the subject area. Mike asked, "Alex, how can they say no collars if we see a sale? We're still cops."

"Yeah, Mike we are, but the job doesn't want the bad guys to get to know us; it spooks them and hinders UC buys. Better to observe, send in a UC and collar the guy after a sale. That way, the charge is heavier, a felony sale verses possession. We don't make jump collars unless it's absolutely necessary. By the way, do you speak Spanish?"

"Very little, why?"

"Well, as you may have guessed, I'm a Latino and if we pass bad guys, I'm gonna chatter in Spanish as if I don't give a crap about what they're doing. If you don't understand me, just nod once in a while. It makes us look like we're part of the neighborhood and not outsiders."

"Fine with me, that really makes good sense."

As they spoke, Mike took the opportunity to get a good look at Alex. The man was maybe an inch taller than himself, his head was crowned with reddish tightly curled Hair cut in a mild afro; he had kind hazel eyes and a close cropped beard that bordered a cultivated five o'clock shadow. In his left ear was a small golden loop earring like the household icon, "Mister Clean" wore. Of special interest to Romano was the apparently well used, multi-color striped carpet bag slung from Al's left shoulder.

In his mind Mike said, *Summers looks like an old fashioned sea captain or Hollywood's version of a narcotics cop. But, there's that bag, bet if that grungy bag could speak, it would have lots to say.*

Curiosity finally triumphed over Michael's sense of politeness. "Oh, that's an interesting shoulder bag you have there. That black rope slung around you that's part of the bag; where did you get ever find black rope?"

Softly Alex responded, "It's human hair. I carried the bag in Nam and brought it home with me." Al offered no further explanation and Mike didn't ask for one.

As the duo walked past the school, they observed no sales adjacent to the school as stated in the complaint. The kite wasn't accurate, but they did observe dealing a short distance away.

After passing the school, the team crossed the street and headed towards the several unofficial car park areas that were tucked between the support pillars for the elevated roadway approach to the Williamsburg Bridge. As they drew near the "lot", Alex chattered loudly in Spanish.

Mike had no idea what he was saying, but acted as instructed and nodded occasionally.

On the far side of the area, tucked between parked cars, were several persons milling about, drinking and smoking.

On the outer perimeter, that bordered the north side of Delancey Street, were two guys sitting on what appeared to be milk crates; their backs against one of the pillars, hiding them from the street.

Mike mumbled, "Now those guys look suspicious."

Summers acted as if he never heard the comment.

In addition, there were several other men moving back and forth in an uncoordinated attempt to look casual.

To a narcotics investigator, they were obviously acting as steerers. It's their job to determine, as best they can, that a potential customer isn't a cop. They also doubled as lookouts. If a steerer feels that a potential buyer is "legitimate", he or she will then 'steer' the customer to the actual drug dealer, the hand to hand man.

As the team passed the group, they observed several persons first conversing with one of the peripheral people, who would then direct them to one of the two men at the pillars. The pillar guy would then reach into a hole at the base of the pillar, withdraw something and an exchange would take place.

Mike had observed similar sales activity like that years ago when he worked in plainclothes on 42nd street. The difference was he and Gino would make summary arrests on the spot, based on their own observations. They didn't have undercover cops working with them.

The new partners continued to walk past the activity, crossing Delancey and stopping behind a parked truck.

While keeping the dealers in sight, Alex radioed, "Ralph, suspicions confirmed. Come get us. We'll meet you at north corner of Columbia and Delancey. Give us about two minutes."

"See you soon. Let Mike know that he picked a good kite."

Two minutes later the two men joined Ralph in the car and drove several blocks away before they stopped again.

Once they were stationary, Ralph handed the kite to Alex, who handed it to Mike with, "Here you go Michael. Write down what we saw, but be accurate because that kite has my name on it."

"Alex, I'm honored that you trust me but it's my first day. Are you sure? You trust me not to screw it up?"

"Yes. Just say everything out loud as you write it. If I hear something wrong, I'll stop you. Keep it simple and accurate and make sure that you correct the kite's sales location."

Mike took a breath and spoke as he wrote, putting down an accurate description of the two hand to hand men and describing the hole at the base on the bridge support pillar. Alex never said a word until he looked over the notes.

"Great job Mike, especially for your first day in the street." He chuckled as he added, "You're gonna make a great narc."

As they rode from location to location, the team passed an optometrist and eyeglass business on Essex Street called Broken Glasses.

When Mike saw the storefront, a long gone happy time flooded his mind. *Wow, I remember coming down here with Betty when we were newlyweds. She would get her eyeglasses there and while they were being made we would always have those terrific sandwiches and fries at Katz's Deli. Later on when Annie was still young we brought her here too until Donnie was born.*

Fondly, with a twinge of anguish, recalled Annie, *trying to manipulate the huge sandwiches and refusing help from either of us. Damn, we had good times. Her whore bitch mother took all that away.* The memory tugged at Mike's heart.

He managed to shake off the pain as Alex announced their next location, "Here we are guys. Hey Mike, are you alright, you look zoned out?"

"I'm good Al, just enjoying the sights," he lied.

Over the next ninety minutes the trio visited several other locations. Only two of them were worth revisiting to work with a UC.

***

Back at the office Ralph announced, "Well Mike, your training is over," and left Mike and Alex to fend for themselves.

Al secured a new diary for Mike from the supply cabinet. The two men grabbed a small corner desk in the team room that was now crowded with half of Sergeant Billing's team members.

Alex showed his new partner how to record the day's activities into it. For the most part, both men made identical entries.

Next Alex handed Mike a blank daily activity report. After showing him his own, DAR, Mike used it as a model to fill out his own report. Alex further instructed him how to extract limited information from his dairy notes and transfer them to the weekly hand in sheet.

When the paper work was completed Summers brought his new friend upstairs to meet the two other Sergeants and whatever members of their teams were present in the building.

Alex even brought Mike down to the basement garage to show him the UC cars. Both UC cars were there.

"Yeah Al, Ralph told me about the cars, but I never saw them. They're really something, especially our team car. I really want to drive that blue pimp mobile."

Romano spent the balance of his tour looking at case folders, paying particular attention to cases where warrants were executed and talking with Alex.

By 1800, Officer Michael Romano was signed out and heading home enjoying the adrenalin rush of his first day experiences and thinking about what tomorrow might bring.

CHAPTER NINE

Thursday morning at 4:30 a.m., Mike Romano, newly assigned Narcotics Investigator, sprung out of bed. Quickly, he completed his morning ritual and hurriedly left his apartment. He planned to catch breakfast at the Annadale Luncheonette. Mike had not seen or spoken to Leona, the owner in almost two months. Now that he was no longer working on Staten Island, Romano felt more comfortable perusing a possible relationship with her that always seemed to linger just below the surface. He also wanted to share his elation about his new assignment and knew that she opened weekdays at 5:00 a.m.

Mike entered the eatery at exactly 5:15 and was disappointed that Leona was nowhere in sight. The early morning, travel to work 'in the City' by the train and ferry crowd had begun filtering in. When he saw that the last stool near the kitchen was still empty, he almost jogged to it. Plopping down on the soft green top, he anxiously awaited her appearance.

Within seconds, Leona walked out carrying two trays of freshly baked biscuits, concentrating on what she was doing and didn't even notice him.

As she passed, he said, "Good morning Miss. Can a guy get some bacon, eggs and coffee here?"

Startled at the sound of his voice, Leona almost dropped the trays. "Michael, I haven't seen or heard from you in forever or at least several months. Where have you been?"

Hearing her voice again, he was struck mute. Mike just smiled and sat there, staring at her and saying nothing.

Before he could answer, Leona shouted to the waitress near the front of the counter. "Millie, please down black coffee, two over easy, bacon and rye toast for my friend here."

In her excitement, Leona hurriedly turned to a glass wall shelf and slammed the trays down almost breaking it. She gasped at the pending disaster that didn't happen, and then rushed over to Romano giving him a bone crushing hug.

He quickly stood and waited for the moment. Finally, enjoying her embrace, he thought, *Wow. I forgot what the embrace of a beautiful woman can do for a man. I hope she feels the same way.*

Mike spoke before she could say anything, "Leona, I hope that together, we might be able to walk through the doorway we spoke about some time ago, the one that led from friendship to something else. What are my something else chances?"

Millie broke into the moment with, "Here's the coffee, the eggs are on the grill and will be ready in another minute," and scooted away.

Slowly, as if deep in thought, Leona loosened her grip. Mike felt the change and thought it was because Millie infringed on their space. It was obviously only part of the reason. Romano was about to learn more as Leona stepped back, and in a soft voice said, "Mike, it's so good to see you again and I have something to share with you."

Romano was slightly apprehensive at hearing the apologetic tone in her voice. "Well, Leona, I want to share something with you too, but please, you first."

Millie had returned again and placed his plate in front of him. Reluctantly waiting for unfavorable news, Mike reclaimed his perch, picked up a fork and poked at the eggs, knowing deep inside, that he would not be happy with whatever Leona was about to share.

Leona put a hand on his shoulder before speaking.

His body twitched in response.

Leona removed her hand, moved to face him with the counter between them as if marking the distance that not separated them.

She felt apologetic as she spoke, "Michael, we were close to opening that doorway, we really were. I'm flattered that you still regard me in that way, but since you were gone, I stepped through the door with someone else."

Mike felt as if he was stabbed in the heart as he held his breath.

Seeing the disappointed look on his face she added, "When you stopped coming in, I thought that I had lost you. Every day I hoped that you would pop in again. You didn't. I'm so sorry. It's someone I knew for years and it just happened. I don't know what to say."

Mike tried to take a sip of coffee and couldn't. The cup rattled as he returned it to its saucer.

Sensing his pain, she tried to lighten the blow with, "I think you guys would like each other. I hope you and I can still be friends. Maybe our daughters can become friends as we hoped and you can meet Roger. That's his name, Roger."

After the attempt at coffee, Mike never moved as Leona spoke. It was as if the eggs had frozen solid and held his fork prisoner. His mind buzzed, trying to sort out a potpourri of emotions; it was as if an eternity had passed.

Then he heard his own voice, lifeless and metallic, as he lied, to Leona and himself, "That's great for you Leona, and yes, we'll always be friends. I can't wait to meet him. Now I should eat my eggs before they get cold. I start my new job in Manhattan as a Narcotics Investigator."

Millie broke in again as she pleaded for Leona to come help with several customers at the front end of the counter.

As Leona moved away, Michael slowly tried to eat his breakfast while agonizing about the one that got away; however, he had lost his appetite and after trying to force down several bites, he finally pushed his plate aside and finished his coffee in one gulp. It went down his throat as if it was a solid mass. Mike rose from the stool, placed a $5 dollar bill on the counter and headed for the door.

Leona was waiting with a smile. Mike never stopped moving and only said, "Bye pretty lady, I'm happy for you. Good luck," and quickly passed through the doorway before Leona could answer.

CHAPTER TEN

During his drive to Manhattan, Mike was lost in thought about how the 'wouldas, couldas, shouldas' had turned into the 'aw shits'. He was surprised to find himself in front of the 4th Precinct, feeling as if he was teleported, like in the sci-fi movies. It took him several seconds to get his bearings before parking his car close to the station house. It was now 5:45a.m. and he was really hungry. Apparently, the ride into Manhattan had retriggered his appetite.

After glancing at is watch, Mike realized that he had plenty of time to kill. Previously, when he was out with Alex and Ralph, he had passed a small corner restaurant that was located only two blocks from the station house. Remembering what Marvin had said the day before, about the team going out to make early buys and not knowing how he could work their meal breaks, Mike decided to try breakfast again.

After two cups of coffee and a bacon and egg sandwich on wheat toast, he felt better, even though his thoughts were full of self-pity. *I try to be a good person and always try to treat people fairly. What's my reward? I lost my home, my children and a possible relationship with Leona. Crap, all I have left is the Job. Just what do God and Saint Michael have in mind for me?*

Mike slowly walked back to the Fourth. With time to spare and in an effort to elevate his mood, Mike went down to the basement garage to get a second look at the blue UC Caddy and liked what he saw. The car's midnight blue paint was offset with glistening chrome. Mike ran his hand along the fenders enjoying the cool metal.

In violation of New York State Law, all the windows of the vehicle were tinted very dark making it impossible to see inside, especially under the dim lighting in the garage.

The second UC car, the Olds, was nowhere to be seen. With his spirits lifted a bit, he went upstairs to sign in.

Sitting at the sign in desk was someone that looked familiar from the series of quick introductions of the day before. Not being able to recall actually being introduced, Mike covered it with, "Hi, Mike Romano here, new to Sergeant Landers team. Forgive me, but I think we were introduced yesterday."

The man at the desk responded pleasantly with, "Louie Vega here, aka, Spanish Mike. I'm one of the shared UC's, but actually assigned to Sergeant Billing's team. I think that I saw you yesterday with Summers. You went out with him and Ralph didn't you?"

"Ralph and who?"

"Ralph and Alex Veranos, the word verano is Spanish for 'summer', so we gave him the name Summers. In this office everyone has a nickname, an alias if you will, and tags his personal cabinet drawer with it. It's kind of a paranoid security measure; you know we try not to use real names outside the office. The nicknames kind of become a habit. RT, Ralph, was working with your team because they were short a man, guess you filled the bill. He's back upstairs with his own guys."

"Yeah, yesterday was my first day. I remember now. I think that I'm gonna like it here. Eventually, I'm sure I'll earn a nickname and have to re-tag my drawer, right now it's tagged Mikey R. I just hope I'll like my new name if and when you people bestow one on me."

Vega slid the sign in sheet over to Mike. Looking at the sheet, he saw that Alex had arrived a few minutes before and signed in at 0635 hours.

"Ola, Mikey," Alex announced loudly as Mike entered the team room. Reverting back to his soft speech pattern, he asked, "Are you ready for your first real work day?"

Within minutes Sergeant Marvin had joined his entire team within the room. They were the only occupants because it was so early. Marvin took the opportunity to reintroduce the team to Michael, however, there was only one team UC present, a petite and pretty strawberry blonde female. Marvin introduced her as, "Ali Sanchez, better known as Alice."

Later that day, Mike noticed that her private drawer was marked, 'Wonderland.' He never asked, yet remained puzzled as to why she was called Alice, thinking, *was it because of the tag on her drawer or because she was called Alice, which is close to Ali, anyway. Manhattan South Narcotics sure is a crazy wonderland.*

Marvin briefed his team as to who was going to 'catch' or 'collar up' (be the arresting officers) for the day, what sets they were working. He concluded with, "Summers, you take the new man with you. You worked with him yesterday, so he's your new partner. Lead him through the paces today." Then in a half serious tone, added, "And let me know if we should keep him."

Mike was not surprised at the comment based on Marvin's prior remarks when Lou first introduced them. He remained silent and continued looking around at the occupants of the room and thought, *well, now I know who B-B Eyes is.*

Alex responded with, "Will do, Boss and don't worry about Mike R, we have it together. The Taz says he's a good cop, so he's a good cop."

He then leaned close to Mike and whispered, "I'll tell you about all the personalities when we're alone. They all have their quirks, but basically we have a good team so don't worry."

Marvin continued, "Since no other team is in, each team sign out a car. I'll take a car alone and Big John will transport Alice in the Caddy. Get your radios and whatever else you need. Go and park someplace near the Port Authority Bus Terminal. Don't bunch up. Be ready to move onto the set in half an hour. Go."

Romano signed out two radios and Summers grabbed a set of car keys. Once outside, Alex handed the keys to Mike and said, "You drive, I'll talk. Head for Tenth Avenue and 40th."

As he climbed into the driver's seat, Mike threw his shoulder bag, an old military sling bag he had used while in plainclothes on the Apple, onto the seat. Alex dropped his striped bag between them. Each man now had a radio, property envelopes, rubber gloves and at least one extra set of handcuffs in their totes. Under their outer clothing the y carried their firearms and one set of cuffs.

Alex began the conversation with, "Mikey, I don't know why, but I feel like we're brothers from another mother and I hope you feel the same."

Romano smiled and replied, "So do I and I know I'm safe with you because your bag hangs on human hair, it's scar y but comforting, because it's not mine. Some day you have to tell me how it came to be."

Realizing that he may have crossed a line with his new partner, Mike tried to lighten the mood with, "But right now, I'm interested in your team tales."

Alex answered, "You're right, the bag's another time, right now, here's the team rundown. Alice is a good UC and a master of disguises. She can alter her appearance faster than any other UC in the office and with better results. You'll often see her with a big dumpy looking bag. She carries her wardrobe inside. Sometimes we even bet five bucks as to who can spot her first."

"Sounds like fun. Who wins?"

I usually win because I spot the ghost and look slightly ahead of him and try to see who he's watching, but if there are several females around it's more difficult and we all have to wait for the ghost to radio us and tell us how she's dressed."

"She's tiny and cute. How can she blend in and buy drugs?"

"You'll soon see, she's terrific. Now, about Marvin, Sergeant Landers; he's friendly and not a bad guy, but he lacks real balls. I don't know how else to express it, you'll have to decide for yourself. Usually he'll team up with the big guy, John O'Leary, obviously known as Big John. Personally, I think, Marvin is chicken and afraid of getting hurt."

"Well, Al, who the hell wants to get hurt anyway? Certainly not me."

"Yeah, but I don't think that you'll take any crap and you'll stand tall. Whenever it gets dicey out there, Sergeant No Balls always stays a few feet behind Big John, you'll see."

"Hey Alex, I know who B-B Eyes is, he's Mike Clinton. Right?"

Mike was surprised at what he thought were negative descriptions of the team members and asked, "But how bad can they be? We all went through the same interview and passed or we wouldn't be here, right?"

Alex responded in his usual soft toned voice, "Don't misunderstand me Mikey, they're not bad people or bad cops. They're just not guys that I would hang out with after work. I'm sure that you'll form your own decision once you're here awhile. I'm just giving you my opinion. The whole office, both modules, refer to the trio as Marvin's Kids though. In time, I think you'll agree with the rest of us."

Their chatter for the rest of the ride was of little consequence.

Finally, Alex said, "Here we are. Pull over on the right. We'll wait next to that tan looking building."

Mike took the down time to look at his partner and studied his face. Feeling comfortable, he asked, "Hey Alex, since we're gonna be steady partners, can I ask you something personal?"

Alex had a look in his eye as if he knew the subject of the question that Mike was about to ask.

"Sure Mikey, ask away."

"It's really two questions. First, did you make that black rope? Next, where did the hair come from?"

Alex smile on his face as he answered, "I knew you would never back down, not even from me. We're gonna be a good team. Well, I told you that I got the bag in Vietnam and that's where the hair came from. I served with a Force Recon team and I don't want to talk about it. Enough said? You're not backing down, just showing respect. Okay?"

Romano couldn't figure out what Al's eyes were saying as he spoke. His new partner's voice was soft and pleasant but his eyes reflected a myriad of emotions. Mike responded, "Sure, good. Just curious because I'm intrigued, that's all. I'll never mention it again."

The men sat in silence for a few seconds that was broken by the crackle of Marvin's voice on the radio. "All MSN teams, please go to tactical channel three. Acknowledge on three."

The tactical channels were separate from the Division radio and 911 dispatchers in Police Plaza. Some cops referred to tact channels as point to point channels.

Narcotics teams preferred to use them because the range of those channels was limited to the range of the portable itself and the transmissions didn't go through the City's repeater system. It was safer if a criminal was using a police scanner to monitor the regular band. They couldn't listen in on anything that was not part of normal patrol services.

Both men both switched their hand held radios to tact channel 3.

Alex acknowledged with, "Summers and Mike y R here on tact three."

The other teams were be heard responding in turn.

Marvin, came back with, "The UC is out. Big John is ghosting the set near a seedy bicycle delivery service just next door to a small food place. Location is the intersection of 44th and 9th Avenue. Alice will try to make a buy. Stay alert. UC is wearing a blue scarf on her head."

Alex turned to Mike, "Here we go, slowly ride to 44th. Stay on 10th and park just before the intersection."

Mike put the car into gear.

"The twins will move in for the collar. We're the backup. If any one comes running down the block at us, we jump out and grab their asses when they get near us. Any traffic will be coming toward us so don't turn into the block."

Less than a minute had passed when the voice of Big John snapped from the radio, "UC just signaled a buy confirmation. Two hand to hands; number one is male white, dark red jacket and blue baseball cap, number two is a male black, red pants, blue shirt and shaved head. Both remaining on the corner of 44th. UC is walking down 9th."

It seemed like only seconds passed before Clinton announced, "B-B here, we have two under."

Sergeant Landers crackled, "First meet me at 49th and 10th to confirm the buy (money match), then run 'em to The South for a good toss (post arrest search) before you put them in a holding cell. Shake your asses and then get back out here. Make it quick, our next stop is Hell's Kitchen Park. Be near the set in thirty minutes on the outside and don't go near the park. Units acknowledge."

All the teams answered.

Alex told his partner, "Now they'll be at least two more collars for the Twins so they can both go Central Booking and process their collars. They will wait to end of tour and go into serious OT (overtime).

"Maybe they're really his kid."

"Watch. He'll even try to get one or two for Big John before the end of our tour. His excuse is that it's against policy for one cop to process more than two collars downtown. He's right, it's a valid safety issue."

Before they went to the next set, Romano told his partner that he would like to circle the block to see the location where the collars came from.

When Alex offered no objection, Mike drove north for two blocks on 10th Avenue, then turned back and came down 9th Avenue.

"Holy crap Al. This place looks as busy the Deuce (42nd Street) as when I worked. We usually got there about ten in the morning, not 7:00. Only difference here is the porn parlors are missing."

Passing the messenger service, Mikey R added, "I've been a New Yorker all my life and never realized how seedy the street people are around here."

Both their heads snapped to the left as Summers asked, "Did you see that, it looked like another exchange?

Mike was surprised that sales activity resumed so quickly after arrests were made.

"Yeah I did. Should we call Marvin and ask for another UC buy or at least a couple of observation collars?"

"No Mikey. Always try to let Marvin call the shots. Take it from me, he's capable of childlike temper tantrums. As long as he thinks that he's in control, the guy is basically easy to get along with. The poor little guy has an ego"

After a pregnant pause, Alex added, "But if one of his kids asked that question, he would probably approve the action. That's just the way it is. Go with the flow and he's never a problem."

"If you say so, I'll manage", was Mike's response.

"Let's go," Alex gently ordered. "Remember we can't go near the park, so pass it and come around from 11th Avenue. Go up on 48th Street, then we can stop and observe the set while we wait for whatever Marvin has in mind. I have a small pair of ten power binoculars in my bag that we can use."

Putting their car into gear Mike replied, "Aye, aye, Cap'n on the way."

Romano was careful to stay to the west side of the road as he neared the vicinity of the 47th Street boundary of the park. As their car approached the intersection of 47th and 10th, the traffic light changed from green to red. Having never spent much time in that part of Manhattan, Mike took advantage of the red light and visually, absorbed the flavor of the area.

The avenue was littered with a variety of small businesses and store fronts. The park itself was on the east side of 10th and ran from 47th to 48th Streets. On the west side of that block was a run-down grocery store and a small print shop that sat next to a coin operated Laundromat. To his right on the south corner of 47th was a seedy looking eatery. The park itself wasn't much to look at with benches and playground equipment in need of some new paint on the 10th Avenue side.

Within the cobblestoned border of the park were two handball courts that faced 48th Street. Of particular interest to Romano was that the park was occupied with only young adults, there were no young children or anyone over the age of twenty five anywhere.

When the light changed back to green, Romano continued on to 49th then drove back around 48th, parking at a fire hydrant on the north side of the street about 50 feet before 10th Avenue and facing the park.

The two men then sat quietly observing the activity and sharing the binoculars.

Finally, Al Summers spoke, softly as usual, "Mikey, watch the group at the handball court. Every few minutes one of them throws the ball at the wall and deliberately lets it bounce and roll to the corner of the fence and then he goes over to pick it up. Do you wanna bet there's a stash there?"

"Yeah, I saw him, then he goes over to talk with the blue jacket guy. I think he's the hand to hand. I suppose we have to sit to wait for the rest of the team. Guess we can only continue watching and try to make all the players."

Ten minutes passed before Marvin's voice crackled over the radio, "Alice is out without a ghost. Stay alert. I don't know where she got it, but Alice is pulling a wiggly old shopping cart behind herself. She looks really crappy. It's her best yet. She looks just like a broken down junkie. Remember, Alice's safety is our upmost priority."

Mike spotted her first, or at least spoke first, "Holy crap, Al, there she is and boy, does she look the part. Look at her struggling with the pull cart. Damn, without the pull cart, I wouldn't know her. You were right, she is amazing."

Alex chuckled and softly said, "You're my partner and I'll never tell you a lie. Now watch her work."

Alice looked every bit like a homeless drug user. She wore worn black pants under a well-worn, battered hippie type dress from the 70's and a ripped brown waist length jacket. Her face looked scarred and filthy under her disheveled black shoulder length hair.

As Alice neared the corner, she stopped at the curb, turned and kicked her shopping cart to accentuate her disgust with it, as if it had a life of its own, before crossing to the park.

That little display of feigned temper and frustration caused almost every person in the park to take notice of her, especially two females who approached her as she mounted the sidewalk on the park side of the street.

"Boy, Al, she's good," Mike remarked. If I didn't know any better I would believe she's just another skell (cop expression for a derelict street person) on the street."

After a lengthy and animated verbal exchange with Alice, one of the women guided Alice to a male who was sitting on one of the benches. Alice could be seen digging into her sleeve and apparently removing money, at which point the bench sitter made an exchange with her. Alice, continuing her act; haltingly walked away and again began battling with her shopping cart. After crossing the street, she slapped her own ass.

Mike knew that it was a buy signal when Marvin announced, "Confirmed buy, move in and grab everyone. We'll sort 'em out on the set. Acknowledge."

Alex keyed his portable, "Summers and Mikey R acknowledge, Boss. We know where the stash is and will hit the handball court." At the word "stash", Mike put the car in gear and shot across the avenue to the thrumming sound of large angel's wings beating in his head. *There it is again!*

As their car stopped on the 48th street side of the court, Al jumped out and rushed the three men inside the enclosure. Two of the men froze with the knowledge that they were about to be arrested.

The third man split away and doglegged past Alex.

"Get him partner," Alex shouted.

Mike was just steps behind his partner and had witnessed the perp's quick footwork. Not wanting to allow the subject to get past him, Romano tensed every muscle in his body as the man approached. With precision timing, Mike stuck his right arm out and sidestepped, clothes lining the fleeing felon across the neck, stopping him in his tracks. "Saint Michael just got you and kicked your ass shithead".

The runner gasped loudly as air escaped his lungs and he hit the concrete with an audible gasp, followed by a thud.

Alex heard the noise and without turning around as he hooked up the two men in front of him, shouted loudly, "Did you get 'em Mikey?"

"Got him good Summers. He's down and I think his brains are still shaking."

"Way to go brother. I knew you were a man after my own heart."

Mike took only seconds to quickly snap on one end of his handcuffs to the groggy miscreant while pulling and dragging him a few feet towards the chain link fence and attaching the man to it. Mike didn't even care if he was conscious. Romano then quickly advanced to assist his partner.

Alex was surprised how quickly and efficiently Mike moved. "Mikey, you're good. You're almost as fast with your hands as I am. What a team we're gonna make."

Mike R just smiled and took control of one of Al's prisoners.

As an afterthought, Alex continued, "Thank you God, I finally have a partner I'm comfortable with." After leaving Big John with their first two collars, together they went back for third man. He was still groggy.

In all, eight people were grabbed at the park. After questioning, three Stop and Frisk reports were filled out and those people were released.

The three males that Summers and Mikey grabbed in the handball courts, would be booked and charged with possession of narcotics with intent to sell. The charge was justified base on the team's earlier observations and because of the recovered stash, seventy five glassines believed to be heroin. It was too much to claim personal use.

The girl was arrested as the steerer because she acted in concert with the hand to hand, and would also be charged with sale.

The remaining guy, the actual hand to hand, would be booked for the sale and possession of narcotics. In all, 92 glassines and $680 would be vouchered later along with photo copies of two previously recorded $10 dollar bills that Alice used to make her buy, the bills themselves would be recycled for other buys.

Marvin was ecstatic even though there were grounds to arrest only five of them.

Everyone arrested was brought to 'The South' on 35th Street and the team began processing the collars. The male collars were strip searched for any possible secreted contraband by Marvin's Kids and the female by a lady Midtown South patrol cop.

The holding cell where the day's first two arrests were lodged was also searched. No additional drugs were found. The first two arrests plus one were assigned to B-B Eyes. The Golfer and Big John took the other four men. John was also assigned to process the female.

Reverting back to three perps for one officer was not the norm, Marvin justified B-B Eyes and John's third person by ordering, "Three of you are going downtown with the collars. Mike R and Summers will assist with the escort until you get there, so there should be no problem with personal safety."

As usual, all team members that were involved in any way with the day's arrests assisted with the resulting paperwork and transportation of the prisoners, including Mike and Alex.

As Department policy dictated, the prisoners never saw Alice. All they ever knew was that they sold to an undercover cop.

After logging the prisoners into Central Booking, Marvin's Kids stayed behind and processed their collars for court, accruing many hours of overtime as just Alex predicted. Mikey R and Summers left CB at 5:00 p.m.

CHAPTER ELEVEN

On the ride back to their office Alex asked, "Well Mikey, what did you think of your first day of 'buy and bust'?"

Romano chuckled, "I liked it. Lots of adrenalin rushes. Good for the circulation."

Alex replied, "Yeah it is, but just wait until you get your first warrant, that's the real rush. Speaking about rushes, gotta stoke the furnace, I'm hungry. Care for a Cubano?"

"Lead on my friend, but it has to be world class."

"There's a place on Pitt and East 3rd that makes the best ones."

"Ready. Let's eat."

"Now don't get nervous when you see it. It ain't Sardis, but they have the best Latino food in this area. If you like their food, tomorrow we get "Pasteles Puerto Ricano'. They're, almost as good as my mom's."

Several minutes later, the two cops walked into, El Casa de Comidas, the Spanish place Alex had raved about. The place was very small and had no tables. It was a takeout only. In the back, there was a small kitchen that was visible through a rickety screen door. To the right of the entrance were two long steam counters for hot food.

The air was permeated with a myriad of spicy odors that were almost visible as they snaked their way around the glass that protected the steam tables as they rose into the air. On the wall behind the counter were two hinged electric griddles and a large butcher block counter for food preparation.

Mike couldn't recognize most of the aromas but found them tantalizing. He chucked inside, as he felt himself salivating.

Scattered around the shop's makeshift aisles were small open crates filled with various tropical fruits, some canned goods and several types of bananas. The little place could have been in a small backstreet somewhere in a tiny Caribbean country.

Mike licked his lips like a kid in a candy store, as Alex ordered, "Dos Cubanos Grande, por favor."

As the counter man acknowledged the order, Al turned to Mike and said, "Mikey, I hope you like the sandwich."

"Can't wait," was all Romano could say as he watched the counterman work.

Mike watched closely as the Latino grabbed two loaves of what looked like French bread and sliced them lengthwise. Separating the halves and almost reverently, he placed them face down, one on each grill and closing the hinged hot plates. As the bread seared, he cut several slices of fresh roasted pork from a huge chunk that he had removed from the steam table.

Romano was rocking on his heels in anticipation.

After an unknown appropriate time, the bread was removed and placed on the work table. One half of each side of bread was stuffed with the sliced pork, thick sliced ham, several slices of Swiss cheese and at least two layers of sliced dill pickles. The sandwiches then were closed and returned to the hot grill and pressed between the two plates for what Mike thought was an eternity.

When the finally emerged, the cheese oozing out from under the toasted bread in every direction. It all smelled delicious. The counter man wrapped them in heavy paper and handed them to Alex.

Alex reached paid form them after receiving the gastronomical torpedoes, "Gracias."

Mike could not contain himself, "We're gonna park someplace and eat these right now, yes? "

"Sure are," Alex replied as he snatched two cans of Pepsi's from the cooler near the door. As the men walked out, Alex turned and shouted back, "Mill gracias hermano," then in English, "See you tomorrow."

"Boy Al, you sure are confident that I'll like the sandwich and want to go back."

"No doubt in my mind. Italians are Latin too know."

Thirty minutes later, Summers remarked, "Guess you liked it. All you said since taking your first bite was, 'Mumble, mummmmm, chew, mumble, chhhhmch' and let fly a burp or two. "

"The was the best damn sandwich ever Alex. I'm looking forward to tomorrow and another gastronomical trip to Puerto Rico or Cuba or anywhere. I can't wait to taste those pasteles or anything else."

Both men laughed as Alex answered, "Para mi hermano" (for my brother).

Their working partnership and what would result in a new lifelong friendship was chiseled in stone.

After consuming their sandwiches, the partners returned to the office to complete the day's paperwork and fill in slips for a few hours overtime, leaving them on Marvin's desk before signing out.

The partners returned to their office and signed out. On Marvin's desk they each dropped an overtime sheet for three hours.

By 7:00 p.m. Mike was home in his apartment sitting in his recliner, puffing on a cigar and sipping a glass of iced Dewars and thinking, *I haven't felt this good since that dirt bag Capelli was sentenced. Wow,, and this is gonna happen every day. Working narcotics is just what the doctor ordered, and an even better, tomorrow because Alex and I catch the collars.*

After preparing himself a small snack, Mike poured another drink and returned to his lounge chair, sat back and flicked on the television. Later after his third Dewars and a cigar, he finally dozed off with the TV showing old reruns.

His sleep was troubled and burdened with the usual reoccurring images of the night he caught his cheating, amoral ex-wife with her lover. Unconsciously, he also forced himself to review the good times, when his children were young. Even though semi-conscious, kept wondering how it all turned to shit.

At 7:00 a. m., thinking that he overslept, Mike fumbled for the lever to return his chair to an upright position and pulled hard and launched himself out of his chair. *My God, now I know what the crap from a shaggy prairie buffalo tastes like. Gotta clean up and get to work. We catch today. Marvin didn't say anything so I guess we do our normal ten by six.. Ouch my neck hurts.*

CHAPTER TWELVE

Mike arrived at the office 9:30 a.m. The sign in desk was unattended. Hearing activity, after signing in, he peered into the team room looking for Alex. Not seeing him, he then headed for Lieutenant Tazzara's office. As he passed Marvin's office, Mike said, "Good morning," not even caring if anyone was inside.

Romano found the lieutenant's office door open. The Taz was leaning over his desk and alone.

Knocking on the door jam, Mike announced, "Morning Boss, do you have a minute?"

Taz turned to face Mike. "Of course Mike, what's bothering you? "

"Nothing Loo. I just came in tell you how happy I am to be here and ask if you were responsible for me getting teamed up with Alex Veranos."

"That was Marvin's choice. He borrowed Ralph from upstairs and asked for a new man, sight unseen because he was a man short. You were assigned as a replacement. Luck of the draw. Is there a problem or something I should know about? "

"No, not at all, on the contrary, I want to make sure that Alex and I stay teamed up. It seems like a perfect match, as if we were made for each other."

Taz rose from his chair, put a meaty arm around Mike's shoulder. "Mikey, I'm pleased as hell that you're happy."

"Thank you."

"If you have any problems while working in this office, come directly to me. Us old Three Two men stick together just like the old days. I'm sure you remember how tight that house was. Got it? "

"Thank you. Excuse me. I should go find Alex now."

"Hey Mikey," Alex said when he saw his new partner. "Today it's our turn. What do you say we try for two each? Maybe even a half dozen."

"Sounds like a plan. Do you know what time we go out?"

"No, we'll have to wait until Marvin tells us what he has planned for today."

One of the twins walked in just as the two men settled into chairs at the long center table. It was Mike B-B Eyes.

"Hey Mike R, the Sarge sent me in with a bunch of kites for you. They're yours to work on when the team is not out doing buys or warrants as a group. Alex can fill you in. Have fun, I think you'll like it here. By the way, that was nice action yesterday at the handball court. Welcome aboard."

Mike thanked B-B and thought, *he seems nice maybe Alex is wrong about this guy,* and then sat down to look over the pink complaint reports. Most of the kites were noted as, "Informed by anonymous", citing drug sales at given locations south of 47th Street. As usual, there was nothing specific on any of the kites with few exceptions.

One particular kite listed a variety store just off the corner of Ave. D and E. 4th Street. The reporter listed was once again, the busy Anonymous, this time, masquerading as a male and giving himself the title of "block watcher."

The report was fairly concise stating the drugs for sale were heroin, the packets labeled Black Ice and two forms of cocaine, both crack and powder. In the report; Mr. Anonymous, also stated that the proprietor lives in the basement and keeps his stash there.

As he read the kite, Mike's mind began to race, *there's the thumping wings again, must be just my heart...Gotta send Alice in and get a warrant. Hope there's*

no kids there when we get inside, then we have to send
them to Child Services and no kid should go there.

Bringing his mind back to the task at hand, he spoke, "Hey, Alex, take a look at this kite. When you get stuff like this is it usually for real or just bullshit?"

Al took the paper from Mike, skimmed over it and answered, "That's why we get time to investigate these things like we did on your first day. We lock a kite in with observations and a UC buy. If it's real, we buy again, and then go see Marvin and tell him we want to apply for a warrant."

"How quickly do you get his permission for a warrant?"

"Landers doesn't like to try for a warrant with just two buys. He's lacks 'cojones' and is always protecting his ass. We may have to get three buys before he'll approve the application and of course, there's the usual confirmation buy just before we go in."

"Holy shit, he sounds like a pain in the ass."

"Don't worry about it. This kite looks good and between us; we can do anything we have to."

Marvin walked into the room. "Team, we have to visit a particular set later today so we won't be going out until at least two or three. Team up with your respective partners and go investigate some kites. I'll be in my office if I'm needed." As fast as he came into the room, he left.

Alex smiled at Mike and said, "Well my friend, looks like we're on our own. Grab some kites and let's go. Don't forget to bring that hot one. I'll go see Alice and tell her we might need her today."

***

When Alex returned, Mike asked, "Al, I really want to try to get a buy in for this new kite. How do we get Alice to work with us if Marvin isn't out with us?"

"Delicately. We improvise, adapt and overcome," he answered with a grin.

"How?"

Alex then quietly explained, "Alice is gonna be out with one of the guys, buying more theater makeup for her disguises and agreed to monitor point to point channel, 5 today. If we need her she'll answer.

Should we get lucky, she can make a buy using some of the money that Marvin gave her earlier just before we left the office for the afternoon."

"How's she going to explain buying without any authorization? "

"Marvin knows that she went out because they took the UC Caddy. She'll say that she just wandered into the location to buy something and an offer was made to her. Being a good cop, she couldn't resist and made the buy. It's not according to the rules but it's been done before. We Latinos stick together."

Mike was both surprised and impressed at her dedication to the team. "Wow, against the rules and without a ghost or backup. The girl's got balls."

"She's got balls to be sure, but she'll also have backup. The guy she's out with is Gus Perone, another of our UC's. He's been on loan to a team upstairs and you haven't met him yet. He'll be her ghost if and when we call. We all take care of each other here, except of course Marvin's Kids; they're usually kind of selfish."

Al Summers and Mikey R gathered up their equipment for their jaunt, including, signing out a 35 MM camera with a telephoto lens. They secured two radios, car keys and hit the street.

The team's first stop, was the location listed on one of Al's kites about possible narcotic sales in front of a variety store that's just off the corner of Eldridge Street and E. Houston.

The report claimed that activity occurred daily, beginning in mid-morning and continuing until the wee hours of the morning.

"Mikey, let's watch the location for a while and jot down what we see. That'll give Alice and Gus time to do their shopping." After twenty minutes, of observation from across Houston, the men moved their car and parked again. Alex, a meticulous investigator, wanted to do a walk-by before leaving the area. Ten minutes later, they were back in their car, made notes on the back of the kite putting details into their 'red books.'

Alex commented, "Well Mike y, did you hear that little guy with the beard talking to me in Spanish?"

"Yeah Alex, I did. What did he want?"

"He offered me crack cocaine. I told him I had no money. Guess there's drugs there, huh? We'll come back and try it again with a UC."

"Sure enough. What's next?"

"Let's go see the place on your kite."

Mike drove to the location listed on his kite, the variety store on East 4th and Avenue D. Alex directed him to avoid passing the subject store and to park mid-block at a fire hydrant on the opposite side of the street. Mike did as instructed, then climbed into the rear seat and lit a cigar.

Once the interior began to fill with smoke, he reached into his trusty shoulder bag, designed for map carrying, and withdrew a large pair of 7 x 50 binoculars, focusing on the storefront and the foot traffic out front. Many years before, Mike had bought the bag and a well-worn CPO jacket from an Army Surplus store on Canal Street just after being assigned to his old plainclothes detail back in MTS. The numerous pockets of the jacket had proven their worth many times on the streets.

After a few minutes of silence, Mike was the first to speak, "Al, there seems to be at least one guy, the guy in red, taking something from people and directing them around the corner out of our sight. Most of the people going into the store don't even speak to him. I heard you clicking away a few times. Did you get any photos?"

"Yeah, Mikey, see action through the camera lens and have a few shots of him. Let's try to reposition and see just what happens around the corner. Ready?"

Mike was definitely ready. He bounded over the seatback almost killing his partner to get back behind the wheel. The voices in his head were saying, *Go Michael. Go.*

"Let's roll. It's too bad Alice isn't here. Should we call her?"

"No. Not yet. We're gonna reserve that call for later. Don't you want to set up your first search warrant?"

"Oh yeah! Thanks. Okay, and then let's get more pictures. He took a deep breath and started the engine.

Summers suggested, "Find a real parking spot within a block if you can and we'll try to get on the roof of the housing building across the street. That will give us a good vantage point and we won't be observed. What da ya say? "

After several turns around the block, a spot opened up near another fire hydrant. Mike pulled in, stopping within three inches of the car in front of him because he wanted to leave the required fifteen feet from the fire plug.

Alex laughed, "Mikey, don't be such a Boy Scout. We just write a quick 49 (Official letter), get Marvin to sign it and any summons is voided."

"Sorry Alex, old habits die hard. Ready? "
"Let's do it."

The two men slung their bags over their shoulders and walked to the towering apartment building opposite the subject corner.

As they approached, Mike's mind flashed back to the Three Two and the night he caught a rapist. That night too, he had to climb the stairwell of one of those towers.

His mind raced. It was as if he was watching a movie; complete with an unknown narrator, perhaps Saint Michael himself: *The Essex complex covered one square block and was run by The New York City Housing Authority.*

The complex stretched from Eight Avenue on the west to Seventh Avenue on the east. West 126th street marked south end and West 128th Street the northern boundary. The development contained seven, fourteen story buildings.

Number 247 was approximately one hundred yards west of Seventh Avenue. As the men entered the building lobby, the portable radio crackled, "Adam, be advised, there has been two more calls on this job. Be further advised that this may be a sexual assault."

Romano's heart began to pound as the vivid memory continued; *all he could now hear was a powerful, surf-like roar in his ears. "Come on Len, let's get there." He punched the elevator button.*

"Shit, it's not working." Although the wholesale assaults on police officers of the early Seventies were over, Len always did everything by the book. He cautioned his partner, "Mike, slow down. We have to take the stairs now. We'll each take a stairway. Use the radio if you see anything and for God's sake, note the floor you're on. Please."

Len then radioed the dispatcher to advise any responding backup units to the fact that the elevator was out and each stairwell contained a police officer.

Mike began his climb in the East stairway, running up the steps two at a time. His heart pounded harder as the exertion began to get to him, forcing him back to taking one step at a time.

Mike's head was swirling as another memory jumped into view, *the little girl in Jackson Heights and his obsession with Brian Wilkey and the crooked cop, Deputy Inspector Dennis Bryan covered for him.*

His mind instantly spun back to the housing project rapist. At the time, he had wished, *if I really was Saint Michael, then I could fly up the stairs. His legs felt like lead weights as he approached the fourteenth floor landing. He was barely able to draw a breath. Silently, he pleaded, please God, if there is an assault, let the guy give up and I can't fight him. Ahead of him, the door to the hallway opened. Mike reached for his weapon.*

His chest puffed like a steam locomotive as two women faced him. It was two women. They spoke in unison. "Officer, this big guy, he's wearing a long dark coat. It's summer, he's crazy."

Then the older one singularly carried on with their tale. "He has this little woman on the roof. They done been drinking wine for a while and he tried to rape her. We called the police and he took her down the stairs."

As he returned to the present, he thought, *Shit I almost had a heart attack that night.*

His heart was still pounding as he shook his head and snapped back to the present.

"Hey Al, I hope the elevator is working. The last time had to climb stairs like this; I almost died from exhaustion and could barely make the collar."

"What happened?"

"We responded to a rape in progress and the guy was back on the street level floor when we got him. I wish that I knew that before going up thirteen flights. There's no way that I want to make that climb again. Maybe we can change buildings if the elevator isn't working?"

Alex chuckled as he spoke, "Don't know if we can, gotta go up to have a full view of what we're after. Not to worry, God is on our side."

Once in the building lobby, Mike was relieved to see that there were two elevators and both were functioning. Less than a two minutes later, the 'narco rangers' exited on the top floor and moved to the stairway. Cautiously they entered the stairwell to the roof.

The walls were typical of those found in ghetto housing; smoke burn and spray paint graffiti, with a scattering of gang tags. The floor was littered with assorted debris and was tacky and it stank. It looked as if the maintenance crews never visited that particular location, maybe out of fear. Alex led the way.

Seeing a broken slide bolt on the roof door, he excitedly turned to Mike, "The door lock is broken, and we have access to the roof."

Cautiously, both men stepped through the door opening. Each man crouched low and moved onto the rooftop in an opposite direction from his partner. They worked smoothly, without conversation. It was as if they had rehearsed their actions. Mike even checked the roof of the stairwell.

After thoroughly checking the entire rooftop, Alex turned to his partner and remarked, "Mikey, you react with the grace and instinct of a man hunter. We're gonna be some team, I love you brother."

"Thanks Alex, let's see what we can see," Mike replied as they moved closer to the roof's edge. It was early spring and there was a brisk breeze blowing.

Alex commented, "Holy crap Mike, please close the refrigerator door will you?"

Mike only chuckled and said, "There they are. We got them in our sights"

They spent about forty five observing the activity below them before leaving the rooftop on the elevator.

Alex asked, "Mike are you comfortable about our observations and ready to call Alice?"

"Sure enough. The hand to hand guy went into the store to re-up at least three times while we watched. The stash has to be inside."

The two men re-entered their car and organized their notes. Alex then switched to point to point channel 5 and in Spanish, called for Alice and Gus to meet them where 14th Street dead ends at the FDR Drive.

Alex and Mike only waited two minutes before the UC car drove up next to them. Gus was behind the wheel. "Hola caballeros. Que pasa?, Gus asked.

Al responded in English, "Did Alice tell you we might ask her to visit a location?"

"Yeah, she did. Is that the new man with you? Did you guys officially partner up?" Looking at Mike he asked, "Mike Romano, Mikey R, is it?"

Romano, feeling that Alex had given him the lead, took it, "Mikey it is. Al told me a little about you. Are you back with our team or still on loan upstairs?"

Before Gus answered, Mike had a chance to assess him. Gus was about five-nine, with a solid build. Mike guessed that he was a weight lifter and worked out regularly. He thought, *Guess little Alice is safe with him as backup. Don't know if I would want to tangle with him either. He's built like a brick wall.*

"Yes, I'm back with the team. Alice and I are ready. Does Marvin know about this potential buy?"

Alex answered, "No Gus, he doesn't, but that doesn't stop bulldogs like us. Alice can walk in, poke around and 'by coincidence' make a buy. It's been done before. We just spent time at the location got some shots of activity on film. After a buy, we'll bring it to the Photo Lab for prints and hopefully convince Marvin to justify starting a warrant case right away. You guys ready?"

In unison the two UC's answered, "Yeah, let's get it going. Fill us in."

Mike answered, "Okay, here's the location..."

After giving the location and describing what they observed, Mike turned to Alex and asked, "Is there anything that I left out?"

With a big smile, Al answered, "No Mikey, you did good. Oh yeah, I hereby christen you, 'Bulldog' as your new office name because you never let go. I've seen it on the set making arrests and now, even though you never set up a buy, you have this one down pretty good."

"Why Bulldog?"

"Once a bulldog takes a bite, he hangs on until the very end. You have that, quality, Como? We call it tenacidad, persistenica; Tenacity and persistence in your language, you're a bulldog for sure."

While the conversation between the men was in progress, Alice had moved to the back seat of the Caddy and transformed herself into a sorry looking druggie.

She emerged, having donned a black wig, leggings with holes in them under her skirt, adding a torn and patched windbreaker that looked like its last owner resided on Skid Row.

To complete her transformation, she used some of her newly bought theatrical makeup to turn her face into a rather unsightly mess, complete with dirt and sores.

With a flourish, she executed a pirouette and announced, "Ready boys, let's go."

Alex and Gus just smiled.

The newly christened Bulldog, was amazed, "Holy crap, if I wasn't here when you looked like you, I never would believe that's you, Alice. You're a damn human chameleon."

Al looked at Mike and said, "I'll drive Bulldog, you pay attention. Gus, give us a three minute start to set up and then come do your thing. Please watch our girl closely, we don't want anything to go wrong especially because Marvin doesn't know about this. See you later."

Summers and Bulldog climbed into their car and returned back to the variety store location.

***

Within five minutes of leaving their tactical meeting with Alice and Gus, Summers and his partner, the newly named Bulldog, arrived on E. 4th Street and were lucky enough to find their previous parking spot in front of the fire hydrant. The red jacket guy was still in business.

Mike, anxious for Alice to make her buy asked, "Al, how long do you think it will be before Alice and Gus show up?"

Summers pointed towards Houston, "There goes the UC Caddy. It just passed the corner heading west. It won't be long now."

Several minutes went passed. Impatiently, Mike asked, "Where the hell are they Alex? It's been awhile now."

"They probably had to spend some time looking for a legitimate parking space. Gus won't let her out alone, especially if he doesn't see us."

Reaching for the door handle, he continued, "You stay with the car, I'm gonna walk to the corner. You make sure your radio is on."

Romano was on edge. He keyed his mike and called, "Gus, are you on the air. Can you hear me? Alex is out looking for you guys."

Barely audible Gus answered, "Keep it quiet will you. I'm very close to the store and the UC is inside. Wait it out and shut the fuck up."

Mike was embarrassed by Gus' response and said nothing.

Summers was next. "Hey shithead, shut the hell up. I can see the ghost and also heard you, he's right. You can get someone hurt. Soon as she exits, I'm coming back." The tone in his voice had a chilling icy tone and was not soft as usual exhibiting his irritation.

Within seconds, Alice came staggering out like, looking a junkie in pain.

Thinking that she was hurt, Al and Gus were ready to bounce to her aid, but she spotted their movements and waved them off. In rapid Spanish, Gus quietly spoke to Alex that she must have made a buy and was doing her act. When she got close to Gus, after confirming that she was fine, Alex turned away and started back to his partner. The radio crackled as Al got close to the car. "

"We're clear. The UC scored", it Gus. "Meet you back at the office, acknowledge."

Mike acknowledged as they climbed back into their car, "Right as rain. See you there."

"Mikey, Bulldog, I know that you were anxious to get a buy in back there, but the safety of the UC is the most important thing here. Too much radio chatter might be heard by the bad guys and put one of us in jeopardy."

Mike just stared straight ahead. "You couldn't see where Gus was and didn't know if any shithead was close enough to him to hear the radio crackle. They're good at their job and know what they're doing, so no more crap, Okay!? "

Romano was as contrite as if kneeling in a confessional in Saint Patrick's Church, " I'm sorry, it won't happen again."

Alex felt sorry for him and wanted to reassure his partner that nothing changed between them. He hit Mike's shoulder and cheerfully ordered, "Okay, 'vamanos'. Let's go James, take us home."

Mike drove back in complete silence.

CHAPTER THIRTEEN

Back in the office, the first thing Alex did was to take his partner aside.

"Listen Mikey, uh, Bulldog, sorry to lose my temper out there. I see you not only as a partner, but as a brother; truly a brother, after yesterday. We must have had the same mother in the cosmos somewhere. We have 'un vinculo', in English, it means a bond. Somehow we're tied together as brothers in the universe. I trust you with my life. I know you can act quickly and decisively necessary, I've seen it. Just slow down a notch, Okay? "

Romano was surprised at the explanation. He paused to search his memory for the Spanish word for brother before continuing, "Alex, Hermano, thank you, I'm honored and couldn't ask for a better brother. No need to explain. I understand why you spoke that way."

As Mike finished the last word, Al grabbed his arm, pulled him forward and gave him a 'man hug' to seal the bond. Indeed, they were now, eternally joined at the hip.

Alex whispered, "Hermano, go fix the name on your file drawer now, you've earned the name Bulldog."

"Yeah, right now", Mike said as he pulled away. "I have a new brother, a new name. I'm having fun and getting Spanish lessons too. What more can a man ask for?"

After a short chuckle, he went directly back into the team room. With a borrowed broad felt tip marker, he stood in front of his drawer, and under Mikey R, wrote "BULLDOG" in large bold letters.

Mike wasn't aware that his partner was standing behind him. He was slightly startled when Alex asked, "Hey, how come you're leaving Mikey R? Any special reason?"

"Because you just named me Bulldog and I think everyone should get used to it. In a couple of weeks, I'll cover Mikey R".

Alex grinned ear to ear as he responded, "That makes good sense."

The two men had just finished expounding their mutual admiration for each other when Alice and Gus walked in. Alice, looked like she had slept on the street for days.

Mike remarked, "Holy crap Alice, I would take you for a junkie in a heartbeat. I really didn't get a good look at you back in the street. You're another person."

Gus sat down, took out his 'diary' and wrote up his observations.

"Listen guys, Alice bought two glassines of something called Black Ice, when she asked for heroin. Give her a minute to clean up and she'll voucher it and tell her story to Marvin when she asks him to sign the paper work."

Al said, "She can take her time while I guide Mike through the paper work on this one. Thanks."

Mike and Al got out their DARS and made minimal entries for the two locations. In their 'red books', they detailed the incident "Were observing the variety store location as noted in a kite and by coincidence, UCs Alice and Gus walked up. Alice went in alone and spent some time inside. UCs later explained that earlier they had seen our car down the block and thought that we might have a kite on the location. UC Alice has informed us that she went inside said location for a snack and someone offered her heroin so she bought it."

"Al, do you think this will fly with Marvin?"

"Sure, he likes Alice, is afraid of Gus and she's a narcotics cop and a UC drugs for a living, so she couldn't just walk out. If we didn't have a kite, she would come back to the office and generate one herself. We just happened to be there. That's her job so stop worrying. It's all good."

"If you say so, I'm good with it too. By the way, Gus looks like he can handle himself. What's his story?"

"He can. The guy is a powerhouse. He lifts weights and competes in the Police Olympics. Yet he's also a very nice person and a quiet guy. One time, there were two guys that tried to rip him off on a set. It was their mistake. He stayed in character and never asked for help. By the time we got to him, the two men were down on the sidewalk and almost unconscious. He's a good man to have around. Whenever he can, he ghosts Alice; it's something about growing up in the same neighborhood."

Alex and Mike returned to finishing the appropriate paper work for their morning jaunt. Romano needed a copy of the voucher from Alice to complete his report and open a folder in the hopes of securing a search warrant for the variety store. Mike was imagining the scene for his first warrant when Alice walked into the room looking like a college girl; pretty and "pure white bread." *My God, she is truly amazing,* he thought.

Alice spoke to them as she handed a copy to Mike, "Okay guys, Marvin bought my 'chance buy' story and signed the voucher."

"Thanks. I'm still amazed," Mike remarked.

"Marvin says that our team is going out to the Washington Square Park area and NYU to work some kites and do some buy and bust. We're gonna try pills and grass. Gus and I will be working two different areas, maybe someone has cocaine too. This should be a fun day."

Alex spoke, "We should be up to catch today. Get us some good collars will you?"

"Hey Summers, I only make the buys. You and your new Bulldog have to make the collars. That's your job."

The rest of their team trickled in just as their conversation ended.

Murray 'The Golfer' Lansky, Mike 'B-B Eyes' Clinton, followed by the illustrious Sergeant Marvin Landers. Close on his heels, was 'Big John' O'Leary and lastly, Gus. Present in the room at the time were members of Sergeant Bill Mathew's team. When they saw Marvin stop at the head of the table, they dutifully moved to the far end of the room.

Sergeant Marvin got right to the point, "Team, we are going to the area around NYU and the park. Alice and Gus will attempt to make various buys near the school buildings. Each UC is taking a different area because the set is so big. Eyes and The Golfer worked late with their collars yesterday, so they'll ghost the UC's. Mikey R and Summers will be catching. We'll hold any collars in the apartment building garage on W. 8th Street, just off 5th Avenue. We'll get uniform to help us with the prisoners if we get too many to handle ourselves."

It was obvious to all present, that even though he waited for questions, he didn't want any and quickly continued, "This request came directly to my desk from Downtown, so let's do a good job.'

Several, "Sure Sarge," mumbles were heard.

"We all meet down in that garage in half an hour. I want multiple collars by 1700 hours. Oh yes, Romano, I understand Alice made a buy inside one of your kite locations today. See me about that later when we get back, will you?"

Once away from their sergeant and the rest of the team, Mike asked, "Alex just how pissed off do you think Marvin is? How should I handle it if he asks, "How did that 'coincidence' go down?"

Al chuckled before speaking, "Mikey, what happened to the bulldog attitude? Did he loosen his jaws? Keep those jaws clenched and stop worrying. I told you our little accidental buy has happened man y times before. You're new, so Marvin is flexing his muscles. If he pushes you, just be yourself. I know you can handle it. Now let's go to the garage and get ready for some fun in Washington Square Park."

Mike relaxed a bit and dug deep inside to give a humorous response, "Well, being the best judge of character I know, I wish to thank you for your faith in me. ROOOWF."

Alex laughed, "Good doggy. Oh, by the way, because of all the activity that's usually there, we affectionately call it Washing Machine Park; you know like a clothes washer, everything is always stirring and spinning around there. If you hear someone use the term, now you'll know what they're talking about. Let's go do some laundry."

CHAPTER FOURTEEN

Alex and Mike rolled into the staging garage within twenty minutes. Two of Marvin's kids were already there, along with Alice and Gus. The blue Caddy was parked in a far corner of the garage almost hidden from sight.

Inside, off to one side was a stairway that led to the building lobby. The building core at that point formed an alcove could serve as a temporary detention area for collars. It was planned, that as usual, Big John and Marvin would remain behind to guard the arrestees until the team was ready to transport them for processing. Within minutes Marvin arrived with Big John.

Gathering his troops, Marvin took the floor, "Okay team, listen up. Gus and Alice will attempt to make some buys. Alice will work near and possibly inside the smaller buildings used by the University. Those buildings house offices, reading rooms or mini libraries and such for the students. As you may know, any building with a gathering room will also have dorms upstairs, so they are always lots of students using them. Any collars made inside those small building are to be very discrete."

Romano knew that NYU had plenty of property in and around the square, but until that moment he no idea that the university owned just about every building.

Marvin was on a roll and continued without asking if there were any questions.

"Gus will kind of tour the park and get whatever he can. Golfer will ghost Gus, and Big John will ghost Alice. B-B will be around to assist if necessary. Once we have a collar, Big John will stay with me in the garage and B-B will then ghost Alice.

He looks like a young student and will fit right in."
There were some remarks about his youthful appearance.

"Summers and Mike R, are up today. Okay let's get cracking. All radios remain on point to point TAC-5 until notified.

" Ten- four Sarge."

"We don't want everyone listening to what's going on. It's 1430 now and I want to have at least four or five collars by 1700 hours. Go, I'll be out there in my car until you have a collar or two. Call for me and I'll pick them up. After that, if you can, securely handcuffed, carefully walk your collars out of the park and to the garage. If you can't do it safely, use regular channels and call for transport to the garage."

***

All of Marvin's kids except B-B Eyes, left the confines of the garage and walked towards Sixth Avenue. Gus who would begin buy attempts, in the vicinity of Washington Square South and McDougall Streets. They would approach the park from Sixth Avenue, allowing them to observe him closely.

B-B Eyes, slowly tailed Alice to the corner of University Place and Washington Square North where she entered the park. Romano and his partner followed about 150 feet behind them.

The park was teeming with humanity. The sheer numbers of the mass of people moving around alone and in groups, reminded Mike of the plethora of pigeons that always filled Trafalgar Square in London, England. He had been there twice and was afraid to look at the sky. He knew that it would be difficult to keep Alice in sight and that he and Al would probably have to rely on her ghost.

"Alex, there's just too many people and too much activity here for me to always keep our team in sight. Is it always like this?"

Al smiled and touched Mike's arm, "Almost every time Brother, almost every time. Now the Bulldog has to learn patience, it's better than charging in; it'll work out. The perps usually don't put up a fight here, but sometimes they will run, then we use the radios, they can't outrun them, can they? Make sure you can hear your portable but don't leave it too loud. We don't want to be made, do we?"

Just as Alex finished his last sentence the team passed two men sitting on a park bench. In a West Indian accent one of them asked, "Yo, my fine gentlemen, anyting you need to party wit the pretty college girls? Bring your ladies sometin' good."

Romano instantly went into mode, his muscles tensed and he planned his next move.

Summers answered, "No, my friends, we're fine." Then in an attempt to be funny, he added, "We be havin' what they need," and giving Mike a gentle shove away from the men as he spoke.

When they were far enough from the men to be out of earshot, Romano spoke to his partner, "Thanks for jumping in Al. I forgot that if I grabbed one or even both of those guys, Gus and Alice would be alone on this end of the park. Sorry, just instinct I guess. It won't happen again."

The two men continued to walk towards the huge circular fountain in the center of the park. The fountain wasn't in operation, leaving the pool dry and allowing people to sit along its walls. Alex spoke, "Mikey, look directly across, about 11 o'clock , there's B-B, sitting on the back of a bench near a group of what looks like students. Do you see him?"

"Yeah, but I don't see the UC. Where is Alice? "

Blending in my boy, blending in; she's probably in the middle of that group of students. Watch the edges of the group, if she bought something, the seller will begin to slide slowly away. If and when B-B speaks, be ready to spot whoever he describes. That's when we move in, slowly, if possible, to avoid a fiasco and a foot race. Be ready, there's no fence around this place like the last park we worked."

B-B turned to look behind the bench as if he had dropped something, then slipped off the bench and dropped behind it, as if he was looking for whatever it was.

Their radios crackled, "UC made a buy." Then it cut off. Barely audible above the din, B-B continued, "Perp scrip is; male Hispanic, close cut afro, white jacket, wearing red sneakers. The actual hand to hand is with him; also Hispanic, wearing a blue jacket and red sneakers. They should be with the crowd to my left."

"Summers and Bulldog received and moving," Al whispered.

"Good to go," said Mike.

The partners then separated as they advanced, keeping about ten to fifteen feet apart. No conversation was necessary. Both men were instinctive hunters.

Romano spotted the blue jacket guy and quickened his approach, trying to act as if he was looking at the abundance of females that were around.

As he got closer to his quarry, in an effort to make Blue Jacket think he was not going for him, Mike quickly formulated a ruse. Speaking loudly to an invisible person he shouted, "Holy crap, Suzie, is that you?" When he was within three feet of his prey, he spoke again to the factitious Suzie, "Yeah, honey, it's me. My God you look beautiful."

Blue Jacket, unable to resist look at a pretty girl, turned around to get a look at Suzie. That's when Romano rushed him.

Quickly grabbing the man's left hand and bending it backwards towards his forearm, Mike applied pressure and announced, "Police, you're under arrest and don't even think of resisting."

The man cried out, "Shit man. That hurts. What jou want with me? I did nothing, just walking."

By that time, Mike had bent the guy's arm into the small of his back and was holding his free to prevent the guy from landing a retaliatory blow.

Menacingly, Mike responded with, "Walk with me quietly and slowly or I'll break it off," as he led his collar towards a large tree. Once at the tree, the Bulldog spun his man to face the tree and applied pressure to the sore arm and kicked his feet rearward to keep the guy off balance.

"Don't move and put your head against the tree." Romano then let go of one of his subject's arms and withdrew his handcuffs from his waistband and snapped them on in one single motion. He then hooked up the other wrist and commanded, "Now stand still and don't move."

Twenty seconds passed before Alex's voice came over the radio, "Bulldog, I got mine. You?"

"Hey Summers, it's two for two. What now?"

Alex answered quickly, "Head for the arch and the street. We'll call for the Sarge."

The partners saw each other as they approached the Arch and smiled broadly. Once together on the outer sidewalk with their prisoners, Alex said, "To celebrate your first collar in the wild, Bulldog, you call the Sarge for transport."

Mike radioed, "Bulldog and Summers here. We have two collars for transport. Do you read Sergeant?" "The response was quick. "I read Bulldog. What's your location?"

"We're on 5th Avenue and standing directly in front of the Arch. Summers is with me."

"Stand by gentlemen, I'm on my way."

Landers pulled up in a midnight blue sedan, the vehicle that he always tried to hold for himself or one of his ' Kids'.

Quietly, Mike turned to Alex and commented, "Kinda looks like the little baby brother of the UC Caddy. Wonder what it'll look like when it grows up."

Alex answered, "Bet it grows up before Marvin or the kids do."

"Okay guys, what do you have?" Marvin asked as Alex and Mike approached with their collars.

There were times when Sergeant Marvin was prone to state the obvious, always having the need to assert his role as supervisor.

Alex gave Mike a quick poke in the back. Mike knew that it was a signal to speak.

"Sarge, we have two under from a UC buy. We gave them a quick pat for weapons, but not for contraband. Can we do it now?"

"I prefer that you all get in the car and do it in the garage. Stuff the two of them into the rear seat. Summers, you sit behind me next to them and the Bulldog gets in the front."

As his men were putting the collars into the auto, Landers notified Big John to meet them at the holding garage. John acknowledged the order.

***

Once in the alcove area, the Bulldog, recited the Miranda warnings to their arrestees. Summers recorded their names and searched them for contraband. Blue shirt possessed several dime bags of pot and over two dozen 10 milligram valiums.

The drugs were put into appropriate narcotics envelopes and marked. Sergeant Marvin witnessed every move and made notes in his work diary.

Red Shirt had two hundred forty dollars in his possession, but no drugs. The sergeant then moved away from the group and reached Alice on the radio. He was informed that she used a ten dollar bill for two valiums.

Marvin reached into his car for photo copies of the buy money to match the bill before returning to the group. After matching a bill taken from Red Shirt, he appropriately marked the sheet and ordered Romano to put it that bill and the photo sheet into an envelope. All the other money would be vouchered separate after counting it all once again.

John still had not arrived, giving Alex and Mike time to make notes in their diaries. Just as they finished, John walked in.

"Sorry for the delay Sarge, it's a long walk."

Landers replied, "You're good John. Stay here with me."

"Sure Boss."

"Al, Mike, go back out there and keep in touch. If needed, you can call Dispatch for transportation to us; we'll stay here with the collars."

Alex answered, "Ten-four, we're gone."

He spun on his hell saying, "Let's go Bulldog Mikey. Now let's get me a couple of bad guys too." He hoped that Marvin noticed the use of a nickname in front of the arrestees and thought, *Marvin is an asshole..*

Summers and Bulldog decided not to use their radios to locate Alice for fear of compromising her safety. As a result, it took several minutes for Al and Mike to locate Alice because she had changed her appearance once again.

When they finally spotted her, she was in front of the NYU Library, a huge red granite building that occupied the entire square block, 68 Washington Square South.

Alice was no longer a blonde; now she was wearing an auburn wig and a mini skirt over maroon spandex pants. On her feet, she sported green sneakers. Their little UC looked like a bohemian art student.

Romano turned to his partner and asked, "Hey Summers, is she married? "

Alex smiled as he answered, in his usual smooth, unhurried way, "Easy boy, I believe that she is and to a Brooklyn Detective no less. Don't even think about doing anything foolish."

"Hell no. I'm not suicidal or planning anything. I just wanted to share a funny thought."

"And that is?"

"Well, if she was married, and now I know that she is, what a lucky guy her husband is. He can never know who will be waiting for him when he gets home, blonde, red head, student or tough sexy harlot. It must keep their marriage young and exciting."

"Yeah, I see what you mean, a different woman every day and never an adulterous moment. Wow, I think I'm jealous."

Romano grinned as he answered, "Me too." Then pointing, he said, "She just entered the ' Library', do we follow or what? "

"We what!"

"What?" Mike was feeling silly.

"We wait until she gives us a script of a seller or says nothing and comes out. The Sarge gives us lots of freedom as to how we work out here, but he's unhappy when an investigator goes inside one of these buildings."

"What's he afraid of? He can't see us and he gives up control?"

"Marv says that it can get messy in if a perp struggles, especially a closed environment like that. He's especially nervous around here; too many big shots and political muscle. The powers that be want us down here, but we were ordered to keep a low profile whenever possible. So we wait. Maybe Gus and 'The Kids' will have some luck."

The two partners spent what they perceived to be thirty to forty minutes trying to act inconspicuous on the outskirts of the park, yet still keeping a close eye on the library entrance.

Alex had smoked a half dozen cigarettes and Mike had lit his second cigar. They began discussing the possibility of going inside to look for their UC, when she walked out and gave a 'no buy' signal by stopping on the sidewalk and tugging at her clothing.

Al spoke, "Well partner, pulling on her clothes like that means, no action, no buy or anything. We'll just have to follow her. Let's go."

They got into motion and their portable crackled. "Golfer here, our UC reports a buy approximately one hundred feet north of the chess tables. We have one under; number two is a white male, five ten, brown windbreaker and blue jeans and was last seen walking deep into the park towards the fountain area."

"Shit Alex, I never heard the UC tell of the buy. I feel stupid. Will our girl go right out and try another buy?"

"Not to worry Mikey, neither did I. Let's go find this guy." Quickly, Al added, "Look across the street at her, she just pulled on her ear. That means that she heard the last transmission."

"What'll she do now?" Realizing the obvious answer, Mike commented, "What a shithead I am, she'll wait. Right?"

"Of course; she's smart and knows enough to monitor the radio and wait until she's sure that we're ready before having another go at it."

Just as Alex finished his sentence, B-B Eyes transmitted, "All MSN units, we have two under and a third perp is running towards the fountain. That perp is the hand to hand and wearing a blue windbreaker. Someone get him."

Mike heard the now familiar thumping sounds start to resonate in his mind after the words "Get him." He went into archangel mode and shouted to his partner, "Here we go!" The two men took off at a trot towards the center of the park.

"There he is Al, over on the far side. I'll run straight at him, you swing left."

As they ran towards their target, the man swung a dog leg to the left and headed for the 5th Avenue arch, shoving his way past people, toppling a few as he ran.

Mike pulled his radio from his bag and double stepped, slowing him down, as he switched over to the Division channel. He keyed the radio and shouted, "Central be advised that plainclothes narcotics officers are in a foot pursuit of a male wearing a blue windbreaker. He's, going north out of Washington Square Park and heading towards 5th Avenue. Please alert all units in the vicinity."

"Ten four Narcotics," was the response.

Then the dispatcher sounded a piercing, attention getting alert signal, before transmitting the chase.

Their quarry shot under the arch and continued north on 5th Avenue. As Mike and Al pursued him, they heard the clop, clackety-clop-clop and knew it signaled the approach of a mounted cop.

The horseman pulled alongside the running pair shouting, "I heard the call for assistance. Where's the bad guy?"

Mike, the Bulldog, was getting winded, yet true to his nickname, he would never give up. He kept running and shouted, "Blue jacket, the man out front if you can."

"Don't worry," the cop shouted over the clatter of his mount's hooves. The horse was flipping his head and dancing in anticipation of the impending action.

The Mountie shouted, "Me and Duke never lost a race yet. We'll get him," he shouted as he led his steed away at a quick cantor.

Alex yelled, "Hey, we got the Lone Ranger on our side, stay with him, Kemosahbee."

Mike added, "HI Yo Silver, away."

Both men then followed the rider, running with renewed energy.

The blue jacketed runner was now at least twenty yards in front of the pursuing cops and turned left on 8th Street towards 6th Avenue.

As Alex and Mike reached the corner of 8th , the partners shouted encouragement to the mounted cop. He was riding in the center of the street and continually drawing closer to his quarry under a cacophony of sound.

They were amazed and puzzled watched the rider clatter about twenty or thirty feet beyond the runner then swing his horse to the left and stop. He had placed his mount dead still across the sidewalk.

When the runner saw the mounted cop pass him, he instinctively glanced back at his shouting pursers.

That's when it happened. The runner slammed into the side of the horse with all the kinetic energy he had left as the mounted cop was just sitting atop his animal with his arms folded across his chest and smiling.

When the man broadsided the animal, the beast moved slightly forward and side stepped, pinning the man against the brick wall of a building.

To Alex and Mike, when they finally caught up, it appeared that the horse was actually holding the fleeing felon upright. The runner looked exhausted, but was still able to curse in two languages.

"We are, Officers Burns and Duke at your service gentlemen," remarked the grinning horseman. "We'll release him when you're ready. Catch your breath first."

Exhausted, the foot cops could only nod in agreement. Alex and Mike, still puffing like freight trains; took a full minute before they were able to thank the mounted man for his help.

Mike spoke first, "Hey, whuuufff, uhhuff, Burns, does Duke always act like he's doing now, auffhh, pinning the perp against a wall if one's available?"

Burns grinned, "Well, he's a cop too and doesn't like to see a bad guy get away. The real truth is, I control him with leg signals, like I'm doing now. That allows my hands to be free in case the perp starts to reach for a weapon or strikes my partner, Duke. If that happens, he gets lumps from me; if Duke doesn't bite him first."

Alex finally caught his breath and commented, "Wow, he's better than my bulldog partner here. But, then again, I haven't seen him bite anyone,,,yet. I'm sure he could and would, given the right circumstances."

Alex had his cuffs out as he spoke to Mike, "Turn him around partner and let's cuff him." It was done in seconds.

As Burns and his animal backed away, he stated, "Gentlemen, it was a real pleasure. We were bored to death a few minutes ago and I think Duke enjoyed it more than I did." At that point, Duke pawed the sidewalk twice and whinnied.

Almost in unison, Al and Mike patted Duke's neck and said, "Thanks big guy, but we gotta go."

The runner, now uncomfortable in the handcuffs as Mike held them, was complaining in Spanish prompting a rebuttal in his native tongue from Alex. He remained quiet.

The mounted man said, "Before you guys go, I need your names and command for my memo to record an assist."

Summers answered, "Alex Veranos and Mike Romano, Manhattan South Narcotics and thanks again guys."

Mike spun the prisoner around and ordered, "Okay. Let's go pushed their collar in the direction of the garage holding area. The reluctant runner had to be nudged along. Summers and Bulldog were just waiting for their collar to cause a fuss. As payment for their earlier physical exhaustion, they felt that a personality adjustment would be justified. He sensed it and didn't give them a chance.

As they brought their perp to the holding area inside the garage, Marvin quipped, "Nice run guys, "I heard about the horse race, seems like the horse won. Is that man the runner?"

Mike already had two collars. Alex answered. "Oh, man, could he run, but we got him. He's less than happy and mumbled all the way here. Something about we cheated and used a horse to get him."

"Okay Summers, toss him and put everything you find into a property envelope. We'll take care of it all later."

Marvin continued, "I want to try for a couple of more collars, B-B and Golfer are already out there. Big John and I can handle this, so hustle back out."

Looking at the collared men sitting against the wall, Marvin made a rare joke. "And if anyone tries something, we'll just call the horse back."

An hour later, Marvin's team was back in at the command processing seven arrests. Romano had two, Veranos, three and Lansky, two.

As the arresting officers were vouchering their gathered contraband, Alice and Gus were vouchering their buys and distributing copies of their vouchers to the appropriate officers.

The buy money found on the defendants was matched by Marvin to the corresponding photo copies. Pictures of the corresponding bills were initialed by the recovering cop and co-signed by Sergeant Marvin Landers.

All other contraband and money was then vouchered and included in the arrest packages that the processing officers would bring down with them to Central Booking and court. The actual bills that were used and unspent money was returned to Sergeant Landers, to be used again the next time the team went out.

Buy money usually lasted two to three months because most of it was recovered from the actual hand to hand dealers. When the supply of bills got low, the team Sergeant would request more money from his supervisor. The module Lieutenant, in turn would replenish his own stash from Headquarters.

As Mike was just finishing his share of paperwork for the day's arrests, he remembered that Sergeant Landers had commanded his presence about Alice's "accidental" drug buy earlier in the day. He was still nervous about it. After assurances from Alex, he decided to tough it out as he entered Marvin's office.

"Sarge, here's all my paperwork for today. I need sign offs. Earlier you said you wanted to see me about the buy Alice made on against kite today."

Marvin spent what seemed to be several minutes reviewing Mike's paperwork before speaking. Without looking up, he spoke with an icy tone.

"Romano, everything seems in order here."

"Thanks Sarge."

Still fussing with the papers on his desk, he continued, "Now about that buy today, tell me again how it went down."

Mike took a few seconds to review his thoughts and began, "Well Sarge, we were checking the location because I had a kite on it and .... ending with, "Alice had seen us and told us that she just bought heroin. That's how it went down."

He felt guilty as he thought, *I take great pride in always telling the truth, no matter what. I told Marvin the truth about the buy, and justified the part about first setting it up. Guess it wasn't actually a lie.* "Any problem Sarge?" he asked.

"No." After a pause, he added, "Romano, when you get a chance, let me know and we'll go out and have Alice make another buy. Next time with Gus along, so we can get the store layout and you can write it up for your first warrant. Lieutenant Tazzara and I already spoke about it."

"Wow. Thanks Sarge."

Seems that he likes you, but remember, I'm still your immediate supervisor, so do not deviate from standard office procedure. Got it?"

Mike felt that there was a definite veiled threat in Marvin's tone as he spoke and thought, *well screw him. I've been through this crap before. Saint Michael never lets me down. You and The Pumpkin can both kiss my fuzzy Italian ass.*

After lodging their collars in Central Booking, Alex and Mike proceeded to the offices of the Special Narcotics Section of the District Attorney's to prepare their affidavits for court arraignment. While sitting around waiting for their turn, Mike told Alex about the conversation he had with Marvin and what he had perceived as a veiled threat.

Al's chuckled and said, "Just remember brother, a bulldog never backs down. Relax. I think he's afraid of you. Sometimes I think that he got his training at Sister Mary Agnes Academy School for Girls."

CHAPTER FIFTEEN

When the investigative teams were not catching, it was normal office procedure that the tour was considered a "down day". It was then set aside for checking kites, running down leads or following any other orders that the team supervisor might issue.

Sergeant Marvin had informed his team that he was authorizing a down day and they should use the time to work on their kites. He added a foot note, obviously for Mike's benefit; that Alice and Gus would be available if needed, but only after conferring with him.

Summers and Bulldog were happy to have an easy day after the last two weeks. The bond between Alex and Mike grew stronger with each passing day. They had processed over a dozen arrests each. They had put in lots of overtime and were tired.

Grabbing some kites, including the "accidental" Alice buy location, they signed out a car, camera, two radios, and left the office. Standard office procedure was to stay on the division frequency while engaged in such work. The TAC channels or point to point was for team communications only when working a set.

During that first day of their third set of tours as partners, while they were out checking kite locations, their radio crackled with an emergency type alert.

The result of that transmission brought two of Marvin's Kids, B-B and Golfer, a hairline away from meeting Alex Summers, the combat seasoned, US Marine. If they had known that the lanyard/drawstring of Alex's shoulder bag was made from human hair, it's doubtful they would have found humor in a near tragic incident.

Summers and Bulldog were sitting in their car, sorting through their kites, when Division Radio chirped an alert.

"Be advised a bearded male Hispanic just assaulted a plainclothes officer on Broome Street between Allen and Orchard. He was last seen on Orchard Street. Use caution, the subject is considered armed and dangerous."

Mike instantly went into hunt and fetch mode. "Al, that's half a block from us, we should go."

Alex already had the car door open and answered, "On it partner, you take one side of Orchard, and I'll take the other and stay in sight." He locked the car's doors, added, "And be careful."

The team tried to remain inconspicuous as they walked quickly towards Broome Street.

They had advanced about twenty five yards when Mike heard, "Freeze, you son of a bitch, or you're dead."

The challenge came from the opposite side of the street where Alex should have been.

Romano instantly drew his weapon and sought cover behind some parked cars. Cautiously peering through the vehicles' windows, he was shocked at what he saw. There was Alex, with looking stunned with his hands in the air. He was standing frozen on the opposite sidewalk and trying to say something. Two men were pointing guns at him. Every time he tried to say something, he was shouted at by two men.

Mike silently prayed, *please Saint Michael, let them be cops.*

Knowing that his partner was in a volatile situation, Mike pulled his shield out from inside his shirt and held it high above his head with his left hand as he stood up. In his right hand was his own weapon.

"Police. Easy guys. I'm on the Job, That's my partner, he's a cop too."

Summers almost felt safe when he heard Mike shout, and true to his sense of humor, asked, "What took you so long partner? Ask these guys if I can put my hands down will you? My arms are getting tired."

Seeing the two men begin to lower their weapons, Mike tried to lighten the gravity of what could have been tragic with humor. "Guys, I know he's not pretty, but he's my partner and my brother, so go easy."

It took a full of minute for the usual cop to cop ritualistic verbal identification exchanges before everyone holstered their firearms. It took the fact that Mike and Alex also held police portables that crackled with calls from the Central Dispatcher, before the cops from the City Wide Anti-Crime Unit completely relaxed.

Initially, they offered no apology for their actions or their negligence for not notifying the local command that they were in the area. Department protocol required it. Nor did they give Mike and Alex any explanation as to why they were in the area .

Several less than courteous tense moments later, apparently deciding that they had spent enough of their valuable time with the two Narco cops, they reluctantly apologized to Alex and unceremoniously took their leave.

Before Mike and Alex could even discuss the incident among themselves, The Twins and Big John approached.

The Twins were smiling, and to his credit, Big John looked solemn. B-B Eyes was chuckling and The Golfer was snickering. Seeing the expression on Al's face wiped the grin from B-B's face.

The Golfer, yuppie jerk that he was said, "Wow guys , that was something, we were coming up the block behind you just as they stopped you; Mike didn't even see us. That was some show. Were you scared Al?"

Mike spoke first, "You shitheads didn't see me because I was watching my partner from behind cover."

Alex held his shoulder bag by the braided rope, looked directly at The Twins, and cold as Death himself said, "If you two dumb fuck assholes ever giggle in my direction again, I'll be adding some length to this. Clear?"

The look on their faces said it all, they didn't know what he was talking about, but weren't staying around to find out. They didn't want to know what he meant either. Turning away, without making a sound, like frightened children running from the Boogeyman, they quickly walked away.

Mike asked, "Alex, you don't like them very much. Even before this little mishap. What's up? You're always so easy going. I know there's a tough Marine inside, but you even scared the crap out of me just now."

Softly he answered, "No, my brother, I don't like them. I don't respect them either. Let's put some distance between us and them before I regress back to the old days in Asia."

***

The team spent the next two hours checking locations and recording their observations. To help pass time, they chatted about everything and anything except the earlier incident. It was never discussed again by either of them during their entire partnership. However it was mentioned once.

Before returning to the office, the team stopped off at the bodega where Mike was introduced to his first Cubano sandwich and brought two more back to the office. They sat in the far corner of the team room, to avoid some of the usual cop humor that followed when anyone brought tasty smelling food into the room. While they ate, they also caught up on their paperwork concerning their morning observations.

The confrontation with City Wide was not recorded anywhere.

Naturally, cops are always cops, and their sense of humor is, at times different than the norm. As usual, when one of them put their sandwich down to write or shuffle papers, someone would slide up to them and reach for it saying, "Hey if you're not gonna finish that, I'll take it."

Alex, with his humor returned after being back in the office for elected himself spokesman and replied, "Hey, leave my lunch alone, I have a gun." He changed it to "My partner has a gun," if Mike's lunch was the target.

None of the potential thieves ever responded, because it was only friendly ribbing, or maybe because Alex never raised his voice, yet could always muster up a look, that could, when necessary, turn water into ice.

The Kids never entered the team room because they were probably still washing out their underwear from their earlier encounter with Alex. Two days later Marvin's Kids collared up. The Bobbsey Twins were the official arresting officers for the day. It was Department policy that arrests were brought to the station house in the precinct of occurrence for booking and processing. That particular day, Marvin's team was working in the confines of the Tenth Precinct.

Alice and Gus disappeared to an inner office, away from the arrestees, along with Marvin, to check buy money and evidence. Marvin previously ordered 'The Kids' to process the six collars upstairs and strip search them as was the policy in Narcotics.

There was an attractive female hand to hand in the mix. The arrest processing room was not very big and Big John asked Mike and Al to please keep the female separate from the other detainees while they waited for a female officer from the command to come upstairs and conduct a strip search.

There was a chance for retribution.

While they waited, Mike had been focusing his attention on the female. They were holding the female in the unoccupied tiny ladies room. After they checked the room, they had her stand just inside the door, propped it open and kept her close to them. He and his partner stood in the corridor for several minutes. Romano almost jumped for joy as he quietly told his partner, "Summers, I think there's an opportunity for payback here for the gunpoint incident."

"What the hell are you talking about?"

Romano grinned. "When the lady cop gets here, stay close and enjoy."

Alex just shook his head and was about to speak as a very young, uniformed female officer nervously walked up to them. She was carrying a pair of latex gloves.

"Detectives, the desk officer sent me up here to conduct a strip search for you. Is that her? Please be help me out, I've never done this before. What do I do?"

Alex saw Mike grinning and said, "Partner, you seem to have a feeling about this, so instruct the officer."

"Well," Mike began after looking at her name tag, "Officer Brady, take her into the ladies room and put her into a stall so she can't move around the room too much. Then put the gloves on and have her remove one article of clothing at a time, hand it to you so you can carefully and slowly check it for contraband. You're looking for needles or whatever. If clean, put it aside, and then order her to remove another article of clothing and give it you for checking.

Mike sensed that her nerves were on edge and emphasized his next instruction, "When she's completely naked, make her squat to be sure nothing drops to the floor. Then make her jump up and down and squat again. When you're satisfied that she's not hiding anything, give back her clothes and let her get dressed. Then bring her and hand her off for processing."

The prankster in him was enjoying her shocked expression.

"What if I find something?"

Alex answered, "Just shout out to us, Found something, and say what it is. Then safely put it aside and continue." We'll be right outside the door or the arresting officer will be. We would come in but there are no doors on the stalls, so to preserve her dignity, we'll follow regulations and stay outside and keep the door closed. We'll only go inside if you call us or we hear fighting. Okay? "

The young cop indicated that she understood by nodding her head and saying, "Okay, let's get this over with." while guiding the perp inside and waited for the door to be released.

Once the door closed, Romano again spoke softly to his partner. "Stay close, in case the kid needs you, I think she's a he! I'm going for the Twins," and rushed off.

Quickly entering the arrest processing room, Mike looked directly at B-B Eyes and asked, "Can you or Golfer come and stand by the ladies room, we have a rookie conducting a strip search on the hand to hand girl and I have to use the head. I got the runs. Summer's there alone." Without waiting for an answer, he quickly turned to leave the room .

Mike Clinton was almost contrite as he asked, "There's nobody else?"

Mike replied, "Can you go, she's your collar, or send Golfer?"

B-B frowned, said nothing. Reluctantly, obviously nervous being alone with Summers, sent Golfer.

Alex was just beginning to enjoy Lansky's uneasiness, when he heard a loud thud accompanied by loud screeching. It sounded like the rookie, "Holy shit, you're a guy! You bastards knew it and set me up. Get your asses in here!!"

Alex held back his laughter and managed, "Your collar, deal with it," he said as he followed Lansky into the bathroom.

Romano, had remained behind some cabinets in the corridor for the last few minutes, stepped out wearing an ear to ear grin.

As he entered the ladies room behind his partner, he expressed disbelief at what he saw with, "Nobody would have guessed that she was a guy. We were all totally fooled."

Little Brady stopped screeching as the three male cops entered, but could only point at the last stall.

Lansky, the spineless shit, screeched to a halt just short of looking in and asked, "Just what the hell is going on?"

Trying to regain her composure, Brady managed to say, "She's a he and his pecker is the biggest I've ever seen. You guys knew it before you sent me in here."

All three cops looked into the stall and there was the perpetrator naked as the day he was born, standing with his hands on his narrow hips, above which were perfect breasts. The pièce de résistance was a male appendage of epic proportions, hanging between his legs.

"What's the matter big bad cops? You never saw a transsexual before? Lock me up for drugs, but don't make fun of me, you shits!"

Brady felt obligated to continue, "I thought he was a girl the whole time and tried not to look at her, him, too much. Everything was fine until I said, "Turn around and squat. That's when it dropped and he turned to face me all at the same time. I lost it and called for you bastards."

As the Golfer began apologizing to the little cop, Al and Mike looked at each other and shrugged their shoulders. Al said, "Well, Bulldog, looks like all's well that ends well. We can go now, he's got this. Lesson learned I'd say."

As they left the floor, Summers and Bulldog enjoyed a High Five. Later, back in the office, they signed out and left for their respective homes. They would be on a swing and scheduled to return to work in two days at 0930 hours.

Mike replayed the incident in his mind all the way home and laughed as he drove. He felt that Lansky had it coming for thinking the Alex gunpoint incident was funny and thanked Providence for giving him the opportunity. *Sometimes even an avenging angel needs a laugh.*

CHAPTER SIXTEEN

It was during his two day swing that Romano, divorced father of two children, attempted to contact his ex-wife. He had hopes of having some quality time together with his children, daughter, Annie and son, Donny, once again, he was disappointed.

When Mike dialed his old phone number, he was shocked to hear a recording; "We're sorry but the number you dialed is no longer a working number."

Over the last few months, due to his emersion in his work, Mike had little time to stay in touch with his former family, except to send child support checks to his former residence.

Confused and getting angry he placed a call to his old friend Rocco Banducci, the paramour of his former sister-in-law, Kelly. Letting the phone ring at least a dozen times before hanging up, Mike became vengeful and agitated and began to pace the room.

Fighting an almost uncontrollable urge to call his former mother-in-law's house, he reached for his nerve tonic, the ever present bottle of Dewars that was in his fridge. Grabbing a glass and pouring three fingers, neat, he lit a cigar and settled into his lounge chair in an effort to calm down and contemplate what to do next.

After smoking the entire cigar down to a stub with the assistance of three servings of his amber nerve tonic and three more attempts to reach Rocco, Romano settled down. He to realized, that the best time to reach Rocco was in the morning. After calling for a pizza to be delivered, he took a quick shower and then phoned Alex and told him what had happened.

As usual, Alex Veranos counseled his partner in his soft easy way. "Now Mikey, I'm that sure your kids are fine and from what you tell me, your lawyer will know where they are. Rest easy until the morning."

"Al, I even called a friend who used to date my sister- in-law. He wasn't home. I'm so pissed off that I can't think. Can I call you again if I have too?"

"Sure Mikey I'm here if you need me. Later."

"Thanks. There's the doorbell. Gotta go."

Even though he felt somewhat better after his conversation with Alex, Mike was still nerved up and after consuming two slices of pizza, he settled into his lounge chair with a large Dewars, clicked on a mundane TV show and finally dozed off.

***

Romano awoke the following morning and first thing, jumped into the shower to wash off the effects of his rather fitful night's sleep. Throwing on some loose clothes, he padded in bare feet into the kitchen to make some coffee. The wall clock indicated that it was 9:00 a.m.

He paced his apartment as the coffee brewed while running several scenarios in his mind regarding his ex-wife and what to do about his kids. He surprised himself by some of his solutions that came to mind. There were a few that violated his personal moral code.

In an effort to occupy his thoughts, Mike turned on the TV news. By 10:15, Romano reached for his telephone and dialed Rocco Banducci's number. On the third ring a voice answered, "Yes, how can I help you?"

Recognizing the voice at once, he smiled at the caution Banducci always exhibited when on telephones. "Hi, my friend, it's Mike Romano. I can't reach my kids and was wondering if you knew where they are?"

As usual, Rocco's answer was guarded. "Yeah, Betty moved out of state, to New Jersey I believe, and sold your house. My suggestion is, contact your divorce attorney and have him supply you with any information that you need. Now, aside from that, how are you doing? Fine I hope?"

Rocco's vague answer took him by surprise. "Huh, ah, yeah, I'm good. Recently got transferred to a new command and I'm doing okay. You?"

"Fine my friend, I gotta go. Call whenever you feel the need. If I'm not here leave a message with my wife and I'll eventually get it. Take care." Promptly, he hung up.

Mike ran the quick conversation over in his mind. *Rocco wasn't his usual friendly self. There was something in his voice. He's always cautious on the phone, but always asks if we should meet and have a conversation, even if I don't bring it up first. What was that, I'll eventually get a message left with my wife if I'm not home? He must be nervous of someone watching him and is too close for comfort. Well, he's right, I should call Arthur. He's my attorney and he'll know what to do.*

"Mr. Slotnick, It's Mike Romano," he began and without waiting for a reply, continued, "I can't find my ex-wife and my kids. What happened? Where are they? "

Slotnick, hearing the tense urgency in Mike's voice answered, "Easy my friend. I was just about to contact you when you called. Just yesterday, I received a written communication from her attorney alerting me to the fact that she sold the house and moved herself and the children to New Jersey. I have the new address; you'll need it for visitation and child support. I can give it to you now and mail you a confirmation letter."

After a second to sort out his emotions, Mike answered, "No, it's fine, just mail it to me. That'll be fine; I'm too busy now anyway. Thanks."

"Mike, my friend, you are not the first person to be treated like this after a divorce. You'll be fine, better than you think. Please don't miss any payments and if you receive any other communications or have questions, call anytime. Be well my friend."

"Thanks Arthur, that helps a little. Thanks and if anything happens, I will call. Bye."

Romano was not a happy camper for the balance of his two day swing and tried not to think about the problem by keeping busy. He went grocery shopping and did his laundry. As a last resort, he even took a ride to Queens and visited Alex and his mom, Anita, for several hours.

While at his partner's house, he recalled the first time that he had met Anita, a vibrant little petite woman, less than five feet tall. She reminded him of the fondness he had for his paternal grandmother. Mike had searched his memory and remembered the Spanish word for Grandma, Abuela. He began calling her Abuelita, little grandma. Each time he used the name; she giggled and blessed him in her native tongue.

As usual, whenever he visited, she cooked. While they dined on a lovingly prepared from scratch, delicious meal of Aroz con Pollo (rice and chicken) Mike forgot his immediate personal problems. After the meal, as Anita tidied up, the two men relaxed outside to talk. Mike was receptive to his partner's gentle counseling. It helped him decide what his next move should be.

On the drive back to Staten Island, Mike made a hard decision. First, he would contact his attorney and immediately obtain the address to send his child support checks. Second, he would forgo any attempt at seeing them. He didn't need the aggravation. Third he would block from his mind the difficulty of not seeing his children. Mike physically shook at his decision.

He felt that there would be time plenty time for that later when they were no longer influenced and controlled by their mother. Knowing that he might not have made a correct decision, even feeling some guilt, he was determined to deal with it and go on with his life.

For the entire second day of his swing, Mike was morose and contemplative, never leaving his apartment.

With the television on, more than an occasional imbibing of Dewars, and several cigars, he spent the entire time in his recliner remembering the old Betty, the woman that he fell in love with. It pained him to remember how he exerted every effort to always conduct himself honorably and her ultimate infidelity.

Mike, in his bitter sweet recounting of his past romances also fondly remembered his feelings for his 'almost' relationship with Lenore. He silently chastised himself for waiting too long to announce feelings to the luncheonette owner.

Mike 'Bulldog' Romano then had an epiphany type realization; he would avoid involvement with women, at least in the near future.

It made sense. After all, he had his work and knew that he could immerse himself in it completely. The Job was certainly an alluring mistress and it could ease the pain of setbacks in his personal life. Steeling his resolve, Mike anxiously anticipated his next day back at work.

CHAPTER SEVENTEEN

When they returned from their swing, Romano and Veranos met at the sign in desk at 8:45 a.m. Each man carried two coffee containers. As if rehearsed, they simultaneously asked, "Is one of those for me?"

Mike answered first, "Yeah, the one with the sugar in it. I'm sweet enough and take mine black as you know."

Holding out the appropriate container towards his partner, Al quipped, "How nice of you. Are you still single? I might marry you myself, here's yours."

"You'd have to shave first," Mike chuckled as he spoke. "No way, stay single."

Alex squinted and asked, "Your humor's back. How are you after our little talk?"

"Not to worry Al, I'll adapt and overcome. After all, you christened me Bulldog and I've got to live up to that."

"Good! Let's go across the hall and see what our fearful leader has for us today. I've been thinking, if there's nothing pressing, maybe we can get another buy for your warrant at the variety store on Houston street where Alice made her accidental buy."

Sergeant Landers had nothing pressing for his team that particular day. Bulldog and Summers requested him to allow Alice return to the location and attempt another buy with Gus as her ghost.

Their request was granted and twenty minutes later Mike and Alex were sitting in a car close to the subject location. Marvin and Big John, were also nearby in a second auto. Department regulations required that a supervisor will verify every UC's final buy.

By noon, having successfully made another buy and the two UC's were sitting with Mike and Al and sketching a floor plan of the interior of the store. They would need it for the warrant application, the pre-execution tactical meeting and again at the actual time of entry.

Marvin signed off on the vouchered drugs that Alice bought and then turned to Alex and ordered, "Alex, show Romano how to prepare a request for a warrant. If everything is in order when you're done, I'll sign off on it and you guys can make a quick run to deliver it for write up. Get cracking but no overtime on this, we all sign out at 1800 hours today."

***

"Wow, Mikey, I'm surprised that he's going for it with only two buys in. But that's terrific because you're gonna get your feet wet so much sooner."

"Yeah Alex, let's get it done. Show me what I have to do."

Alex sat down with one of his previously executed warrant folders and handed it to his partner. "Mikey, you're a sharp guy, look this over while I run out to get us two burgers. Do you want yours with all the trimmings?"

"Thanks and yes, I sure do." Romano opened the old file as Alex left.

The folder was assembled in the OCCB prescribed format. On the right side of the folder was everything noting action taken by the investigators and the UC. Included on the right side was a copy of the warrant. On the left were any vouchers, photos of buy money, properly marked and initialed. Also on that side was a sketch of the subject location and vouchers that were the result of the warrant.

Everything contained in the folder was fastened at the top using a two hole four inch stainless steel slide fastener. On the outside of the folder, in addition to all other case info was the warrant number and date of its execution.

Alex returned within twenty minutes and walked up behind his partner. "Wow, Mikey, you're a quick study. It appears that you're almost done sorting all of your paperwork and separating it."

"Hey Al, yeah, I think so. Give me my lunch and I'll eat it while you check my work. If you're not finished when I am, then I'll eat your burger too." He laughed and continued, "But I'll be nice and leave you the fries."

Alex gave Mike's paperwork the once over and said, "Put the fasteners in, it's nice work, especially for the first time. You follow instructions well, and didn't try to touch my lunch."

Both men enjoyed the tit for tat chiding between them, especially Alex, "Nice to see you back in the groove Bulldog. Let's get Marvin to approve this and then we'll go downtown and have fun. Wait until you meet the chick that does the warrants."

Sergeant Landers took half an hour to review the application before approving it and handing everything to Mike.

"Okay guys, go down to Special Narcotics on Worth Street and drop this off at the warrants office. Alex knows where the room is." Turning to Alex, he added, "Don't come back late. No overtime."

Outside Mike asked, "Alex, what the hell is up his ass? Is he always like that?"

"Mikey, who knows? Maybe one of the twins wanted to do a warrant too and we got to him first. I don't give a shit.

Mike had been to the fourth floor offices of Special Narcotics many times to meet with Assistant District Attorneys to formally prepare affidavits for court following an arrest. This time was different. He was applying of a search warrant and his senses tingled.

In the elevator, Mike watched as Alex pushed the fifth floor button and asked, "What's on five Al? I thought that everything was on the fourth floor."

"The fifth floor has the important stuff; our own Tech Services, Investigative ADA's and the man in charge, the Narcotics Special Prosecutor. The warrant office is also there. After we drop off your application, I'll give you a tour."

Exiting the elevator Romano noticed that security was tighter. There were no metal detectors on the fourth floor. After identifying themselves to the cop at the security desk and were waved through, Alex led Mike to room 525. Finding the door wide open, Alex announced, "Warrant request," and walked in followed by his partner.

Sitting to the right of the doorway was a blonde female in street clothes. She was totally engrossed in what she was doing, looking up at a computer monitor as she typed. Mike stood still; trying to remember if he had ever met her before. Without looking up from her work, the blonde said, "That sounds like Alex Veranos, from South Narcotics. Is that you Al?"

"Indeed it is. Sophie, meet my new partner, Mike Romano, here for his first warrant. Mike, meet Detective Sophia Kaminski."

Sophia stopped what she was typing and turned to look at Mike. With a big grin she spoke quickly, "Well, well. Look who's here. I remember you. Have you been sleeping well lately?"

She then turned to Alex, "Alex, watch him. If he's bored, he'll fall asleep and that could get you hurt on the street."

"Not to worry Sophie, he's the best partner I ever had. He's sharp, quick and tenacious. I call him the Bulldog."

Kaminski pushed her chair back and stood, extending her hand toward Mike, "Well, nice to meet you Michael Bulldog. If Alex likes you, you must be worth the effort, so I like you. Take care of my friend Alex."

Mike took her extended hand. Laughing heartily, she added, "As long as you don't sleep on the job, Welcome to Narcotics."

Mike, remembering their first encounter, came back with, "I'll never nod off around Alex, he's not boring like some of the people I've met."

"Alex," she responded, "Now I know why you call him Bulldog, he never backs down. Just make sure you have a tight hold on the leash. I think we're all gonna be good friends."

Reaching for the folder in Mike's hand she asked, "Okay Romano, what do you have?"

Sophie, removed everything, skimmed and through the warrant application. She then returned the folder to Mike.

"Well, Romano, I still have the one I'm working on now and one in the wings. So, I think that sometime in the morning I'll be ready to submit yours to a judge for signing."

Mike came back with, "Is that considered good time?"

Ignoring his question, Sophie asked him, "Do you want me to call you when it's ready or send it up to you through channels? Channels, usually adds a day. It's your choice."

The two men exchanged glances and Alex nodded his head at Mike to indicate that it was his choice to make.

"Well Sophie, It's my first warrant and I'd like to get it done, so call me and we'll come down to pick it up. Thanks."

"Fine, leave your papers on the PAA's (Police Administrative Aide) desk for log in. Okay, fellas now I have work to do. Excuse me."

"Alright Mikey, on with the tour." Alex led his partner through the corridors, past office upon office, assigned to the ADA's, there were eighteen in all.

Alex explained that it was these ADA's, that took turns manning the complaint room downstairs, where the court affidavits are written for all narcotics arrests in Manhattan. All the ADA's have their actual office on the 5th floor. There's a similar group in each borough. There were a few ADA's assigned in an investigative capacity to work with cops on heavy cases.

As they walked, Mike asked, "Alex, where's Tech Services? I'd like to see their office."

"You didn't see the sign on their door when we left Sophie?" he asked.

Mike quickly answered, "No, I didn't." To cover his embarrassment he added, "I was thinking about the first day I met Sophie. I never told you that I nodded out during her lecture on warrants, resulting in a friendly exchange like the one we had today. I knew we would eventually meet again and get along but it certainly was an unexpected surprise to see her today."

"Well, we'll go back to Tech and ask for a quick tour," and turned around to retrace their steps.

"By the way Mikey, I know her a long time and I can tell you that she likes you, you know."

Romano didn't respond.

Within seconds, Alex announced, "Here we are, the office of Tech Services. "

The door to the office was closed; Alex knocked and went in, followed by Mike. Inside were three men, one at a desk and two others who were hunched down over something at a work counter.

Alex knew two of the men. He pointed to the man seated at the desk, then to the men working at the counter.

"Hey, guys, this is my partner Mike Romano. Mike, meet Barry. Jim, meet Mike. Mike, Jim. Sorry I don't know your work partner."

Jim responded as he waved his arm, "Alex, nice to see you, guys, this is Neil", indicating the man next to him.

Barry stood up and offered his hand to Alex and Mike respectively, "Al, Mike."

The two men working at the counter returned to what they were doing without a word.

Barry asked, "Guess you're a new man in Narcotics and would like our dollar tour?"

"Sure would," answered Mike. "Are you guys part of TARU?" (Technical Assistance Response Unit)

"No, we're not. We have all our own equipment, even an OP van with a periscope and cameras to film operations when necessary. We can even film at night. It's kept in the garage under One PP."

Mike's eyes kept trying to peer into the adjoining room. Barry caught it and offered, "Like to see some of what we do? Come on, let's go."

Barry led the partners into the room that was filled with rows of electronic equipment. There were reel to reel tape machines, what looked like equalizers, various radio receiving sets, cassette players, earphones, cameras, and a myriad of carry bags and cases.

Mike asked, "Is this where the equipment came from for the video they show the new narcotics people during orientation? "

"I don't know what they showed you when you attended, but sometimes they use our stuff. I know they show you how a dog works, and that's from Special Services in Flushing Meadows."

Mike was getting worked up. "Yeah the dog was cool. Hey, they showed us a night-scope. You have one here?"

"Yup and we also have infra-red cameras like they do and so does TARU. Our work is confined to narcotics cases and because of the danger and secrecy involved, we prefer to do our own work and use our own equipment, there's less chance of a leak. You know, the less people involved, the tighter the security. It's very rare that we have to use equipment or personnel from outside of Narcotics."

Barry gave Mike a quick demonstration of what some of the equipment did and after fifteen minutes, he announced that he had to get back to his desk.

Alex and Mike thanked him, and left to return to their office. First they stopped to say goodbye to Sophie. She was so busy that she just waved them off.

***

Back at the office, Mike and Alex stopped in Marvin's office and informed him that the warrant was submitted. They expected a phone call to pick it up the next day, sometime in the morning.

As usual, Marvin exercised his authority by telling Mike, "Well, Romano, you can pick it up if we have nothing going on otherwise you have them send it through Department Mail. Got it?"

"Got it Sarge. Not a problem. Just anxious to get my first warrant that's all and execute it is all."

"It'll happen sometime during this set. Don't worry, you'll break your cherry", was Landers' curt response.

Alex saw his partner's jaw tighten at the rudeness exhibited by Landers. Quickly he and put his hand against the small of Romano's back, saying, "Come out into the team room Mikey, I want to show you something."

Outside in the hallway, Mike said, "Thanks for moving me out of there. He's beginning to really twist my shorts. I Wish he was just a cop like me, then I could adjust his personality."

"Mikey, don't let him get to you. Just wait it out. Someday he'll step on his tongue, or his Johnson and fall on his ass. It's only a matter of time. Remember, he's still your immediate supervisor."

"Yeah, Okay. Let's go do our DARS and talk about Marvin's Kids until it's sign out time."

He thought, *those wings are beating in my head again but there's no danger...........or is there. Alex is right, I got to calm down.*

Romano wasn't completely satisfied with the outcome of that quick conversation and continued, "Hey Alex, I seem to remember that in the warrant in the model case file you gave me to follow, had a seventy two hour limitation for serving it. First, I'd like to know if that's on all warrants and second, do you think Landers will let mine expire?"

With a smile on his face and a soft voice, Alex said, "Wow, Mikey, you got that all out in one breath. Kind of wired up are we?"

"Well, yeah and I want to get a warrant under my belt but it seems to me that Sergeant Marvin is against it."

"Do you believe in re-incarnation Mikey? " Mike was surprised at the question, "No why?" "Well, if it exists, you were definitely a bulldog in your first life. You always keep your teeth in and never let go."

Mike threw up his hands at the remark.

Alex chuckled at his own joke and continued.

"No, my friend, he will not try to allow the warrant to expire, to answer the second question first. He'll get his ass from the Taz on up. It would be hard to explain because he signed off on it. Once he signs off on a warrant, it becomes his responsibility to get it done."

"Good. Maybe he'll show some balls and do it quickly."

"Now, back to the first question. The signing judge can put a time limit on the warrant if he chooses. No-knock warrants are given to us because it is assumed that if we used regular warrants and announced our intent to search, evidence could possibly be destroyed."

Mike nodded slightly to indicate that he understood.

Al continued, "The judges put a time limit on it because of the nature of the business, dealers move their stash and change locations often. That's another reason we make a confirmation buy just before busting into a place. Any other questions you want to ask?"

"Just one, do you think the lieutenant will go with us when we work the warrant, especially because it's my first one?"

Al smiled his knowing smile as he answered, "He's an old friend of yours, he likes you and he sees the tension between you and Marvin, what do you think?"

"Yeah, that wasn't too smart of me, of course he will."

"Mikey, Taz likes the action, especially breaking down doors. He usually goes with us on all our warrants. You're his man, so of course he'll be there."

Finished their logs and paperwork, Al and Mike went to sign out. As they leaned over the sign out log, Sergeant Landers walked in.

"My team. Be in at 1000 hours tomorrow, we have orders to work the New York Public Library at lunchtime."

CHAPTER EIGHTEEN

Mike signed in at 1000 hours the next day as ordered. Anxiously, the first thing he did after signing in was to check the incoming mail basket in anticipation that his warrant had been signed and returned to the office.

Not finding it, he sought out his Lieutenant, Lou Tazzara and asked, "Loo, by any chance did my warrant come in? Did you see or hear anything about it?"

"Well, good morning to you too Mike. What, no hello or anything?"

"Sorry, it's my first warrant and I'm a little anxious. Good morning Boss."

Lou chuckled then continued, "Mike, you've always been a good cop and so far your work here is just what I expected from you. But, let me give you a little advice, follow orders to the letter. This detail is not like patrol, there's constant monitoring. The bosses even watch us supervisors, so don't push too hard."

"Boss?"

"You have a terrific partner in Veranos, absorb some of his style and learn to go more slowly. Now get out of here and go to work. I'll watch for your warrant and we will execute it together. You're dismissed kiddo."

Alex also had a habit of arriving early and brought in some breakfast. They were sitting in the team room munching on egg sandwiches and slurping coffee by 10:00.

"So that's what he told me Al." Romano attempted to keep a straight face as he continued, "Oh, by the way, he also said you're a terrible partner."

With an ear to ear grin, Summers answered, "I'm sure he did, but you're stuck with me. By the way, what makes you think that I'm happy with you as a partner?"

Both men chuckled like little boys.

"Hey Al, do you have any kites for the Library? I've never seen any."

"No. The area is usually covered from upstairs by Sergeant Lopez, one of Lieutenant Aloe's teams, why?"

"Well, yesterday Marvin said we're going to work the library today. I was wondering about it because, he said that orders came from downtown. Why us, if it's another team's area? "

"Mikey, you think too much. Besides if its orders, then he'll probably have his Kids catch the collars so they can look good downtown. It shouldn't matter to you because you want to work your warrant as soon as it comes in. Right?"

"Yeah, if it comes today, I hope we can do it tomorrow. I'm excited, it being my first one and all."

"Cool it, here comes two of the children."

In walked Lansky, "The Golfer" and "B-B Eyes" Clinton. They were followed by "Big John" O' Leary. To his credit, only O'Leary actually spoke to Mike and Alex.

"Hello, good morning guys."

The other two only nodded at Alex from several feet away and mumbled something unintelligible to Mike.

When the entire team, including the two UC's, had gathered, Marvin briefed the assembly.

"Okay team, here's what we have for today. The Chief (of OCCB) informed me that he wants collars and summonses today, in and around the public areas of the Fifth Avenue Library."

Muffled comments were heard from the group.

"Even though it's Lieutenant Aloe's area, we got the job because we're hardly ever there and shouldn't be made as cops. The catchers today are Clinton, Lansky and Big John." He paused to draw a breath before continuing.

"You will all assist each other when making collars and you all are expected to issue marijuana summonses for smoking. Make sure you each have a summons book and plenty of envelopes for each team. I'll be inside the   park attendant's building that's on the 43rd Street side. There's an empty equipment cage in there that we can use for collars. When we're filled up, I'll call for a wagon to transport our collars. Does anyone have any questions, comments or by some miracle any suggestions? "

Receiving no comments, Marvin continued, "Be low key today. We don't want to cause any undue notice to our operation. That strong request reportedly comes right from the Mayor's Office."

Moans and groans erupted from the team.

"Knock it off. The Office of Public Relations claims that they will announce the arrests and summonses after the fact in an effort to scare off future dealers."

Looking directly at Mike, he asked, "Does everyone understand the meaning of low key?"

Mike turned to his partner and whispered, "Al back when I worked in Conditions on the Apple, we were in that park almost every day.   We made dozens of arrests there every month. We the unit even made the cover of New York Magazine. I may come up dry because there's always the possibility that someone may recognize me. Anyway, you can't stop that crap. Are they kidding?"

"Go easy Bulldog that was a long time ago. Those people must have moved on by now, so let's be quiet and just do our job," Alex cautioned.

"Yeah, you're right. Every time you call me Bulldog, I know you're just busting my balls and it's time to take a step back. Is that why you do it? "

Al smiled as he asked, "It works, doesn't it?"

Twenty minutes later, the teams gathered inside the W. 43rd street garage of the New York Telephone Company as ordered by Landers and received their final instructions.

The entire team hit Bryant Park by 12:10 p. m. Within five minutes, the first arrest, a single hand to hand, was brought to Landers. It was for sale of Placidyls, also known on the street as Jelly Beans, or Pickles because of their dark green color. Even he was surprised.

As Mike and Al walked the park watching for the UC's and waiting to jump into arrest mode, they passed a small group of men; some sitting, a few standing. As the team strode by, one of them spoke in a thick Caribbean accent, "Hello, Officer Romano. Do you remember me at all? "

Mike instantly tensed his muscles and readied himself for any defensive move that he might have to take.

Al sensed his partner's reaction, rather than saw it, and whirled to face the speaker.

"Easy maan, there be no need to get jumpy. Your friend taught me a life lesson and I wished to say thank you, is all. We all be good maan." The speaker was smiling broadly. Even his eyes were smiling.

Seeing the man's full face, Mike's adrenalin rush subsided. I was Stanley Livingston, an old collar, crescent scar and all. Stanley was extending his hand toward Mike.

As he accepted the friendly handshake, Mike quickly assessed the other men in the group.

Alex keyed in on the hesitation and took a small step to the rear and prepared himself to assist his partner if necessary.

Romano, either by instinct or divine whisper, felt no threat and took Stanley's hand and paraphrased a famous literary quote, "How nice to see you. Mr. Livingston, I presume."

Stanley only continued pumping Mike's hand and smiling.

"You're not back to your old trade are you?"

"No, Sir. I be telling the boys about the copper that arrested me one time in this here park when I be with my wife and child and his promise to do it again and you did."

Livingston proudly pointed to the bright pink crescent scar, on the side of his face. It seemed alive against his dark brown skin.

After taking a breath, he continued, "Giving me this little reminder proves that sometimes people be keeping their promises, especially bobz (police) that do good work for da Maker of All Things."

Stanley waved his arm at the group as he added, "Gentleman, this be the fine poooliceman what put me on da straight and narrow. Sometimes a person need to be hit upon da head to be wake up and do da right ting. Dis man be using a building." He touched his scar and pointed across 42nd Street to The Grace building. There was laughter in his voice.

Alex began to relax a little and listened as the conversation continued.

Mike asked, "Stanley, if you're not into you old business, just what are you doing now to support your family now and just what are you doing in the park?"

Stanley shook his long dread locks, smiled broadly. "Well, I'm here wit me friends on a lunch break. We be working nearby designing ads and tings for an agency. It be fine satisfying work and we all make music at nighttime and weekends."

Surprised, Mike asked, "Stanley, you have a band?"

"For sure Mister Romano. The band name be, Quintessence. We all be from Saint Lucia or Saint Vincent and make fine music wit true island flavor. We be known downtown in The Village."

Mike shook Stanley's hand again. Secretly he was pleased with himself that by arresting him twice, he put Stanley on a righteous path.

" Stanley, I sincerely wish you well and good luck. Stay straight because I'm always out here."

"I be knowing that Sir."

Mike then excused himself so that he and Al could continue on with their work.

Alex asked, "Just what the hell was that all about partner? You obviously locked him up, twice, and he likes you. How did you put that bright pink scar on his face?"

"Yeah, let me tell you about it." Mike went on to give his partner an abridged explanation about first arresting Stanley, his wife and baby. The second time when Stanley ran and the building that got in Stanley's way, giving him the scar.

"That's an interesting story Mikey. Maybe you should have a new nickname, The Shoemaker, a mender of souls."

"No way Mr. Summers, Bulldog is fine and it fits my personality. Beside, is makes me sound tougher than I really am."

***

Alice and Gus made five buys between them that afternoon, netting seven arrests that were split among Marvin's Kids. The team wrote a total of eight summonses for marijuana smoking, Alex and Mike responsible for five of them. Landers was pleased.

The best part of Romano's day was when the arrestees were transported to the precinct of arrest, Midtown South. After bringing the arrestees into the Arrest Processing room to begin assisting with processing of the collars. He ran into some of his old Conditions Team members.

From the doorway came, "Is that the infamous Mike Romano that I see?"

The voice was vaguely familiar to Mike and he turned quickly, expecting to see someone that he knew. It was a very old friend, someone he knew as a teenager and former Conditions team member, Jimmy Carter.

"My God, it is Mike Romano," Jimmy gleefully stated as Mike turned to face him. "I thought you fell off from the face of the earth when you went to Staten Island. The whole team did."

All Mike could get out was, "Great to see you Jim. You still look the same as when we were kids."

Jim continued, "Michael, they were talking about your challenging exchange with the old CO, Bryan the day you left. The whole damn command thought that he would harpoon you and use his weight to ruin your career. How did you escape that? "

"It's a long story Jimmy and this is not the time to get into it. Enough to say that I got lucky and wound up in Narcotics, working in Manhattan South and it's all good."

Even when we were kids, you always had a way to come out on top. Do you remember when you dated the old Police Commissioner's daughter?"

"What about it?"

"Remember when he used to have you followed sometimes?"

"Yeah, but I never did anything wrong Then after the make out party in your basement, we moved away so it didn't matter. Maybe we can reminisce over a couple of beers sometime soon. Say hello to the guys for me.

Sorry to cut you short but we have lots to do."

Jimmy walked up to Mike and gave him a man hug. "Sure thing Mike. I still owe you for saving my ass that day on 43rd Street. If you weren't there, no telling what would have happened. The drinks are on me."

While Mike and Alex were assisting their team members, four other members of his old team stopped into the processing room to say hello.

Romano especially enjoyed how Marvin's Kids paid close attention each time one of his old working buddies happily greeted him. Mike felt that the Kids only tolerated him and he thought that perhaps they were curious as to why he was so well liked.

Mike reveled in the fact that his old friends made such a fuss over his entry into OCCB Narcotics. He knew that Pride was one the Seven Deadly Sins, but he couldn't help himself. Mike justified his emotions by thinking; *I'm not a prideful person. I'm only taking pride in my accomplishments.*

As they worked, Alex could not hold his curiosity in check, and returned to Carter's last remark. "Mikey, when we're alone on the drive back to the office, you gotta tell me about that saving Jimmy's life thing."

Slightly embarrassed, Mike answered, "Sure Al, later. But it was nothing. Not like your stuff, you're a Marine and a Nam vet. You carry a bag that has human hair as part of it and all."

"Brother, something tells me that you're no slouch either. Don't forget, I'm a trained investigator."

"Yeah, yeah," Mike responded laughingly to cover his embarrassment.

Three hours later, after dropping some of the collars off at Central Booking, the team of Bulldog and Summers were driving back to their office.

"So my brother, Mikey, please tell me about the Jimmy incident."

"Well back when I was in the MTS Conditions, we were working the Library steps and Bryant Park and Jimmy made a collar. He had the guy up against a van when............as they passed me, I capped a few rounds and............."

"Bulldog in action. I see."

Mike tried to make light of the story. "It was stupid and I got lucky."

"No such thing my friend, you acted like a true warrior. Your team member was in trouble, you took action and both of you were none the worse for wear."

"It wasn't much. I couldn't think of anything else."

"That's what it's all about. Real warriors don't always have to act dramatically, they just have to act and you did. You truly are my brother."

Mike's face flushed with embarrassment but he also had a grin as wide as Park Avenue. The two men did indeed love each other as brothers.

***

When Mike signed in the following day, he was called to Sergeant Lander's office.

"Romano, your warrant has been delivered. It arrived yesterday while we were in Bryant Park. We have three days, the rest of this set to execute it."

"When can we do it? Tomorrow?"

"After the collars yesterday, I want our team to take a down day and be here at 0900 hours tomorrow for a pre-warrant tactical plan. I'll notify the rest of the team. We'll review again the following day just before we go out. You and Al go out and do some kites. Oh, by the way, no more accidental buys, got it? "

"Ten-four Sarge. You got it, and thanks."

Mike sought out his partner; grabbed some kites and they spent the day checking locations. Their day was filled with anticipatory conversation about the upcoming warrant. Mike's was like a kid expecting the arrival of Santa Claus. The rest of their tour was routine and uneventful. Both men signed out on time.

CHAPTER NINETEEN

Mike Romano was in 'Bulldog' mode when he signed in the day of his first warrant execution. In his head he heard the throughmp - throughmp of large birdlike wings.

Next to him was Alex Summers, "Well, Mike my boy, today's the day, your first warrant. Good luck, but then, hard work produces its own luck. Let's get 'em."

As Alice and Gus entered the room followed by the other team members, the partners settled into two chairs on the far side of the table. As usual, Alice carried one of her many huge shoulder bags. Gus was dressed in scruffy clothing, looking like a street panhandler. It was his warrant ghosting getup. The Golfer and B-B Eyes took positions as far away as possible from Alex and Mike.

Sergeant Landers filed in, followed by Lieutenant Tazzara who announced, "I will be going with you people today to personally see how this team works with the new man."

Gesturing towards Mike in the rear of the room, he continued, "Mike Romano, Mr. Bulldog, is our newest team member and this will be his first warrant execution and by coincidence, it's also his warrant."

The Taz then turned to Sergeant Landers, "Marvin, it's your meeting, let's see how it's going to go down."

Marvin began, "Okay team, yesterday it was a quick review, now we do it for real. On the chalkboard I drew a sketch of our target location. It's a variety store on the corner of E.4th Street and Avenue D. The number 355 is displayed on the front door. Romano and Alex will be team one, Clinton and Lansky are team two, myself. Big John and the lieutenant are team three. Teams one and two will take a position on either side of the store."

Moving up to the chalkboard, Marvin continued as he drew, "Team one will park somewhere close, not more than fifty yards away on E.4th. Team two will park within the same distance on Ave D. Team three will also be on Ave D, but, south of E.4th and in position to watch the action if possible. When the UC's enter the location, Alice will attempt to make a confirmatory buy. If the buy is made, the g h o s t will signal us and if h e can, give u s additional intelligence as to who is in the store and whatever else he can tell us. Nobody moves until I say so. Naturally, I'll carry the warrant. Any questions?"

Mike asked, "Sarge, who does the searching?"

"In this case since it's your warrant, you do Romano. Summers records everything and you will not pick up anything unless I'm there to witness it. Got that?"

Mike didn't like his tone but answered, "Ten-four Sarge."

Taz chimed in with a humorous, "And of course, I'm there for support and backup."

Sergeant Landers cut the meeting short. "Okay team, gather your equipment, get to the location and setup as instructed. Stay out of sight and use point to point Tac 5 only for communication."

Mike walked up to the lieutenant and quietly asked, "Loo, we don't need a ram because the place is opened for business but should we carry one anyway or something else?"

"Michael, that's one of the things I like about you. You're always thinking. Carry a ram and a couple of pry bars in your trunk. You never know."

"Will do Boss, see you on the set." Within fifteen minutes, all teams were in position. Alice and Gus had entered the target location.

To Mike Romano, now in his Bulldog persona, it seemed like an hour passed before he heard Gus on the radio.

"Alice made a confirmation buy. Be advised that the hand to hand is wearing a blue tee shirt and took the package from an unknown who came out of a trap door in the floor behind the sales counter. There are also three additional males loitering in the shop. We have no further info on the basement. UC's will remain close by if needed."

Marvin responded, " Ten-Four. UC. Remain out of sight and stay in your vehicle."

"Ten Four"

Marvin barked, "Okay team quickly now, let's go, and be careful. GO, NOW!!"

***

All team cars pulled up to the shop at once. Doors swung open and erupted with officers carrying drawn weapons who ran into the store. The occupants froze as a chorus shouted, "Police."

To make sure that everyone understood, Alex added, "Policia, usted no mueve."

The interior of the shop was organized chaos for a few seconds. Taz grabbed someone on his left who was trying to get to the door.

"Hey, go easy. I got nothing to do about here. I only come to here for to buy something. Go easy, ju gonna broken my arm," he shouted in accented English.

Big John and Marvin pushed a man against some shelving on the back wall directly opposite the entrance door causing some items to topple to the floor as they quickly snapped on handcuffs.

Alex swung to his right and charged around the sales counter that was to the right of the entrance to grab the man in the blue tee shirt.

Mike pointed his weapon and shouted, "Hands, put your hands above your head."

As the man raised his hands, he stomped his foot down twice on the floor. Instantly, Mike vaulted the counter and knocked Blue Shirt against the window mullion. The man moaned in pain.

Alex quickly snatched the guy and forcefully held him while Mike regained his own balance and then rapidly applied his Smith and Wesson stainless steel charm bracelets.

B-B Eyes and The Golfer went to assist the lieutenant who ordered, "Take this jerk, pat him down and keep him away from the door."

As they took charge of the prisoner Tazzara, barked, "Somebody lock the front door, this place is closed. Nobody gets in or out unless I say so."

Once again feeling as if his authority was pushed aside, Marvin ordered the obvious, "Golfer, help get all these guys to the back of the store and you, Summers, pat your man down and then move him to the rear. Mike, just what the hell prompted that jump over the counter? You ain't on TV you know."

Mike thought, *you piece of crap. Am I wood? Use nicknames, you bastard.* He then quickly answered with annoyance in his voice.

"Hey Sarge, didn't you hear the UC? There's a trap door. By stamping his feet, he was obviously signaling someone downstairs and I just wanted to stop him."

Before Marvin could answer, Mike issued a challenge, "Any problem with that?"

The lieutenant heard the exchange and decided to intercede, "Bulldog, Sarge, stop. I'm in charge here so stop that crap and let's get downstairs. Summers, ask that shithead what's down there!"

Alex questioned the man. Blue Shirt explained that he lived downstairs with his family. He had a wife and small child and they're down there now.

Alex informed the lieutenant.

Blue Shirt continued in accented English, "Please they did nothing, don't hurt them. Let me say to them you are the police and will not harm them and we are coming down. Please, Patrones, por favor."

The Lieutenant told him he could make his announcement but not without permission. Marvin took a long look at the trap door. When fully opened, it could rest against a counter that was under the window.

Finally he bent down and slowly began to lift it. Standing to the side of the opening, No Balls Marvin opened the door only about six inches and stopped, tapping the blue shirt guy on the shoulder and said, "Go ahead tell her."

Blue Shirt first looked at Taz, realizing that he was obviously the man in charge and waited for a head nod.

He began in English, "Cara Mia, we have police in the store. We are coming down." In Spanish he added, "Ir al la parte posterior y cerrar la caja fuerte."

Alex pushed him away hard and shouted, "He just told her to move to the back and close the safe. They're hiding something."

He then turned his head towards his trusted partner, silently stating that he was ready and had Mike's back.

"Mike nodded and said, "Let's go," while bumping against Marvin and fully opening the door.

The sergeant took a step back as Mike squatted down on the first step, pointed his firearm, and peered into the area below.

With false bravado, Marvin ordered, "Let's go Summers."

Mike moved quickly yet cautiously, descending into the basement, with Alex right behind him.

True to his nervous and spineless nature, Marvin never moved and was pushed aside by the lieutenant as he also began his descent.

***

Down of the basement floor, partners stood, back and tactfully paused to look around. Cowering in the far corner, Alex saw a female holding a small boy and began to softly assure her in Spanish that they meant her no harm but not to move or it could get messy.

Mike took stock of the basement itself. It was one very large room, similar in layout to a typical loft; sleeping area, eating area and what must of served as a living room/sitting area with a decrepit stand-alone dry bar. In all, the furniture in the place could have been in any lower middle class apartment in the city. On the far side was a partially opened door to what appeared to be a bathroom.

"Summers," Mike called out. "Ask her if anyone is in the bathroom."

Her reply was, "No." The Taz checked to make sure.

Marvin had been watching from the steps. Finally he mustered enough nerve to go down. Clinton accompanied him.

Looking at Marvin with disdain, Taz ordered, "B-B, take the woman and the kid upstairs and, call for a female patrol officer to search her. Leave them there and come back down. I'm sure Big John and Golfer can watch four handcuffed prisoners and a kid.

As Clinton began to ascend, Taz added, "Bring lots of property envelopes and a Polaroid, if one of you dip shits remembered to bring one."

It was obvious that Tazzara didn't respect The Kids much either.

Sergeant Landers took the slight pause the action to once again bolster his fragile ego and disrespect Mike by not following his Lieutenant's use of nicknames.

"Okay, Romano, we'll start on the left side, where the woman stood and swing right down along the wall. Keep going and spiral towards the center of the room in our search. Summers will record what and where you pick something up and you reach for nothing unless I'm standing next to you. Remember even though the lieutenant is here, I still have to sign off on it all. Alright, let's get cracking."

Mike was pissed at the use of his actual name and thought about letting Marvin know about it. He held his tongue.

Slowly and methodically, Romano began to check every nook and cranny and piece of furniture he came upon, followed by Alex and Marvin. The Taz, a hands on guy, also got involved by turning over the bed and two sofas, finding nothing.

The payoff occurred when Mike got to the dry bar. Under the well-worn counter top was a shelf that contained several glassines of what was believed to be heroin. They were stamped, Black Ice and bound in bundles of five with rubber bands. Along with those packets were at least fifty unmarked glassines of white powder and an old cigar box containing vials filled with what appeared to be rock cocaine, commonly known as crack.

Romano couldn't contain his enthusiasm and not knowing how close Landers was, without looking up, shouted, "Loo, Sarge, we hit paydirt, come on over here!"

Marvin said, "No need to shout. I'm right behind you and don't pick up anything until we photograph it first. Where the hell is Clinton?"

Mike smiled inside. *He's a real jerk. He just called B-B Eyes by his real name too. Maybe he's just stupid.*

B-B Eyes had been following the lieutenant and hustled over like a butler at the sound of the master's bell, "I'm here Boss, here's the camera."

After photographing the three items in and marking the back of the Polaroid's, Marvin ordered, "Alright, Romano, initial the photos, and count the stuff."

Marvin was on a roll and also included Alex in his disrespect, by using his real name. "Alex, write down everything; what, where it was found, time and today's date. You will carefully put the stuff in properly labeled envelopes, no mistakes. Take your time. When you're finished, we'll continue."

Mike had reached his tolerance limit. "Okay Landers."

Alex just grunted.

While Romano was still processing Marvin's slightly nasty tone, he dropped a couple of crack vials and bent down to get them. They had rolled under a string mounted makeshift curtain that covered the entire area below the shelf. Becoming irritated with Marvin's disrespect towards himself and Alex, he wanted to return the favor. Without waiting for Marvin's approval, Mike slid the curtain aside.

Under the shelf and hidden by the curtain was a small safe.

"Holy crap, I found the safe that the guy was talking about."

Again without approval, he attempted to move it. It didn't budge, "Probably bolted to the floor," he remarked aloud.

Marvin, obviously upset, replied, "Romano, don't touch it. Finish what you're doing. I'm the supervisor and I'll tell you what to do."

Taz, anticipating an explosion of the tension between Mike and Marvin jumped in and again reminded his subordinates, "Hey, once again, let me remind you two dickheads that I'm the ranking officer here and I'll tell both of you what to do. I have the final say here!!"

Mike and Al both snapped their heads in the direction of the lieutenant's voice and saw Sergeant Lander's face. He looked like a small boy who had just been chastised by one of his parents. They shared a smile and continued what they were doing. Neither of them had any special fondness for Landers and his egotistical style.

The Taz asked, "Bulldog, is it open? "

Mike responded, "Don't know Boss, the door's closed. Do you want me to try it? "

"Not yet kid, first finish what you're doing."

Marvin, with lost dignity, kept his back to his supervisor and spent the next few minutes closely monitoring the partners' actions.

After all the shelf evidence was 'bagged and tagged', Marvin asked, "Lieutenant, are we read y to open it?"

The burly Taz answered, "Photo first Sarge. Then you go ahead Bulldog and try to open the door."

Sergeant Landers photographed the safe, and then said, "Attempt to open it please." It was locked.

Taz ordered, "B-B Eyes, go bring the woman down here. Only her and do not say anything to her but first find out if she was searched. If yes, bring her down. If she wasn't get it done. We'll wait. Tell the girl cop to stay upstairs."

Like a small child seeking approval, Clinton scrambled upstairs to fetch her.

The woman came down the steps slowly. She was having a hard time with her balance because she was rear cuffed. Clinton had to assist her. Once clear of the steps, she looked around and mumbled something in Spanish.

Landers, finally catching on to the error he was making, asked, "What did she say Summers?"

"She's complaining about the mess and wants to know why she was brought down here."

The Taz asked, "Has she been searched yet?"

B-B Eyes answered, "Yes. Nothing was found and the cop is staying on top."

"Summers, show her the safe and tell her that we need her help to open it. Explain that if she agrees, we might let her stay here with her son tonight."

Alex translated.

"Yes, she can open it and thanks you for your kindness."

"Ask her the combination and write it down along everything else she may say, in English naturally, after you tell us what it was."

As the door swung open, she began sobbing but remained silent. The lieutenant motioned for her to be returned to street level. B-B took her.

Inside the safe was: a shelf that contained several bundles of cash, what appeared to be a kilo of powdered substance and a white metal, matte finished .380 Colt Mustang semi-auto pistol. On the floor of the safe was loose cash, assorted glassines, a container marked Lactose and a plastic bag containing numerous almond size pieces of what everyone believed was crack cocaine. The shelf and floor of the safe was littered with white powder residue.

Tazzara loudly ordered, "Nobody touch anything without gloves on! Somebody bring some down here forthwith!"

Marvin hurried to the stairway and shouted to Clinton, "B-B, on your way back down, bring some gloves. We'll need several pairs."

To subjugate Sergeant Landers, the Lieutenant ordered, "Marvin, you seem to like the Polaroid. Take multiple pictures of the of the safe's interior."

"Sure thing Lou."

Marvin took two photos, one of the interior and a second shot long enough to show where the safe was in relation to the dry bar. Both photos showed the items that were inside.

Taz then spoke directly to Romano, "Bulldog, get down there and start emptying that thing out. Put the gloves on first. Summers, accurately record everything and identify it. When we get back we'll make copies of the photos, mark each recovered item and label the corresponding pictures too."

Mike had to wait until Clinton returned with some rubber gloves. While he waited, he squatted down and examined the contents of the safe, drawing a bellow from his lieutenant, "I told you not to touch anything, so don't."

"Easy Boss, I'm not deaf, only looking."

"Make sure that's all you're doing. Damn it, learn to follow orders."

Mike turned around to find B-B Eyes grinning as he approached, obviously enjoying what had just flowed from the lieutenant's lips.

Romano reached for a pair of gloves and without a word, pulled them on.

"Ready, now Lieutenant?"

Annoyed at Mike's obvious insolence, he came back with, "Yeah, go and give Summers time to write."

Mike first removed the firearm, handing it to Marvin, who had previously snapped on a pair of gloves. With shaking hands, Landers, clumsily removed the rounds and handed everything off to Alex who recorded the serial number, number of rounds and bagged it. Next he removed the cash bundles. Behind them was an unmarked video cassette.

To nobody in particular Romano commented, "Hey, we've got a video tape here. Maybe it's porn."

Slowly, the tape and the other contents were removed from the safe, tagged and stored in envelopes for transportation.

"That's everything," Mike announced as he prepared to stand.

"Hold on, there's a 718 phone number taped to the back of the door on this thing."

He began to remove it, but froze in response to a bellow from the Taz. The lieutenant was pissed and forgot protocol.

"Leave the damn thing alone Romano. I'm the Lieutenant and I say what we take. It's probably worthless. Leave it!"

Alex bent close to Mike's ear and whispered, "I used to work in the Bronx and that's a Bronx number. When he's not looking, grab it and hand it to me. Once I bag and tag it, it'll become evidence; even The Taz won't screw with it then. I trust your instincts my brother."

Mike thought that he was hearing noises in his head again, but it was the Golfer came stomping noisily down the steps catching everyone's attention.

He asked, "The prisoners are getting restless. Are we ready? "

"Now", Alex whispered.

In one smooth motion, Mike removed the phone number and handed it off to his partner.

Marvin asked, "We're done, right Lou?"

Still upset, Taz asked, "Romano, Alex, are we ready to go?"

Mike answered, "Yeah, Boss. We're good to go."

Alex turned his back toward the lieutenant, "Yeah Boss, just marking my last envelope. To maintain a proper chain of evidence, Alex and Mike carried all the recovered evidence back to the office in their shoulder bags. The prisoners were herded into cars and transported back to the station house for processing.

Romano thought he heard the celebratory fluttering of wings as everyone left the set.

CHAPTER TWENTY

When he returned to the office after serving his first warrant, Mike felt like a conquering hero; a Roman Centurion from the distant past.

Bulldog and Summers entered the team room to begin the lengthy task of counting drugs and money, initialing everything, then preparing vouchers for the lot. Included with the recovered money was everything from the store's cash register and personal pocket money from each perp. The case against them would be a shoo-in because Alice's buy money was recovered from the cash drawer.

Lieutenant Tazzara announced, "Alright, nice work people. Sergeant Landers will stay here with you. The prisoners are being processed downstairs in the command's arrest room. I'll be in my office to verify everything after it's all completed and first signed by Sergeant Landers. There's a lot to do, so get to work."

It took the team over two hours to properly mark, record and voucher, all the recovered contraband from the variety store.

Landers ordered that of Lansky and Clinton bring the firearm and narcotics directly to the 5th floor lab in the Police Academy.

With hardly a glance, Marvin mechanically put his signature on everything put before him, reports, vouchers and lab requests. He never even asked about the video tape.

Mike had not handed in the voucher for the video tape.

Romano asked, "Sarge, I have a funny feeling about that tape and want to look at it before we seal it up. What do you think? We should check it, after all it was in a safe and probably isn't just a family video unless it's porn."

With some annoyance Marvin agreed. "Yeah, okay. Once you get into something, you never let go. That nickname, Bulldog, sure fits. Why can't you be like your partner? Remain quiet and follow orders"

Alex chuckled at that comment drawing a quick disapproving glance from the Sergeant.

"Alright, stop breaking my balls. Go to the desk and sign for the key to the ICO 's office (Integrity Control Officer, usually a Lieutenant) and roll out the VCR and TV. I'll meet you and Alex there in five. Remember, regulations state that prisoners must to be brought to Central Booking within two hours of arrest and we're way over that limit now. We're not spending too much time on that tape."

Alex quietly asked, "Mikey, are the angels talking to you again? You look as fired up as a Roman Candle about to pop on the Fourth of July."

"I don't know what it is Al. Maybe they are. This is a have to. Let's go watch the damn thing and see what it gives us."

***

Mike and Al were ready when Marvin walked in.

"The Lieutenant is on the telephone with One PP and they say not to wait. Let's get started Romano"

Mike turned on the TV and slipped the cassette into the player. As the video began, it looked like an innocent gathering of friends or family, all males. As first they saw nothing special. About one minute into the video, one of the men was recognized as the hand to hand they had arrested at the store.

"Holy shit, it's him," Mike shouted.

"Yeah. Shut up. Let's see what we have here before you get all worked up." Marvin spit the words out.

Alex cautioned, "Easy guys. Let's watch."

The men were next seen climbing into cars and waving goodbye to unknown persons who were out of view. At first the tape resembled a travel video. There were highway shots of the approach to Washington Bridge, followed by views along Route 80 in New Jersey, ending at Teterboro Airport. Then it got interesting.

As the video continued, it showed those same men boarding a Lear Jet at the airport. The aircraft's tail markings were clearly visible. The tape flashed twice, then the cops watched a short segment of the plane obviously flying above the clouds.

After a few short seconds of blank tape, the disembarking of several men in fancy flowered shirts and exchanging several suitcases came into view. Behind them could be seen the word Miami atop a hanger. All of the men appeared to be Hispanic.

Alex commented to nobody in particular, "Damn it, there's no sound on this thing."

No one else spoke as the video progressed. Apparently the plane had been airborne because the screen showed some of the men inside the plane's cabin, and then panned to a window. They were landing in a different airport. It looked small and might have been private, except for a small well-worn sign that read, "Welcome to Cabo Rojo."

"Holy shit, that's in south eastern Puerto Rico", Alex shouted, several decibels above his normal speech.

Mike lost it and felt the need to erupt, "Damn, they're all drug dealers."

Sergeant Landers ordered, "Stop the tape and go get the Lieutenant. Do it, shake your ass!"

Mike pushed the stop button as Alex rose to get Tazzara.

Landers continued, "It seems that you may have gotten lucky with this one and you were just assigned to this office. You're a stubborn bastard, but lucky."

Romano wanted to argue with his supervisor, but remained silent. *You're an ass. You're just jealous. You have the rank, but I'm the better cop.*

In less than a minute, The Taz, followed by Alex, rushed into the room. "Marvin, Summers, said that your hand to hand guy and some other men are flying around looking like major dealers and it's on the recovered tape. Let's see it."

Marvin ordered, "Turn it on again Mike."

As the tape resumed, the next scenes showed the store subject getting off the plane wearing a fancy Hawaiian type shirt, followed by three other similarly attired men. They milled about, apparently waiting for someone.

They were all met by a man, possibly in his mid-thirties. He looked like an advertisement for something, dressed all in white with a Panama Hat on his head. He was a heavy weight because he was flanked by two huge Asian looking men. They appeared to be no nonsense guys and were possibly his bodyguards.

'The Hat' personally greeted each man as he exited the aircraft. The big Asian boys just nodded and looked intimidating as they were introduced.

Tazzara commented, "Now I see why you got all excited. Mikey, your collar is probably meeting with his supplier; but let's just watch."

The tape continued, next showing the interior of what was obviously a club of some type; complete with more men in fancy flowered shirts including some of the men from the previous scenes. Most all of the men appeared to be Hispanic and had girls hanging on them except the hulking Asians. They were seen lurking in the background and watching everyone.

Alex once again commented, "Damn it, there's no sound on this thing."

After another second of blank tape, the next location shown was what appeared to be an expensive residential complex with several out buildings. Everyone seen in the video seemed very happy to be there.

The camera panned to show various buildings and a mixed variety of people. Just before the final scene, the Hat, the obvious host, was shown opening a corrugated carton and removing what looked like a kilo of white powder. The photographer moved forward and showed the stuffed interior of the carton. It was loaded similar product. Then it moved back and panned right and left showing several similar cartons. The taped ended with a longshot showing cartons being loaded into a Lear. For a second, the tail marking was visible.

Taz said, "Holy crap. I think it's the same number as the first plane."

Just before the video went blank, the host was seen handing a video cassette to each man that was in the very first scene, including the variety store collar.

Tazzara spoke, "Look at the dumb bastards; filming their enterprises and handing out copies of it. That jerk in white linen must have the biggest ego in the world; it even eclipses his common sense. Mikey, this shit is gold. Great find."

"Thanks, Lou. I just got lucky."

"Get this tape to Tech Services and have them make two copies. Voucher the original before you go and keep a chain of evidence. When you get the copies, give them both to me. We're going to the Feds and giving them a copy of everything."

"Just waiting for you to view it. I already prepared a voucher for the tape."

Taz then turned to Marvin, "Notify the DEA that we have a live one in custody. They'll probably want to interview him. Get me all the vouchers so I can to sign off on them."

When Taz saw the voucher that listed the cassette tape, he bellowed, "Romano, I told you to leave the damned phone number alone and you took it anyway. Are you fuck'n deaf? "

Mike felt that an answer was necessary, "No Loo, I'm not deaf or stupid for that matter, and don't you be. By your own statement, this stuff is gold."

Tazzara fumed at the insubordination exhibited by Romano. "I'll kick your ass if you ever speak to me like that again and I'll kick you back to uniform too. Got it?"

The volume of the exchange brought Alex to rescue his partner. "Loo, Mike's just excited; he didn't mean anything by it."

Tazzara began to calm down. "He had better not. Are you two guys joined at the hip or what? " His face had softened as he spoke.

"No Boss, we're just a damn good team, that's all."

"Well, teach this Bulldog to take smaller bites and calm down. I hate to have to hurt him."

Mike saw that his lieutenant had mellowed and decided to test the waters. "Hey, Lieutenant, anytime you want to go at it with me, we can go into the station house gym and do it."

Mike knew he was no match for the powerful man and added, "If you can catch me."

The waters were calm and comfortable. Louie Tazzara chuckled and said, "Maybe we will but right now get your ass moving."

Alex and Mike went to do as The Taz ordered.

Once out of earshot, Alex commented, "Mikey, don't screw with Taz. I know you go way back, but he's still the boss and strong as hell."

"Not to worry my friend, it's just an Italian thing. That's the way friends in the old neighborhood interact, we're fine."

***

Copies of all the day's existing paperwork were made, including the four arrest reports. Lou Tazzara had lied. He ordered that Child Services was to be called to place the woman's child for at least one night, until she was arraigned in court.

Marvin confirmed that the DEA was on their way and ordered that a Spanish speaking cop should remain with the prisoners until the DEA arrived to prevent collusion,.

Clinton and Lansky had returned and were ordered to arrange for prisoner transport then stand by. When the interviews were concluded, Big John would accompany them to Central Booking. Then while they logged the prisoners in, he was to deliver the vouchered cash directly to the property room in One PP.

Mike and Alex headed out to make copies of the cassette.

After stopping alongside 25 Worth St, Romano asked, "Alex, are you coming in with me? "

"No my brother, this is your warrant and we don't have a parking permit with us. So, I'll stay with the car. Don't be too long. I'm getting hungry."

Mike grabbed the cassette and went in. Once on the 5th floor, he flashed his ID as he passed the security desk and went right to Sophie's office.

She was just leaving for the day. "Well, if it isn't Mr. Romano, how did your warrant go?"

"I just stopped by to say thanks for getting it signed so quickly. We executed it a few hours ago and scored a winner. There was lots of coke and heroin, along with some crack and a gun recovered." He excitedly left a pregnant pause hanging in the air.

Sophie was sharp and knew there was more. "Heroin, Coke and Crack is not so unusual. Neither is a gun. They all go together, it's expected. How many perps and what else? I'll bet there's something more you have to say."

Mike waited, enjoying the moment before he answered.

"Sophie. You've been on warrant executions, right?"

"Yeah, lots."

"Did you ever get a video of the perpetrator with his supplier showing where he gets his goodies from and who supplies them?"

Her eyes widened, "You're shitting me."

"No. We recovered one. That's why I'm here, to get two copies made. Can Tech Services do it? Now? "

The thumping of those angel wings in his head was enjoyable.

"Sure they can. I was just leaving. Come on, I'll walk you in. Just wait a minute while I sign out and lock up."

Seconds later, Sophie and Mike entered Tech Services. Barry was hunched over a piece of equipment and looked up from his work when he heard their voices.

"Hello again Sophie, and you're Romano, right? "

Sophie answered, "Yes, it is. Mike just executed his first warrant and found something interesting. Tell him about it Mike." She was obviously used to being direct and barking orders.

Mike began by explaining the viewing the video tape back at the South, leaving out very few details.

Sophie couldn't resist, "Likes to talk doesn't he?"

Romano continued his litany and finally got around to the reason for his visit, "Barry could I get two copies of this tape made right now because my lieutenant is waiting.

"Yeah Mike. We can do it on the quick copy deck. It'll take an hour or two depending on the length of the recording. Can you wait for it?"

"I'll come back. My partner is downstairs. It's been a long day and we're hungry. We'll come back and wait if necessary, after we eat."

Sophie dropped her hand on Mike's shoulder and said, "Okay, Romano, I gotta go, so I'll walk you out. Seems like you're getting enough sleep after all."

To maintain a proper chain of evidence, Barry signed the back of Mike's copy of the voucher as receiving the original tape. Stuffing the voucher into his shoulder bag, Romano left the office with Sophie. The two new friends exchanged stupid cop jokes on the way down to the street.

Once on the sidewalk with Alex, Mike said "Listen Sophie, we have time to kill, so before we eat, let us drive you home, it beats the subway and it ain't our gas."

"Are you guys sure?"

Alex replied, "Narco Taxi at you service Miss. Address please?"

" Hope you have change of a hundred."

After dropping Sophie at her place in Stuyvesant Town, the two men went to China Town for a leisurely meal before returning to Barry and picking up their tapes.

When they finally got back to the office, it was almost deserted, except for a team that was getting ready to go out. Even Marvin and Taz had left for the day.

Mike asked, "Alex, what should we do with the tapes and vouchers? I don't want to carry them around and we can't leave them unsecured."

"Well, we can ask the desk officer downstairs to put them in the command's safe for Lieutenant Tazzara to pick up in the morning. We'll leave a note on Taz's desk telling him where they are."

"Great let's do it."

Mike dropped a note on his lieutenant's desk, and both men signed off duty. Once downstairs, Mike and Alex stopped at the Desk and explained what they wanted done The desk officer made a blotter entry for safety and added his signature to the back of Mike's copy of the voucher. Satisfied, the partners left the building.

Tomorrow was going to be a busy day. In what was fast becoming a tradition, the team slapped a high five and went their separate ways.

CHAPTER TWENTY ONE

Mike awoke at 6:00 a.m. the next morning, excited and in a rush to sign in at Narco Court and prepare the affidavits for his warrant collars that would be necessary for the prisoners' arraignment. He was in Manhattan and clocked Worth Street in by 7:30 a.m. Then he signed on with his office by calling in.

Mike smiled as he heard the voice on the other end of the phone. It belonged to Delores Richards, a cute coffee colored Puerto Rican female from upstairs. She was cute as a button and had a better, show stopping derriere than "Fran the Can" from his Police Academy days. Besides her physical attributes, Delores was reported to be an ex-biker who grew up in the tough streets of the South Bronx. It was said that she could hold her own in any situation. Fascinated by people that he assessed as, enjoying and surviving a good scrap, he found her interesting.

"Romano, there's a message from The Taz for you. It reads, 'Don't take all day with those collars. Call me before you leave court and that's an order!'"

"Wow, it sounds serious. Thanks Delores, if you see him, please tell him I'll hurry along. See you."

Mike went directly to the ADA's intake room and logged in. The DAs rarely got there before 8:30 a.m., so he went to visit Sophie.

Her office was locked. Disappointed, he turned to walk away and heard, "Romano, if I knew you were here, I'd have brought you a coffee."

There was Sophie, advancing with what he could only think of as, *a female swagger, yet still looking feminine. That chick reminds me of me, without a male package.* She carried a cup of coffee in her left hand.

"That's fine, we can share yours," he responded.

Sophie unlocked the door, entered and offered him a seat. "Sit", she ordered. "Tell me why you're here. Did you get your tapes yesterday?"

He took the empty chair in front of her desk and sat down across from her.

"Yes, we got the tapes about two hours later. Barry good took care of us."

Sophie rummaged around in her desk and came up with what appeared to be an unused paper cup and put it on her desk. Then she removed the lid on her coffee and was about to share some of her morning beverage before Mike stopped her.

"Hey, Sophie, thanks anyway. I'm good. Besides, I only drink coffee black and I see you're regular."

"Romano, if we're going to be friends, let's agree on something. There's nothing regular about me except my coffee."

I knew that the day we met."

After a short chuckle, Sophie continued, "And I'll bet you're far from regular too."

Mike laughed heartily and answered, "Well, I like to think so."

They sat back and exchanged the usual cop to cop banter, exchanging views on The Job and the bosses.

Romano enjoyed exchanging cop talk with one of the few female friends he had ever made on the job. It was always different, getting a women's point of view.

Forty minutes later, Mike made his excuses. He explained that his boss wanted him back quickly and went to draw up his affidavits.

The ADAs were ready to begin their work day. Because he was the first to sign in, Mike was the first cop interviewed. Two hours later he signed the completed affidavits and was ready to leave. As instructed, just before he signed out of court, he telephoned his lieutenant.

The Taz was in a good mood as he spoke, "Hey Bulldog, you're a pain in the ass but I love you. Even though you didn't follow orders and vouchered that phone number yesterday, I had it checked and you got lucky again."

"How so, Loo?"

"The damn number comes back to the desk of the Bronx Borough President's chauffeur. I don't know why it would be in there but we're gonna find out. Double time back here and we'll have a look at it."

"Sure thing Loo."

"You and Alex are gonna be busy. Move it."

The phone went dead and after clocking out, Mike almost ran out of the building and to his car.

Less than twenty minutes after hanging up the phone, he and Alex were standing in Tazzara's office.

The lieutenant began with, "Now, Romano, you and Veranos are going to take a copy of the warrant, all the vouchers, and the video tape from yesterday to a special prosecutor at 26 Federal Plaza."

"When Boss?"

"Right now. I've already notified our CO and he gives his blessing. You will also inform them as to who the vouchered telephone number comes back to and that our Department will cooperate with them in every possible way."

After a pregnant pause he continued, "Mike, the collars are good but of course you know that our collars are local and OCCB will not pursue the Bronx connection because of politics. The Federal prosecutor can if there's any connection there."

"Okay Boss, but who are we going to see?"

"The special prosecutor is actually an Assistant United States Attorney. Her name is Connie Whitehead and she's expecting both of you. Her office is on the 10th floor. Get moving and good luck. If there's any problem, call me." The partners knew by his tone that the lieutenant wanted no more questions and they were dismissed.

***

It was to be a first for both of them. Neither Alex or Mike ever had contact with a US Attorney regarding a criminal investigation.

Alex did the driving as they talked about what might happen once they met Whitehead. Of paramount concern to them both was the hope that the Feds would keep them in the loop should they actually open a case.

When they were finally ushered into the office of Connie Whitehead, they looked at each other as if to say, "I didn't expect this."

Ms. Whitehead was a tall, blonde woman wearing a white tailored blouse under a sky blue business suit. She appeared to be in her late 40's to early 50's and reeked of a sterile sexuality. She looked more like an actress than a prosecutor.

With practiced formality, Whitehead extended her hand as they approached her desk.

"Good morning gentlemen."

"Ma'am." Each man answered as he introduced himself and returned the handshake.

Whitehead, without missing a beat, continued in a very no nonsense manner, "Your supervisor has informed me as to the reason for this visit. Do you have the video and other material?"

Alex answered first, "Yes ma'am, we do."

"Fine, then will you both please follow me to a conference room please? Some people are waiting for us there and we have a television and video tape player at the ready."

She led them to a conference room several doors down from her office. Once inside, Whitehead indicated that they should take a seat around the oval table. They were alone. The partners took adjoining chairs.

Calmly, she loaded the cassette and turned on the television, just as two men walked in. They wore no suit jackets and only one man had a firearm on his hip.

Whitehead made introductions, pointing to them in turn, "Mike Romano, Alex Veranos, please meet my assistant attorney, James Wagner and my Special Investigator, Paul Sparta; Gentlemen."

Whitehead began with, "I have been informed that officer Romano initiated this case, so please, Mr. Romano tell us all, in your own words what happened before we view the recording."

Mike turned to his partner, "Alex, please stop and correct me if I make any mistakes."

"Will do Buddy, go ahead."

Romano spoke without interruption or even noticeably taking a breath for several minutes ending with ….. and we came down here to meet with you."

Whitehead was all business. "Fine, let's see the tape."

She punched the power button on the player. The TV screen that had been only glowing, sprung to life.

The Special Prosecutor paused the tape only once; asking Mike to identify the man he had arrested, otherwise it ran without interruption. When it was finished, Connie thanked them for bringing the video and all other pertinent material. Moving out of earshot, she had a quick discussion with her assistants.

She then addressed Mike and Alex, "Thank you both for your input and professionalism. We'll take it from here and call you if your assistance is necessary."

To their dismay, for the second time that day, they were unceremoniously dismissed.

Alone in the corridor, Mike asked his partner, "Well, do you think anything will come of that and if it does, will we be notified?"

"Can't say Mikey. Good looking broad, but she sure doesn't waste words."

They were back in Tazzara's office within two hours including travel time.

"Alright guys, what happened?"

"Not much Boss," Mike replied.

"She's all business Boss and doesn't waste words. She didn't even ask us any questions except to have Mike identify his collar in the video."

It was Mike's turn again, "The last thing she said was that her office would call The Department, this office I hope, if they needed us and that was it."

"Okay, I'll notify the Chief, go do something until end of tour. Tomorrow we go back to normal."

The months that followed for Mike and Alex were typical; kites, investigations, some buy and bust and an occasional lecture from Tazzara directed at Mike for failure to follow orders exactly as given.

There was an occasional exchange of personnel between teams, due to vacations and such, bringing closer interaction among the entire office, with the possible exception of Marvin's Kids. They were too shellfish and only worried about themselves and how Marvin took care of them. More importantly, the bond between Alex and Mike grew stronger.

CHAPTER TWENTY TWO

As the months passed since Mike's visit to the Federal Prosecutor's Office, both he and Alex had let the incident slip into the far recesses of their minds. They had forgotten about it and moved on. One afternoon they were called into Tazzara's office.

Taz began in a very friendly manner, "Alex, you're one of the best men in this office, you're quick thinking, bi-lingual and a former Marine like me."

Alex, being a sharp guy thought, *Mike's in court, Taz calls me into his office and begins with a friendly snow job..... What's he want?*

He waited and then it came, "Go upstairs and see Sergeant Ortega. He wants to have a talk with you. It seems that one of his informants developed some good info and they need you. I told them you would be happy to help. Was I wrong?"

Alex, being a good soldier answered as expected,

"Not at all, I'll get right on it," and off he went.

Sergeant Vincent Ortega explained that a member of his team had a registered informant who had developed a strong relationship with a major cocaine dealer in uptown Manhattan on 146th and Broadway. The area, once an up and coming middle class area in the 50's through the late 70's before the latest influx of a heavy minority immigration, had become a haven for drug dealing gangs.

It also had been declared a no man's land for men and women in blue for the past several weeks. The local drug dealing crew had issued a statement that any cops seen within their area would be shot.

Until the Department could determine what they wanted to do while trying to not cause any unrest, all foot patrols in the area were canceled. Patrol cars are being used sparingly and response to any 911 calls are answered by two teams, even sick calls. Reportedly, those orders came directly from City Hall.

Sergeant Ortega wanted to work his information and couldn't use anyone known in the area, nor did he want to use officers from Manhattan North. He felt that because the info came from his CI, he didn't want to give it up.

After conferring with both Lieutenants, Ortega expressed the need for an older UC investigator, bi-lingual and who could think on his feet and adapt to changing conditions. Because the investigation would undoubtedly be dangerous, the most important asset the investigator needed was a solid set of balls and the ability to back it up if necessary.

Lieutenant Lou Tazzara chose Alex Veranos.

Ortega explained, "Alex, when Tazzara told me that he would send you to me for this assignment, I was overjoyed. Your record in this Department and the military is extraordinary. It's my belief that you can pull it off. Here's what we have in mind...."

Alex interrupted with, "Hold on Sarge, who partners up with me?"

"As far as I'm concerned, you can have anyone you choose."

Alex happily responded with, "That's great, go on."

"Our informant told the target that he has a friend who is looking for a new supplier for his trade in the Wall Street area. You and whoever you choose will be introduced to the main player, Carlos Pria and his crew. The perp is a successful middle man as of now and wants to become a supplier."

"After lots of discussion thinking, the   Lieutenants and I, feel that someone who is older than most of our investigators, with some grey in his hair, would get over better. You don't look like a young buck and would pose no threat to the target. Carlos and his crew are notorious and probably responsible for the current threats to cops in the area."

"Our job will be?"

"You'll be   introduced   as Wall Street dealers, looking for a new supplier. Do you feel comfortable doing it? "

"Yeah, but first let me discuss it with my partner, Mike Romano, you know, Bulldog. If he's in, I'm in."

Ortega smiled broadly, "Great, get back to me ASAP. We gotta strike while the iron is hot."

Back downstairs, Tazzara asked, "Alex, how does it sound? You get to play drug dealer and get the bad guys."

"Sounds good to me, Boss. I told him I would get back to him tomorrow. There's something I gotta do first."

"Fine, let me know what you decide."

***

The following morning, when   there was nothing special for do, Alex asked Mike if he wanted to go out and do some kites. B y the tone in Alex's voice, he knew that something important was on his mind, but remained silent.

In their vehicle, Mike asked, "Everything alright Alex, how's Momma? " (his mom was over 80 years old.)

"She's good and says 'Hello to Mikey'. It's about something that Sergeant Ortega asked me to do and I won't do it without you as my partner."

"You look serious, what is it? Do we have to kill someone?"

"Maybe."

"What the hell are you talking about?"

"Ortega wants us to play major Wall Street drug dealers who are out looking for a new supplier. He wants us to work a case uptown on 146th Street and Broadway. They want older guys, so we were asked."

"Yeah, if you're doing it, I'm in. After all, we're partners."

"Hold on, there's more to the story. The target is in what is right now a no cops on patrol zone. City Hall pulled all uniform foot cops because of threats. We'll be in a dangerous situation. Do you still want to do it?"

Mike's grin said it all. The angels were talking to him. "Exciting isn't it? They'll never know what hit 'em."

"Okay partner. I wanted to see you first. I'll tell Taz and Ortega that we'll do it."

***

"What do you mean, I can't use Mike for my partner in the Ortega case. You asked me if I would work a case and play drug dealer. Ortega said that you and he agreed that I can pick my own partner for the case. It's my ass and I pick Mike Romano."

"Easy Alex, let me explain."

Alex turned his back started pacing the floor. Taz had never heard Alex Veranos raise his voice except to announce "Police, you're under arrest". Now he was challenging his superior officer, something that a Marine never did.

"Look at me when I talk to you. Who the hell do you think you are, Marine?"

"Sorry Lieutenant." Alex was dancing around like he was ready to explode.

The Taz thought better than to get into a war with Alex and tried to calm him down.

"Listen Alex. Mike is a great investigator and a good partner, but he doesn't always follow orders. For an operation like this, one that could end badly for the undercover cops involved. Unfortunately shit like this has gone bad in the past. The cops involved must be able to follow orders without questions or deviations."

Alex decided to push. "I only want Mike."

Tazzara was getting upset and ready to blow but controlled himself.

"Do you know that Pria's crew threw a UC out of a third floor window? The guy spent sixty days in the hospital. Six of Pria's crew have served time. For this kind of operation, orders must be followed to the letter. Your Bulldog is too head strong. What if he screws up? Are you willing to risk your lives?"

Alex froze, "Listen I've been there and back in the military and I know a good man when I see one. Mikey's one of the best. Stubborn, yes and like a bulldog, he won't give up and he's got balls. You can't order me to do this. It's a voluntary assignment and my ass. I won't risk my life without him. No Mike, no me. Think about it."

Taz shouted, "Are you sure that's the way you feel? This could help your career. There are other guys. You can take Gus from our team. He's a tough guy and bi-lingual like you."

Alex steeled himself, standing ramrod straight, almost at attention in an effort to control himself.

"No Mike, no Alex. Get back to me."

Then executed a military style about face and walked away.

Tazzara, dumbfounded and speechless by Alex's, actions. In a weak effort to save face, he shouted, "We'll talk again."

Veranos found his partner and related the conversation he just had with their lieutenant.

"Gee, thanks Alex, but you can go ahead and do it. I'll be alright and I'm sure you will be too."

"Yeah Mikey, but will I? I'm comfortable with you, you're like my brother. Besides, I need those angels you carry around in you carry around with you in your head. Let's see how desperate the bosses are."

Two days later, Tazzara called the team of Summers and Bulldog into his office.

"Alex, against my better judgment, I'll let you have Romano, but both of you will follow my orders to the letter or all bets are off along with disciplinary action. Got it?"

"We got it Boss and thanks," Alex responded.

"Okay, we meet with Ortega in the precinct muster room in twenty minutes. Tidy up whatever you have going on. You'll be working off schedule as needed, get moving."

Twenty minutes later, Alex and Mike met with Lieutenant Tazzara, Sergeant Ortega, Investigator Jerry Collins and his confidential informant, a guy known as Rico. They moved to an empty room and closed the door.

Ortega spoke first, "Gentleman, this is Rico." Ortega did the formal introductions. It was obvious to all that Rico was nervous.

After polite hellos and handshakes all around, Ortega continued. "Rico had a relationship with our target. For personal reasons, wants to help us nail Pria. He told our target that he has two people from downtown who lost their cocaine supplier and were looking for someone that could supply their needs."

Rico interjected, "Can your two men be trusted?"

Ortega looked at Alex and Mike, pausing before he answered.

"With my life Rico. With my life. Now let me continued please."

Ortega return to supplying the UCs with case background.

"Rico explained Carlos that he was close to you Summers, because you used to date his sister, until you found out that you were cousins. He added to your credit, that you had old Puerto Rican values, you stopped dating her when you found out. Our target, Carlos Pria was impressed and wanted to meet you. Got that so far?"

Both men answered "Yes."

"Good. Rico has set up a meeting for tomorrow. The exact time is uncertain right now. He'll make introductions, then drop out of the picture. You two will have to carry the ball. We already passed the word along the street that Rico is running from a rival dealer because he was bringing you to Pria. It explains his absence. Still good?"

Alex answered, "Yeah, do we make a buy right away or what?"

"If you feel that it's necessary to make Carlos a believer then do it. You'll be given some buy money tomorrow before your first meeting."

At that point, Tazzara broke in, "Here are my orders. You guys dress the part, jewelry and stuff. You will carry no ID. Walk softly at all times and don't challenge the crew. We want you back. Alex, you'll have a pager that will send a signal to your backup team who will shadow your trips to the target area. Should there be any problems, push the button. Mike, you'll act as his driver and second. Alex, for this, you will handle most of the action. Mike will follow your lead."

"Ten-four Boss."

Taz addressed Ortega with, "Sarge, can Rico go or is there something else we have to discuss?"

Ortega answered, "Only that once he sets the meeting, call me to let me know it's done and our boys will pick him up. That's it, Rico?"

The informant answered, "All good. I'm going now and will call soon. Nice to meet you guys, good luck." Rico rose and left the building.

Without Rico present Tazzara continued, "Every time you go out, I and another team will be sitting on W. 125th Street near the meat packers on 12th Avenue. Mike, have a portable in the front seat of the vehicle with you at all times and keep the volume down . Keep it hidden and out of sight. Remember, keep your radio on at all times in case you have to transmit. Always keep it on point to point channel 6....We will use that for the entire operation. We don't know if these guys have a police monitor or not. Got it? "

"Yes, Sir."

"When you leave your meetings, you'll use the radio to notify me. If I ask for you, you will respond at once to the market spot. That's standard orders Mike."

Romano knew that he had better answer for the team, "Will do, Loo."

"Okay, now go do whatever you gotta do to get ready, gas up the Caddy. You'll be using it exclusively for this case and don't make me regret my decision."

The two partners went to the underground garage to discuss their plans in private.

Alex took the lead, "Mikey, I speak Spanish so most of the time I'll do all the talking. My game plan is to tell them that you're my driver and bodyguard. I intend to also tell then that you're crazy. I'll add that they can't approach me unless I ask for them or you'll kill them."

"How the hell am I gonna know when it's alright? I don't understand much Spanish."

"Besides giving them permission, I'll also use my hands. Don't worry, it'll be clear to you."

"Now, tactically, you must always face the target and his men. It will make them believers. Always stay close by with your back to me and always watch them. Act quiet and alert, as if you're always ready to do damage or something like that. As part of our act, we gotta dress up our weapons too. I have a cowboy type gun at home. I'll carry it. What do you have?"

"I have fancy stag horn grips for my service revolver. They look really cool. I'll put 'em on tonight and use an ankle holster for my off duty as a backup."

"Great, I have a double barreled derringer, my backup. Now for dress, we're playing dealer that are wanna be major guys, so let's dress the part, but not flashy. No sneakers, pressed dress slacks, nice shoes and nice shirts. I have several Guayberra shirts. They're native to Puerto Rico. We can use those and buy some more. They're made to be worn outside the pants. They will hide guns and look kinda classy too. Being the boss, I'll wear lots of gold, rings and stuff. What do you have?"

"I have a couple of rings, one gold one silver."

"You're supposed to be below me in the food chain, so only wear silver. I'll bring some more silver stuff tomorrow for you to use. Let's go gas up the UC car and drive up to look over the set before we start working it. You're getting your wish. You get to drive the UC car."

They grabbed a radio, signed out the UC car keys and drove uptown with great anticipation. Mike drove because he was an old Harlem cop and familiar with the area and in case they were noticed and he was after all, supposed to be Alex's driver.

West 146th street, just off Broadway looked fairly nice, consisting of old three story brownstones that reflected a once proud area.

Broadway itself, was lined with various businesses and teeming with people. There were even benches on the street's center island that had a smattering of occupants.

Not wanting to draw unwanted attention, they only made one pass through the subject block and headed back to MSN.

During the ride back, Alex and Mike agreed on UC names. Alex would be Ramon and Mike would use the name, Tony. Tomorrow couldn't come fast enough for the team. They were stoked up like an old coal fired steamship boiler and raring to go.

CHAPTER TWENTY THREE

The first day of their journey into the world of undercover cocaine buying had arrived. After signing in, Mike and Alex went directly upstairs to Sergeant Ortega.

As they exited the stairwell, two of Ortega's men were in the corridor with him. He couldn't help himself, "Holy crap, you two look like half of a Mariachi Band. Where's your instruments?"

Alex and Mike looked at each other and nodded, then lifted the front of their shirts exposing their handguns.

"Right here, and we're master musicians." They both responded as if it was rehearsed.

Everyone laughed. Ortega kept up the jokes.

With had Sombreros, you'd look like that Bandito who advertises potato chips. Are you sure you're really cops?"

"We can be anything we have to be," came from Alex.

The sergeant then got business like. "Okay guys, you pick up Rico in front of Katz's on Houston at exactly noon today. These two fine gentlemen will be your backup."

Pointing to each man in turn he said, "Alex, Mike, you already know Jerry Collins. Meet his partner Dave O'Grady. They're assigned to shadow and will be no more than two blocks away at any time. When you stop, they're to move closer if possible. Are you two ready? "

Mike answered first, "Ready and geared up."

Alex added, "Like the man said, let's rock and roll."

The two UC's went to get their gear.

"Holy shit, our backup men are blonde Irishmen. I'll bet they won't stand out too much."

"Not at all Alex, almost like marshmallows in hot chocolate,"

At noon sharp, the UC Caddy pulled up in front of Katz's and found Rico standing there.

Alex was in the back seat and opened the door, "Hola mi amigo, vamanos."

Rico joined him in the rear seat. "Nice wheels," he said in English.

"Hey Rico," Mike said.

Rico was very anxious and spoke rapidly without taking a breath.

"When we get there, Carlos Pria will probably be standing on the street, a little bit back from the corner. He will be guarded closely by at least two men. There will be more close by. Cuidado hombres, please do not make any sudden moves because they are crazy. Let him come to you, if he shakes your hand, it's a good thing. I told him you want to buy a couple of grams of coke today and have it checked for quality. Okay?"

Alex answered, "Yeah, that's good, we have some money to spend."

Mike turned around and asked, "Hey Rico. You never answered my hello. Why? You got right down to business. Something wrong?" His tone was accusatory.

Rico was nervous when he answered, but not because he was double dealing.

"Officer Romano, I know you don't completely trust me. We have, how do you say, no simpatico? But I'm afraid to death of the people you are about to meet."

Mike asked, "Then why are you doing this?"

"Venganza, in English, you say revenge."

"Why? What happened?"

"Pria and his people did not know that one of the many people they have killed in the past was a cousin of mine. The money that your police department pays me for this does not matter. I do this because I hope you have to shoot them and they die. That's why I am here, to avenge a death and I am not able to do it myself."

Mike was totally surprised at the explanation.

Alex and Rico began a long and intense exchange that Mike couldn't understand. It lasted for several minutes.

Al filled his partner in, "In short, Rico is scared shitless of these guys. They have a street reputation that says did away with three people and a cop. Maybe the cop was the one that UC Ortega told us about."

"Yeah and they think he died," Mike interjected.

"Yeah, Rico wants revenge, but he only wants to make the introduction then disappear. He hopes that we have to shoot and kill them."

"Guess I could do that if I had to." Mike answered.

"Mikey, this could turn into a be a big shit storm and if we're gonna run with this one, we'll basically be on our own without ever seeing Rico again. Are you still in?"

"Sure. I understand completely. Let's get it going."

Alex said, "Don't worry Rico, you'll never hear from us again after today. We're gonna surprise the crap out of Carlos Pria."

Mike could see in the rear view mirror that Rico's face had begun to relax but his hands still twitched. He hoped that their informant could control himself during the street meeting.

The men rode in almost total silence as they journeyed uptown to the stronghold of Pria and his men. When they reached the corner of W. 146th Street, Romano turned right into the block and stopped twenty feet beyond the corner.

Immediately, two men walked up to the car and tried to see inside past the blackout windows, while a third man studied Mike through the windshield. Romano remained motionless with his hands in sight on the steering wheel.

Rico, still in the rear with Alex was sitting on the curb side. He powered the window down revealing the interior as he greeted the two men in Spanish.

From a position against the building, a man, who Rico immediately referred to as Senior Pria, came to the car.

Peering inside, Pria swept his arm in a grand welcoming gesture and asked both men to come out onto the sidewalk. Alex translated for Mike.

Once they were on the sidewalk, Rico quickly gave introductions. Alex, aka Ramon, tapped on the car and told Tony (Mike) to join them on the sidewalk.

Mike played his part to the hilt. He exited the auto slowly and carefully surveyed the men on the sidewalk. Then he stood with his back to his partner and began to slowly swivel his head, watching everyone in sight. Alex gave a glowing litany in Spanish about his driver's loyalty and personality. Then he turned, smiled and used a hand signal to get his driver off high alert status. The three Latino men again engaged in a conversation that Mike didn't understand.

Rico then formally introduced 'Ramon' to the two men who were closest to Pria. With Pria's approval, Rico spoke to one of them who, maneuvered himself behind the car to block his actions from the street. He then reached into his pocket and produced a small packet of cocaine. There was more conversation that Mike assumed was about the cocaine.

Alex then reached into his own pocket and withdrew three fifty dollar bills. He gave them to Pria after receiving the packet.

"Mil Gracias."

Pria responded with a short, rapid exchange in Spanish before turning away.

Several seconds later, both Rico and "Ramon" climbed into the rear of the car. Mike scurried around and climbed in, quickly started the engine and slowly drove away.

Ramon and Tony had successfully completed their first buy.

The partners drove Rico back to Katz's Deli. As Mike stopped the car at curbside, Mike had feelings of nostalgia and celebration. He wanted to go inside and relive some of his past, if even for a moment. Mike worked to convince his companions to go and try his favorite Katz sandwich, Pastrami on rye with French fries and wash it down with celery soda.

Rico and Al expressed enjoyment concerning the sandwiches but reserved their decision about the drinks.

***

Back in their command, Alex and Mike made detailed entries into their daily log books, completed their DARs, filled out a buy report and vouchered the cocaine. After explaining everything that transpired during their encounter with their subject to Sergeant Ortega, they went downstairs to tell Tazzara.

Alex asked, "Hey Loo, why must we have the blonde cops tailing. They and maybe us are gonna get made. The damn area is supposed to be off limits? They kinda stand out don't you think?"

In his usual style Taz answered, "Because that's who is assigned to you, that's why. Did Romano put you up to this? It sounds like something he would say. "

"No Boss, he didn't, and it's our asses if those guys think we're cops."

"The way you two look, they're gonna think that 'The Man' is watching you. Stop bitching and do the job you agreed to do. The fact that Pria sold you a couple of grams is good and he probably thinks you're exactly who you claim to be."

"Yeah I guess so."

"When is your next buy and how do you contact him?"

"He gave us the telephone number of the booth in front of the coffee shop of his corner on Broadway. We're supposed to call him there and order up if we liked his quality."

"Great, put a rush on the lab work."

After delivering the buy to the lab, Alex and Mike spent the balance of their tour reliving the events on 146th Street. They also put together a game plan together for the next day.

Alex said, "Listen Mikey, these guys are bad asses. We should have an emergency word or something. What'd ya think?"

"Yeah, we can ask something. The question has to be worlds away from drugs. Maybe, does anybody have any candy?"

Sounds like a winner."

"Then what happens next Alex?"

"Well, if one of us feels like the shit is gonna hit the fan, he has to ask that question."

Mike knew the answer to his next question, but needed to hear it and asked, "Then what's next?"

Alex got real serious as he answered, "Mikey, my brother, are you comfortable shooting a man face to face?" Cold as ice, Mike answered, "If I have to."

"Good, then if either of us asks that question, grab the man next to you and put him down because it's them or us, and we gotta go home. I pray we never have to ask that question."

The partners had decided that a reconnaissance was in order before they tried another risky buy.

***

The two "dealers" signed in at 0900 the following day and asked if any lab reports had arrived for them. Getting a negative answer, they went to obtain approval from Ortega to visit the set on W.146th Street before another meeting with Pria. Their plan was to obtain and develop possible intelligence. Ortega agreed with them.

Mike drove up Saint Nicholas Avenue passing through his old command and then doubled back down Broadway, parking across from Pria's corner. From under the front seat, Romano pulled two pairs of binoculars and handed one to Alex in the rear seat. Mike was forced to slouch down in his seat, remembering when Pria's man stared at him through the un-tinted glass on the day of their buy. Mike quickly scanned the opposite corner.

"Al, I don't see Pria but some of his guys are on the block."

Alex, in the dark rear seat, could afford to take his time.

"Mikey, I think I see him curbside, in front of the second building talking to some black people in a Green Jaguar sedan. Nice car."

"Sorry brother, I can't look again. Too many people looking at the car They might see me."

Al continued, "Pria seems comfortable with them, especially the man he's talking to."

Alex chuckled and continued, "Maybe it's his supplier. That would be hot shit. Wouldn't it?"

"Think we wasted enough time here Al? Maybe we should go. We can't see much or hear anything"

"Hold on Mikey. The guy that Pria was talking with, wearing the suit, just opened the Jag's trunk. Two young girls are getting out and going to the trunk. Mr. Suit is handing them paper shopping bags. The kids are having trouble carrying them. They must be heavy. Is today Sunday?"

" No. Why?"

"Because everyone is all decked out like they're going to church or visiting relatives."

"Well, it isn't Sunday. Can you see the license plate?"

"Naw, it's a little dirty. I think there's someone in the passenger seat, maybe a woman. Anyway, Mr. Suit is now taking out two suitcases. They look heavy too. He's handing them to one of Pria's men. The guy he had trouble with them at first. I could see his face, like he didn't expect so much weight. Now everybody except the person in the passenger seat are going into a building. They're all going inside together. We gotta wait this out."

Several minutes later, the kids and the suit exited the building empty handed and alone. The youngsters climbed into the rear seat as Mr. Suit, got behind the wheel. Seconds later, the car drove off. Both cops accurately recorded the time and details of the incident in their diaries.

Mike said, "It really would be hot shit if that was his supplier."

The partners returned to their command and went to find Ortega. He wasn't around so they went to fill in Tazzara. The lieutenant listened to their narration and opinions with mild annoyance.

Alex asked, "What do you think Boss. Think that we have something here?"

The Taz spoke after they finished, "Okay guys. Nice observation but don't get caught up in any imagined drama. Stick to the game plan. By the way, your labs came back and your sample is high quality coke, almost pure."

"Wow. We scored good."

"Now call your man and offer to buy an ounce or two. Let me know when it's going down. Beat it."

Once alone and away from their boss, Mike commented, "Holy crap, he is one giant pain in the ass. Why does he have to push away everything we say?"

"Because we call him Lieutenant and his ego is bigger than ours. Let's go make our call."

Alex dialed the phone booth from the office safe phone.

It was answered on the fourth ring by a male who spoke only in Spanish. After some quick exchanges that Mike didn't understand, Alex hung up.

"Okay, partner, we're on for three this afternoon. Let's go tell our backup guys and The Taz. Our next mission is to find something to eat."

They walked two blocks to the luncheonette where each man ordered a burger and fries. At 2:30, they were heading uptown to buy up. The blonde backup team was sitting on Broadway and 144th Street. Tazzara and his team were at their 12th Avenue location.

Once on the set, Mike directly pulled up in front of the second building on the right side of the street. As the car came to a stop, a tall man walked up to the car and motioned for the window to be rolled down.

The new player introduced himself as Tony and claimed to be Pria's second in command. Carlos Pria then walked out of the building flanked by two men. Across the street, two men additional men watched them closely. Carlos approached and gently nudged his man aside.

Joe DeCicco

Pria then greeted Ramon in Spanish. Switching to English, he said, "Good afternoon to you too, Tony. This is my best man, mi compadre, my number one man. You two have something in common. You share the same name, Tony. Perhaps, in time you two can become friends." Both men cautiously exchanged a handshake.

Pria waved his hands as a signal of some kind, then had a lengthy conversation with Ramon, after which he indicated that they should sit in the car. Ramon told his Tony sit behind the wheel. Mike tensed.

Once the car inside, Pria spoke in English, "How did you like your sample? Your friend Rico spoke highly of you. So, you will be treated like a trusted friend."

"Thank you Carlos."

To show that he still ran the show, Pria added, "But not too trusted." Please do not disappoint me because I do not take disappointment very well."

The not so subtle threat was obvious to both cops.

Alex picked it up. "Not to worry, as long as we can supply our customers with quality cociana, we will never disappoint you."

Pria asked, "You liked the quality from yesterday and you wish to buy more. Yes?"

"We would like to buy something more, three or four grams to determine if the quality is consistent. Do you have some available now?"

"Si. Come back in an hour, and I will have it for you. What do you want to pay?"

"As little as possible. The most is, maybe two-twenty-five or two-fifty."

"Bueno. I see you later." he said as he opened the door and left the vehicle. He was quickly joined by his number two.

Mike and Alex drove away and notified Tazzara by radio that they would have to return in an hour to make the buy.

226

"Go take meal someplace far from the set and let me know when you're back and ready."

"Ten-four Loo. Will advise."

For the entire hour, Alex and Mike discussed the possibility that they were made. They were prepared if anything went wrong. It didn't.

An hour later, Pria's man, Tony walked up to their car and took $250 from them in exchange for almost four grams of cocaine and returned then to the command without incident.

Ortega and Tazzara expressed how please they were as they signed off on the buy voucher.

CHAPTER TWENTY FOUR

The next step in the world of serious undercover drug buying is to buy up. To purchase substantially more weight. The team's next attempt in a day or two would be to buy half a kilo of cocaine with $13,000 of the Police Department's money.

Alex and Mike thought that adding some dressing to their role as drug middlemen would be a good idea. They discussed it and agreed that an attractive female would fit the bill.

After listing the physical attributes and persona of the office they decided on Delores Richards. The feeling was that she could play Ramon's girlfriend and make their status as wanna be major drug dealers much more believable.

She was a bi-lingual attractive head turner. Both of them enjoyed her tough as nails attitude. But before they could present the idea to the bosses, they had to speak to Delores.

After explaining the operation, Alex added, "Yeah, Delores, it'll be a hoot. You're gonna be eye candy to throw them off the possibility that we're cops, and you're an extra pair of eyes. What'da you say? "

"If the bosses say yes, I'm in."

"Thanks, Dee, I'll get back to you ASAP."

The first approval was given by Sergeant Ortega.

"Sure, if she agrees. Did you ask her yet? "

"She said, 'Yes,' and couldn't wait to get started."

Ortega answered, "It's fine with me, I'll convince Lieutenant Aloe. You handle Tazzara, after all, you work for him."

"Sure thing."

Alex let Mike know the idea was approved by all except The Taz and they themselves, would have to run it past him.

An hour later, the crack UC team of Summers and Bulldog were standing before their lieutenant. They had expected to have some trouble convincing him of their plan. He approved their request before they even finished explaining why they had chosen Delores.

"Lieutenant Aloe has told me all about what you two guys want to do. Dee is one of his people and if he's good with it, I'm good with it too, so go out and have fun."

Before they could thank him, Taz added, "Let me remind you that, Dee is a cop but a woman first. Don't let her get hurt or be degraded in any way."

Alex said, "Don't worry Boss. I'll treat her like she's my kid sister. Thank you."

Outside in the corridor, the team celebrated their success with a jubilant high. Five. They located Delores and told that everything was a go.

"Oh, boy am I gonna have fun."

Alex explained that they wanted to visit the site so she could see it. The Caddy was out, so they had to use the Olds UC car. They did quick drive through the block without stopping.

***

The following day Mike and Alex signed for their buy money. Both lieutenants were present. The Taz, in his usual style lectured them and safeguarding the large sum Aloe uncharacteristically made a joke to the surprise of all.

"You two jokers, use your real names to sign for that cash, not the Summers and Bulldog bullshit."

After signing for their buy money, Alex and Mike went to meet Delores in the garage next to the Caddy.

They were deep in conversation, they never saw her approach. They were more than surprise when they saw her.

"Hi fellas," she cooed.

When they turned, to face her, all that could be heard was a duet of , "Holy shit Dee!"

Officer Richards was dressed to kill anyone with a weak heart. She wore a very short, pink tube type halter top stopping just below her ample breasts displaying them quite nicely. To complement the top, she was wearing a tight, short flower patterned mini-skirt and red spaghetti strap high heel shoes. To finish the ensemble, large hoop earrings were hanging from her ears and lips were adorned with kiss me quick bright red lipstick. Both men remained silent for several seconds.

Alex finally said, "My God, Dee, you could stop a train or raise a dead man in that outfit. None of those boys will even see us. They'll all be looking at you."

Mike, always a gentleman, yet still typically male added, "Alex told Taz that he would think of you like his sister. I think that he's about to go straight to hell. Wow, you'll get the job done. You look awesome and should be called Lola, you know like 'What Lola wants, Lola gets'. Alex, do you like it or have any other suggestions?"

Al just grinned gave a thumbs up sign, "Lola it is."

Delores shook her head to flick her short sassy haircut and smile.

Coyly she replied, "Well thank you boys, you're so kind slowly turning around for effect. You sure know how to sweet talk a lady. Are we ready to go?"

She spoke smooth and sweet as maple syrup as she moved to the rear of the Caddy. As Dee climbed into the rear seat, she slithered like a snake stalking its prey. She was all legs and ass and moved ever so slowly.

Both men whistled.

Dee replied, "Go easy boys, I always carry a knife. It's a hidden switchblade and I know how to use it. I'm just practicing my moves is all."

The two partners, just look at each other as if to say, "Where could she possible hide it?"

Alex then joined her in the backseat.

Once they left the garage, Mike notified the backup team and the Taz before proceeding to meet Pria. During the ride uptown, between discussions about the buy, Mike and Alex made a bet about where she hid her knife.

Delores giggled and said, "Either of you two out of line and it'll cut you before you even know where it came from."

As Mike drove uptown, the team discussed possible various outcomes for the upcoming meeting with Pria and his men.

They arrived at the intersection of W.146th and Broadway, Mike didn't pull into the block, instead he stopped even with the corner remaining on Broadway. The attention of most of the men in the block focused on the Caddy as expected, after all they were Pria's little Army.

Ten seconds later Mike put the car into gear and pulled around stopping at their usual spot. Pria's man, Tony and another henchman walked up to the car.

Alex lowered the window.

"Hola Ramon," Tony said.

Looking inside, he spotted Delores felt compelled to say, "Me gusto chica," (I like that girl).

Delores squiggled in the seat, smiled and remained silent.

Alex responded by slowly stroking her face with the back of his hand and saying, "Mil gracis, yo tambien." (Million thanks, me too).

There was a rapid exchange in Spanish and Mike could only understand that Alex was asking for Pria. Seconds later he walked out of the building, flanked as usual, by two men.

"Hola Ramon" Pria greeted as he approached the vehicle.

Alex answered. Then in English, he said, "Excuse me, we're tired and need to stretch, everybody out."

Mike exited first, keeping a watchful eye on everyone as best he could. Then he came around and opened the door for Alex.

Alex got out and held his hand out for Delores who took it and slowly unfolded herself from the vehicle.

It was quite a spectacle; first one shapely leg, a hesitation, then a second, then more of both legs and so forth. The act ended when she was on the sidewalk. Being a smart aspiring actress, Delores wasn't finished yet. She finalized the show by slightly flexing her knees, and ever so slowly bending from the waist to "fix" her shoe. The men on the sidewalk appeared to turn into stone.

Two men from the other side of the street, eager to see what had everyone's attention, began to cross over. They earned a rapid guttural Spanish, a sharp, reprimand from Pria. The men froze instantly and then returned to their posts.

Delores was good at her job. The smile on her face was probably genuine as a result of enjoying the role play. Acting like a typical proud and slightly jealous Latino, Alex pulled her close.

There was a short rapid exchange between Alex and Tony. Then second back and forth between Pria and Alex. Delores continued acting as if she hadn't caught a single word.

Mike, as usual was waiting for Alex to translate as usual. He thought that trouble was brewing and was ready but his celestial voices remained silent.

He learned what the conversation was about when Alex ordered, "Tony, stay here with my Lola and wait for me. Senior Pria and I are going inside to conduct business, I'll return quickly."

Instantly Mike heard the thrumming of large wings in his head. He began to worry and tried not to show it.

"Sure Ramon, we'll stay right here." His mind raced, *I have the money and he didn't ask for it. What gives? Saint Michael please protect Alex.*

As Alex and Pria disappeared into the building, Mike tensed and whispered to Delores, "This is not in the game plan be ready for anything. Just in case you need it, I put a gun inside the car. It's in the center of the backseat cushion."

Mike noticed that as he backed away from Delores, Pria's man, Tony, never took his eyes off her. Romano thought, *if the shit hits the fan, he's one less to worry about. He'll be so busy drooling over Delores that she'll probably cut his throat and take his gun before he even moves. I hope.*

Romano was trying to determine how much time to allow before going inside to find out what might happened and join his partner. He was about to move in, when Alex and Pria walked out laughing and rattling away in their native tongue like longtime friends. Alex was carrying a paper sack.

When he got close ordered "Tony, please reach into the car and get the money envelope. Then hand it to Lola. Mr. Pria wants her and only her to hand it to him."

Alex helped Delores into the car, then he and Pria followed. Mike got into the front seat then slowly drew his weapon placing it between his legs for quick access. Then he adjusted the rear view mirror to watch the action behind him. Once satisfied that there was no immediate danger to his partners, he took a quick look at Tony on the sidewalk. He was lighting a cigarette and looked relaxed.

After Delores counted every bill of the $13,000, she handed it to Pria who slowly stroked her arm as he took it.

Alex, in a threatening tone said, "Cuadio amigo, cuadio."

With legendary Latino machismo, Alex had just reaffirmed his claim to Lola. Even though his Spanish was limited, Mike understood and touched his forearm as he turned to face the rear.

Pria responded in English for all to hear, "Sorry Ramon, I am just appreciating how beautiful she is. Believe me, I meant no disrespect. I am but a weak man when it comes to woman. Are we still good my friend?"

Mike relaxed as Alex answered, "Yes she is and thank you. Please excuse me, I'm late for something and must leave now. Thank you once again. We'll see you soon."

As the door closed behind Pria, Alex said, "Count to five this time Mikey. Then let's get out the hell of here, but not too fast."

Delores spoke first once the car was rolling, "Wow guys that was fun. What a rush, when do we get to do it again?"

Mike was next, "Dee, you sure put on a show. I think we could take them down without a fight if you were here for them to look at. You played your part so good."

Alex spoke next, "I don't know about you guys, but my nerves are still tingling. Mike, please call the Taz and tell him we did it. Thanks."

"MSN special team, mission accomplished."

The Taz answered, "Special team and backup, respond to rendezvous point. Acknowledge."

"Backup team, Ten-four"

The UC's didn't answer. Mike had been focused on the rear view mirror.

"Alex, you know I love old Mustangs and always look closely at them. Well, a red one has been following us since we left the set. I don't think we should go to 12th Avenue. What da ya say?"

"I agree, try to lose 'em if you can."

Delores twisted around to look through the rear window.

Mike, had been watching the Mustang in the rear view mirror, caught a look at Delores' best asset and almost lost control of the car. "Hey Dee, please stop moving, you're gonna get us all killed."

"Hey, smart ass, you'll die happy," she answered as her rump moved from side to side causing her skirt to ride higher and hinted it at the treasure that it almost revealed. She sat down and quipped; "Now you can keep your eyes on the road."

They all laughed loudly. Alex and Mike enjoyed working with her. She was a good looking woman with a man's sense of humor.

The Mustang followed them for twenty minutes as Romano piloted the auto like a broken field runner in a football game; twisting and turning through the city streets. Adding to the tension, was the fact that the Taz, getting impatient had called them two more times. Both times, Alex only responded with, "In route".

Seeing that he couldn't shake the Mustang in local streets, Mike headed uptown. He then got onto the Hudson River Drive. He headed south to the foot of Manhattan and swung around Battery Park to the FRD Drive going north, exiting at East Houston and stopping on an overpass just south of the Williamsburg Bridge at E. Houston and Avenue D. From there, he was able to see 360 degrees for several blocks and could no longer see the Mustang.

When the team agreed that the car was no longer a threat, they returned to their offices.

Before they could even sit down to gather their thoughts, Tazzara stormed in and bellowed like an enraged bull, "Romano, Veranos, in my office, now, forthwith! Leave all the stuff with Delores."

As they walked into his office, The Taz bellowed, "Someone close that door and only speak if I ask you to."

They must have moved too slowly for the angry Tazzara, because he shouted again, "Close that damn door, now!"

Their attempt to sit brought another outburst, "If either of you two shitheads sits down, I'll knock you both out."

Tazzara's face was bright red and his chest muscles pulsated as he continued, "Romano, just who the hell do you think you are? I ordered you two to return to our meeting point. Not only did you disobey, but you lost your backup team. I'm pulling you off the case. If you open your mouth, I'm writing you up and shipping you out."

Mike started to answer, but a look from Alex stopped him.

"Lieutenant, can you excuse my partner? I would like to speak to you alone, solider to soldier, Marine to Marine."

Taz responded. "You heard your partner Mike, get your arrogant shit stained ass out of my office and close the door behind you."

Mike was crushed and went to find Delores. She had pulled a long, loose dress over her "drug clothes" and was sitting in the far corner of the team room with their half kilo buy in a brown paper sack.

"You look upset Mike, what's up?" she asked.

"The Taz is pissed and wants to dump me from the case because we didn't meet him."

"Did you tell him why? "

"Never got the chance. He even threatened to write me up and send me packing. Alex is with him now, talking with him and trying to calm him down."

To keep busy, Mike prepared a buy voucher in Al's name and waited for what seemed like hours.

Actually it was about twenty minutes before Alex found them in the downstairs team room.

In his usual calm fashion he began, "Mike, my brother, it took some time but the lieutenant knows why we acted like we did. He now knows about the Mustang and I explained had the radio because you were driving to protect us and the drug buy. It was my responsibility to answer and not yours."

"Damn straight. I was too fuck'n busy trying to stay away from that Mustang. He's a pain in the ass."

"I also reminded him that we've been accepted by our target as drug dealers and told him again, no Mike, no Alex. Without Mike there's no case. The bad guys will smell a rat."

"What did he say to that?"

"He understands our actions and almost apologized. But you know, the Italian bull that he is had to woof anyway. Taz says that if that happens again, we better radio him at once of else. He never said what of else would be. The man has an overabundance of testosterone. Anyway he finally agreed to leave the status quo. We're back."

"Thank you for saving my ass. Oh, by the way, I had time to kill while my fate dangled in your hands. I vouchered the half kilo in your name. Here you go. Now all that's needed is for you to sign your name and make a buy report and lab request." Mike forced a nervous laugh as he finished his statement.

Delores chimed in with, "Good work Alex and he had no choice because we're an unbeatable team."

Later they spent hours trying to decide if the Mustang was actually a tail or a coincidence.

CHAPTER TWENTY FIVE

Three days later, the team returned from a swing. Sergeant Ortega, Lieutenants Aloe and Tazzara called a meeting. Mike, Alex, Delores and the two backup cops were in attendance. Tazzara, as usual, was the spokesman.

The Taz began, "Okay team, the lab report from that last buy states that it was almost pure cocaine."

"Holy shit."

The Chief has authorized us to now go make a two kilo buy. Now listen up: having my cops running around the city with $50,000 in buy money and no ID gives me the shakes. In that light, we really have to set up good coordination for this round. First, I want some pictures of the players in this operation. Alex, Mike, go get a camera and try to get photos of everyone involved on the block. How you do it is your business, you seem to be very resourceful."

Alex answered, "Sure Boss, we'll start today."

"When you think you have enough, get three sets printed then bring 'em all to me. Once we have the photos, we'll set up the next buy. Get going."

In the corridor, Alex turned to Delores, "Dee, get into costume. Mike get a camera with a couple of lenses. Make sure that one of them is suitable for long shots. I've got to hit the prop locker for something. We meet in the garage in ten."

Romano was already at the UC car when Alex arrived carrying a wooden crutch.

"Just what the hell are you going to do with that? Do you need it because Delores makes you weak in the knees?"

"She sure does, but not enough that I need this thing. It's to rest the camera on. We don't have a tripod and the damn thing gets real heavy with a telephoto lens attached. It's necessary to steady my hands."

Delores arrived looking even sexier than her last dress up excursion.

When they neared the set, Mike pulled the Caddy to the curb on the southbound side of Broadway at W. 146th Street. They had a good view of the entire subject block. In the rear seat, Alex collapsed the crutch shortening it as much as possible. It would just clear the bottom of the car's window. Then he fitted a 400 mm lens to the camera. Steadying the camera by gripping the top piece of the crutch he snapped away a rapid pace.

"Mikey, soon as I change film and lenses, go around and pull into the block, I want to try something."

"Sure Al, what do you have in mind?

"Well, if Delores is ready to play her sexy girlfriend role, I'd like to get her on the sidewalk and shoot past her to get some close, face photos of Pria and his crew. Delores?"

"Sure Alex. I'll do my very best hot and slinky girlfriend impression."

Mike wasn't sure. "Holy crap Alex, do you think that plan is gonna fly? Those guys will probably take the camera."

"Hope not. Pria and Tony are fascinated with Delores. They act like moths to a flame. Maybe, just maybe, they'll jump at the chance to put their arms around her for some photos to show their friends."

"What do you think Chica? Do you think you can resist slicing them up for touching you and get this thing done? However, I would love to see where you hide it. I would make my day."

"Yeah, I can pose all day long if I have to and if those dummies want to take a picture with me, I can play my part, but they better not get too grabby or you guys will see where I hid it. Let's do it."

Several minutes later, the blue Caddy pulled up and stopped in front of Pria's building. As usual, first Tony approached, then Pria and a few of his men.

When the rear window rolled down, Delores, fetching as usual, was fawning over Alex in the rear seat. The men momentarily froze and then rapidly chatted in Spanish between themselves.

Alex, wearing his winning smile, motioned for Pria to come close. Then he softly explained in Spanish that Lola is all keyed up over being involved in this deal and turned on by all the attention she's getting. She wants to pose for some pictures with her admirers. He added that he would give Pria copies for himself. He spoke rapidly to accentuate a sense of urgency.

Pria was cautious yet fascinated. Alex could sell fancy underwear to nuns.

"Well, I don't like 'fotografia', especially of me. But if Lola desires it, I will allow it. But we stay right here on the street. Who can say no to a beautiful woman, especially one as beautiful as your Lola?"

Even though she understood every word, Delores asked, "What did he say? Can I get my picture taken with these macho guys sweetie?"

Alex got out, followed by Delores. As usual, she had everyone's attention as she slinked out of the car and stood on the sidewalk.

Feigning annoyance with his woman and standing like a matador about ready to engage a bull, he answered.

"Yes, you can have pictures with our friends, but stay near our car and don't get too crazy or you'll be punished."

Dee squealed, "Ohh! I just love it when you're angry."

Alex moved around her and took some shots allegedly of her standing next to the Caddy. He actually shot past her and snapped as many of the drug crewmen as he could. The bad guys never noticed. They were too busy watching her every move as she manipulated her curvaceous body.

Alex, nervous about staying too long with a camera ordered, "Okay my little chili pepper, time to go but first some photos with our friends."

One at a time, she posed for two photos each with Pria, then his Tony. Apparently the other men wanted to get into the act, because Pria muttered something and waved them off.

Before leaving, Alex told Pria that he would be back in two days for a large order and would call first. The stage was set.

***

Before going to the office, the team delivered two rolls of film to the Photo Unit in the basement of One PP. They put a rush on them and requested three set of prints. When the lab attendant complained, he was told that the Chief of OCCB had ordered the pictures. It worked.

Back at the office, Alex went to Tazzara and told him what transpired and that the prints were promised for the following day.

The Taz was pleased. "You know Al, sometimes, I think you're as nutty as your partner, but you guys do good work. Sign in by phone tomorrow and pick up the prints on your way in. That was good work and compliment the other two crazies for me too."

The next day was spent reviewing and marking the photos, identifying the players and buildings. The Taz, Ortega and the three UC's worked out a plan about just how the team would buy two kilos of cocaine and still be protected. Tazzara and Ortega were personally going to pick up the $50,000 buy money just before the buy itself.

Alex telephoned Pria using the safe line and ordered two kilos for noon on the following day.

Pria requested that Alex phone from the street just before the buy, "To make sure there are no cops or 'Federales' around." The actual buy was to be inside Pria's apartment. He cautioned that no exchange of any kind on the street and was setup for noon. They were told to make no attempt to bring Delores or anyone to the apartment.

The last statement from Pria caused the team some concern. It was previously decided Mike would go with Alex into the apartment and that they would bring Gus for added security as he was physically strong and bi-lingual. They were hoping that Pria would allow Gus inside.

Now with their latest demand, should Pria balk, it would be up to Alex to convince him otherwise. For a buy of this magnitude, there would be an additional Hispanic team that would monitor the pager's broadcasts.

Delores would remain in the car as extra eyes and ears.

The UC trio spent the afternoon forming a game plan. It was decided that Delores would drive and Alex would sit up front with her with Mike and Gus occupying the rear. Everyone agreed that with Delores doing the driving, she would be safe behind the wheel when the men went inside. Delores was to drive off if she saw the backup teams roll into the block or if she felt threatened. She also had the radio under her seat for an emergency.

The UC team was comfortable with their plan.

The following morning arrived too slowly for the buy team. However, it arrived too quickly for Tazzara and Ortega. They wanted more time to review everything for a second time. Disappointed, they resolved to live with it.

At 1000 hours, the two bosses went to the Puzzle Palace for the buy money. Everyone else left the office to meet at the 12th Avenue location.

At 1100 Tazzara notified the team that money was in hand and he was on his way to their rendezvous location. The four occupants of the Caddy bristled in anticipation. Alex signed a receipt for the cash package at 1145 and then the team drove off to find a payphone and called Pria.

The conversation was in Spanish. "Hola, Ramon, do not come."

It was 1155 hours, Alex asked, "What problem? You have what I want?"

"Si, mi amigo. But there may be police around, call again in an hour."

The team was disappointed and drove back to advise Tazzara. After hearing what happened, Tazzara ordered all support teams that the buy was delayed.

Then he ordered his buy team to take off and wait out the hour far from the scene of the oncoming action. However, he insisted that the both backup teams follow the UC's wherever they went to protect the cash. Alex and Mike were against being followed by the blonde guys. After some back and forth, Taz gave in and agreed that the Hispanic team would be adequate.

The UC team was always concerned about being made as cops. Subsequently, they decided to drive up to the Cloisters Museum to hide and wait. They felt comfortable that Pria and his boys could not possibly be interested in a celebrating medieval art and architecture. Their feeling was that however effective his network might be, they would never look for them there in the event that was spooked.

Exactly an hour later, Alex walked up to a street phone on the edge of a landmark, Dunnellon Square, at the intersection of Saint Nicholas Avenue and W.149th Street. There was a man who had been leaning against the booth while sitting on a bicycle. As Alex got closer to the phone, the man, straightened up and rode off. Alex thought it odd and watched him head crosstown as he dug in his pockets for change.

Pria answered after two rings and said to come ahead, everything was good.

Alex climbed back into the car and notified everyone that Pria was comfortable buy was a go. The Caddy was proceeding to the set.

He commented, "Wonder why that bicycle guy left when we pulled up?" He got no response.

Once at the target building, Tony met the UCs at the curb. He was surprised to see Ramon in the front seat and Lola doing the driving. The extra man in the rear with Tony puzzled him even more.

"Hola, Ramon. You called from a payphone at Saint Nicholas and 149th Street. You were close by Si?" Not receiving an answer, he continued, "How come La Chica is driving?"

With a hint of annoyance, Alex answered, "That's my business my friend. Besides, a woman must do something besides looking beautiful, no? Today she drives."

Dee's mini skirt was unusually high as she sat behind the wheel. Tony leaned forward to get a better look at Delores' legs and nodded in agreement saying, "And she does it well."

Alex, ignoring his remark and acting as if he was still insulted at the previous question, asked, "You don't trust us amigo, you had us followed? Where is Carlos?"

Tony just shrugged his shoulders and came back with, " Can you tell me why you have another man with you today?"

"He's my cousin and we're carrying a lot of cash today. You are so many and we are so few."

Tony backed away and pointed to the building, "Vamanos amigos."

Alex led the way as they entered the building. He carried the money with Mike on his heels. He in turn was followed by Tony. Gus, ever vigilant, remained in the rear. The four men slowly climbed to Pria's apartment on the second floor. They were watched from below by two of Pria's men until they hit first landing.

When Carlos opened the door for his expected visitors, he looked surprised when he saw Gus and asked for an explanation.

Tony repeated everything Alex had just told him.

Pria, ever cautious, stated that Gus could stay in the building but was required to remain outside in the hallway. One of his men would remain with him. The entire conversation was in Spanish. Alex interpreted for Mike who was not happy as an ethereal voice in his head cautioned him to remain on high alert.

When the steel lined apartment door was locked, both cops became nervous. Mike's mind was reviewing the 'buy gone bad video' that shocked everyone during the orientation process.

He thought, *Shit. This time there's no backup team in an adjoining apartment and Gus is outside, behind a steel door.* In his mind Mike was running scenarios and silently prayed, *please Saint Michael, I don't want to kill anyone today. Please let this go well.*

Alex remained calm, yet still in character, as he spoke to Mike with gentle sternness, "Tony, relax, it's fine. These people are our friends. Don't go crazy and hurt someone."

Pria's two remaining henchmen nervously moved around seeking a tactful position to closely observe Mike.

Pria motioned for Alex to sit on the sofa and examine what appeared to be two kilo bricks of cocaine on the coffee table. Alex sat down.

Tony turned to Mike and asked, "What's the matter Tony? Don't worry, you're among friends. You and your boss are safe and your big man is on the other side of the door to protect us all. Suave mi amigo. Relax my friend. "

To free his hands, Alex handed the money to Mike and got down to business. Alex and Pria spoke only in Spanish. Ramon, knowing that 'his Tony' was only able to understand a word or two; translated some of the exchange for him as they spoke.

Finally, Ramon the drug buyer, in a very icy and professional manner, took out a field test kit then made a small cut in the wrappings of one of the bricks with his knife and took a sample for testing.

After adding the coke sample to a small glass vial of liquid, he replaced its top and shook it.

He studied it and smiled. The results indicated a presence of high quality cocaine. After resealing the package, the two men shook hands. Alex asked Mike for the large manila envelope and then handed it to Carlos.

Tony and Tony remained standing alongside the sofa, next to their respective leaders and watched the action.

The dealers never suspected that Mike's pager was transmitting every word to one of the backup teams who were recording it all.

It took Pria, almost thirty minutes to count the money, twice, before again shaking Al's hand and officially seal the deal.

As Carlos counted the money, Mike thought; *wonder if they have to change the tape?*

As Alex rose, Pria asked, "Do you have my pictures of me and Lola with you today."

"No, sorry, the next time we come again for some product we'll bring them, maybe in four or five days. As usual, I'll call first."

Pria nodded to his man standing next to the door. Both cops hid their relief when it was pulled open. Gus cracked a quiet smile, as they walked into the hallway, then turned towards the stairway and led the way out. Not one person followed them out to the car.

Delores sensed their tension as she pulled away and tried to relax everyone by asking, "Hey, how come my fan club never came back out? Did you guys kill them?"

"No. For a while, we thought they were gonna kill us."

"What happened?"

Mike continued, "They made Gus stay outside in the hall while we were locked in behind a door that was reinforced with a sheet of steel. I think for all of us, we're happy to be away from there."

Alex finally spoke. "Hey, girlfriend, head a few blocks uptown and then head south to meet Tazzara while I tell him the good news."

"What about our backup? Want me to take my time."

"No, they'll hear my transmission; they'll know that everything is okay. I know you want to play, so whatever you want. Just don't crash the car."

Delores mashed the accelerator of the powerful car and was at the 12th Avenue meeting point in four minutes. They all laughed.

Control freak that he was, Tazzara, refused to let the two kilos out of his sight once the team arrived. He insisted on riding in their car for the trip back to the office. Gus rode with Ortega. To their dismay, he wanted to know everything. Alex did most of the talking as Mike drove with Dee in the front seat.

Back in their office complex, after a through debriefing, Tazzara and Aloe complimented the team for a job well done. The Taz supervised all the preparation of their paperwork and signed off on everything. Sergeant Ortega and two of the backup men took the evidence directly to the lab for analysis.

Every team member was required to write a statement as to what they witnessed and the roll they played. It would all be included in the case folder. The tape recording made by the backup team was reviewed and a voucher prepared. Taz ordered it brought to Tech Services for three duplicates.

For the balance of the tour, Mike, Alex and Delores remained buried under a myriad of paperwork. Several hours later, as they signed out, they were tired, happy and wondering what the next move would be. They discussed it over several celebratory libations inside a cop watering hole near the courthouse.

* * *

Only a day had passed before there was more action regarding the W. 146th Street case. It seemed that the DEA had been working the area too.

With the success of the two kilo buy, the ranking officers of both departments decided it was time for a coordinated assault on the block. That red mustang that bothered Mike so much was theirs. They tailed Mike to determine what he was doing with Pria. After the plate was run, One PP confirmed that the Caddy was assigned to a narcotics module.

OCCB explained to Taz that the Feds had opened a parallel case against Pria as a result of information from the Bronx. Their investigation implicated the driver of the Boro President as part of the group. In fact, he even drove a green Jaguar.

When Tazzara informed Mike and Alex, the Bulldog almost jumped out of his skin.

"We told you about the green car and there was that phone number from my warrant, we were right all along."

Lou down played the comment. "I guess those things happen. Now listen up."

After making sure that he had their full attention, he continued, "Tomorrow, at 11:00 a.m. , the DEA is going to hit several locations on the same block as our Pria case. He was with the green Jag guy that our Bulldog was so careful to report. Base on that they're rushing us a warrant for our apartment. The plan is for both agencies to storm all the locations together."

Mike exclaimed, "Way to go!"

"Romano, your instincts are uncanny. You got lucky again. I just wish you could follow orders, you pain in the ass."

"Do we keep our collars or will the DEA grab them up?" Mike asked.

Alex jumped in with, "If we keep the collars, are they prosecuted like they are on one of our Federal Days? Shit they're federal warrants, aren't they?"

Ignoring their questions, Taz continued, "Our boss wants you two there to act as spotters only, from an off street location."

"What? Are they crazy? We broke our asses."

"You are only to act as spotters, telling the street teams who to grab. The raid will be coordinated. The DEA will use one of those do it yourself moving trucks to transport their teams."

"They will stop mid-block and empty the back of the truck. The arrest teams will pour out the back like clowns from one of those little circus cars. We will use our own cars. As they jump out and hit their places, our people will rush Pria's apartment and crash the door in grabbing whoever is inside."

"While we just get to watch, like at a football game. That's not right, Boss. This sucks."

The lieutenant continued to ignore Mike.

"Our street teams will be directed by you two guys. You men will call out anyone you recognize as members of Pria's crew. Needless to say, when the truck opens and everyone jumps out, the people on the block will scatter, you better be alert and ready. The cops will all be wearing vests labeled either DEA or Police."

Taz paused for questions. Dead silence.

"Lieutenant Aloe's entire module will be deployed except for Delores. It should be fun and remember, you two are not to go near the set. We've already secured an OP for you guys in an apartment overlooking the set. When you give scripts, don't talk over each other, it's gonna be confusing enough. Later, when the dust settles, you'll be notified to go back to your car and leave the area and park that blue monster far from the set. Got it? "

"Guess so Boss. But we would like to be in on the collars. Would you change your mind?"

"Alex, you keep your bulldog on a short lease tomorrow and I'm not kidding."

Mike answered, "Okay Boss, I got it; we're not welcome on the set."

The next morning, all players gathered on 12th Avenue to re affirm everyone's job. After they parked the Caddy several blocks from the set, Paul Schneider one of Aloe's Sergeants, escorted Mike and Alex to the OP. His orders were to remain with them during the entire round up. Tazzara, Aloe and Ortega would be on the street with their men.

At exactly 11:15 a.m., the truck rolled intoW.146th Street and stopped midway down the block, right in the middle of the street.

Instantly, three cars from MSN quickly slid in to the street and bounced to a halt. The rear door of the truck opened vertically at least a dozen officers wearing vests emblazoned with DEA jumped out, some carried automatic weapons. Several street people were grabbed as the bulk of the men entered two locations.

Lieutenant Tazzara and several men ran into Pria's building carrying a large ram. Mike and Alex were at the OP directing the remaining NYPD cops as to who to grab. Four of Pria's men, trying to act as interested pedestrians. They were identified from the OP, detained and handcuffed. Tony, Pria's number two, slid away in the confusion.

Within minutes, Ortega announced, "Subject apartment is secure. We have two under arrest. OP can return directly to base."

Mike and Alex were disappointed that they had only minimum input after all their work. Reluctantly, they left when ordered and sulked back in the direction of their auto.

After walking two blocks, Mike and Alex smiled at each other. In the distance they saw Tony and a woman sitting on the steps of a building.

Mike almost shouted to Alex, "Saint Michael did it again, there's Tony. See that and you think the noises in my head are just static."

Alex responded, "Yes, he sure did. Now be very careful and follow my lead. Remember, Bulldog, listen before you bite."

As they drew near, Tony acknowledged their presence, "Holy shit, did you two come to see Carlos? Where's the little chica? There's Policia, Federales. Shit, they even had SWAT. They got everybody. I think they got Carlos too. It was crazy; I got away in the mess."

Alex answered in Spanish. "Lola is waiting for us in my car."

Wanting to grab at least one collar. Alex played his trump card. It worked. At the sound of Lola's name, Tony smiled at the thought of seeing her again. Alex now had his full attention and moved closer .

"We gotta go. Do you need a ride somewhere? My Caddy is only a few blocks away. Lola must be jumpy by now."

"Sure, will you drive me to the safety of my mother's house?"

"Fine, but let's go. I don't want to stay in the area too long."

Tony stood, got off the stairs and took two steps towards Alex.

"Hey Tony, you know something that's funnyabout all this today? "

Tony looked confused as he answered. "Ramon, funny? I am not laughing. There is funny today."

Alex smiled, "Police and you're under arrest."

Mike grabbed him from behind and said, "Now that's funny."

The girl ran down the block mumbling to herself.

Alex and Mike entertained themselves as they walked Tony back to the apartment in handcuffs and telling him, in two languages that if he struggled in any way, they would tell his boss that he was an informer.

The guy was terrified at what Pria might do to him without waiting for an explanation and was almost meek all the way back to the apartment.

Tazzara heard Mike and Alex talking with the man stationed outside the apartment door and began to fire up. Taz began formulating one of his screaming lectures, but stopped as they pushed their collar into the room in front of them.

Carlos Pria saw his man in cuffs and shouted, "Madre Mia, holy shit."

The duo quickly explained to their lieutenant how they managed to grab Tony. They had to be quick. It was necessary for their survival. They had disobeyed a direct order.

After shooting a strong disapproving look at his number two, Pria turned to former customers. "You two fuck'n guys; never before in my life did any cops get close to me. You guys are really good. Lola too?"

Tazzara had listened enough. Reverting back to his normal testosterone fuelled personality, he bellowed, "You two, get the hell out of here. I'll see you later."

Alex handed Tony off to the closest cop and left without argument. The former UC's walked to their car. The partners happily reviewed all the good times they had regarding the case on the drive back to the office.

Mike and Alex filled in Delores about what went down. For two hours the trio relived their antics regarding the case.

"You guys were terrific and we had fun. When can we do another one?" she asked as Sergeant Ortega, followed by Lieutenants Aloe and Tazzara, walked into the team room.

Ortega spoke first, "You guys did a terrific job on this case. You can transfer to m y team any time. I already have Delores. You'd both be a welcome addition and if I'm loaded, I'll transfer people out to make room for you."

Aloe only said, "Terrific job people."

Tazzara was next, "You guys did great. Someday, Romano is even gonna learn to follow orders. You don't have any idea how pissed off I was seeing you walking into that apartment. I was gonna kill both of you with my hands, Romano first."

Mike snickered and walked right up to him saying, "I don't go down easy and I've got a tough battle tested Marine to back me up."

Alex chuckled. "Always have your back Mikey."

"You're forgiven Loo, because you didn't know we had the number two man in tow."

To avoid a potential Italian pissing match, Alex asked, "Hey Loo, who took the collars, us or DEA?"

"We assigned three men from Ortega's team to process them and because we had the DEA with us, they are getting "Federal day" processing on our case. The DEA men took their own collars."

"Oh, Alex replied, "We were hoping that one of us would have gotten Carlos."

"You guys, go do your paperwork and sign out. Tomorrow you're both back with Sergeant Landers and its business as usual. You'll be notified if you're needed in court."

Mike answered the obvious dismissal, "Thanks Loo for leaving me on the case. Alex and I will do it again, anytime. See you."

Both men returned to their team room.

Two days later, the buy team was informed that among hundreds of thousands of dollars recovered from locations within the block, all but $2000 of their two kilo buy money was identified and returned to the Police Department.

The following weeks went by with Landers team performing their normal duties, investigating kites, buy and bust, DARS, arrests and court.

One morning, Alex told Mike, "I'm taking two weeks off. I've got some personal business to attend to and while I'm gone, don't get in any trouble."

"Enjoy your time off Alex and don't worry, I'll be fine."

CHAPTER TWENTY SIX

Mike teamed up with Big John whenever he could while Alex was away. Marvin wasn't happy because he lost his security blanket. There wasn't too much he could do about it because Mike was temporally without a partner. Unlike The Twins, John was always cordial and respectful towards Mike. They got along well enough. Sergeant James Billing sat behind Marvin in the office. It made the occasional drafting of Romano to work with one of his man easy.

On the first morning of his second set, Jim Billings called Mike over and announced that one of his investigators, Henry Colombo, was retiring at the end of the set. Jim added that his men, in a last minute inspiration, put together an MSN only, going away dinner and party to celebrate his retirement. It was to be held at Feng Shui, a high class restaurant in China Town. The dinner party was to be held only a few days away on Friday night, October 28th.

Billings was about to post the announcement, and wanted to know if Mike was interested. Anyone attending was expected to donate $20 to cover the festivities.

Mike said yes immediately. With Alex away, he felt the need for some fun time.

The next afternoon, after returning from a post arrest interview with a Narcotics ADA, Romano found Sergeant Billings and asked if he knew the restaurant's location. Jim directed him to one of his men, Benny Lopez, who was organizing the gathering.

Romano gave his contribution. Benny asked, "Do you know where the place is Mike? If not, I'll get the address for you."

"No; but the name's Feng Shui, right? Not to worry. I know a detective in China Town and I'll know where it is by Friday night. I haven't seen the flyer, what time is this thing getting started?"

"The dinner should start at about 7 p.m. Of course, the bar will be opened. Come early and have a few with the boys."

"Will do."

On Friday morning, the day of the dinner party, there was a note posted at the Sign in Desk announcing new location a for the Colombo dinner party. "Due to unknown problems at Feng Shui, the dinner party for Henry has been relocated. It will now be held at Dennis' Restaurant and Tavern. Location is one block south of the First Precinct at the corner of N. Moore and Hudson Streets."

Additional information stated that the actual dinner would be served at 6:30 p.m. There was also an announcement from Sergeant Billings that his team was scheduled to work a nine-to-five tour that day. He added that anyone attending the dinner would considered to be 'working a down day' in the office. It was all approved and endorsed by Lieutenants Tazzara and Aloe.

Romano had no idea that Providence was about to step in and alter the circumstances of his personal life forever.

***

Romano was looking forward to hanging out and meeting the entire office crew. He had carried a change of clothes to work on Friday. Before signing out, Mike put on the clean shirt and a sport jacket he had hanging in his car just for that night. He signed out and arrived at Dennis' shortly before 6:00 p.m. As was his nature, before entering, he gave the place a quick look over.

The entire exterior façade had an old New York charm. He especially liked the old wood framed double glass doors out front.

Inside, across from the entrance, at two o'clock, was an old wood trimmed bar of reasonable length, completing the old fashioned turn of the century look. In front of it were about a dozen bar stools, six of them were occupied.

Directly to the right of the entrance door was a jukebox. It stood dormant with cool blue lights gently flashing. Just to the left of the entrance was a baby grand piano with the top closed. Stools were placed around most of it, defining the instrument as an intimate satellite bar. Tickling the keyboard was a thin, pleasant looking, dark haired musician.

Between the piano and the bar was an open area of approximately 20' x 20' that may have acted as an impromptu dance floor at times. The place looked cozy and had a friendly feel to it.

The old wooden decor continued beyond the entrance area another fifty feet to what was obviously the dining area. Mike could see a line of eight tables in the center extending toward the kitchen doors at the rear.

Two men were setting them up and placing "Private Party" placards on each table. Midway down on the left side was a coat room. It was being attended by a cute young woman in her mid-twenties.

Romano lingered a minute, enjoying the ambience that all the old wood gave the place.

After ordering a Dewars on the rocks, he slowly began socializing with members of MSN. Mike eventually found Colombo, bought him a congratulatory drink for his upcoming retirement then joked with the man for several minutes.

Standing at the bar was a young cop, Guy Santini. Mike went over to say hello.

During the time he worked on the 146th Street case with Sergeant Ortega's team, Mike had become friendly with one of his men, Guy Santini. Guy was at least ten years younger and generally a happy go lucky kind of person. Young Santini also sold jewelry on the side and often teased Mike that he had no woman because he was a cheap SOB and never bought anything to give a girl.

In response, Mike always gave the same answer; that if he found a girlfriend he would call on Guy to purchase gifts to impress her.

At 6:45 p.m. Dennis himself, announced, "Dinner is about to be served for the lucky man that is about to retire and relish in the fact that his poor friends must continue to be employed."

After some cat calls and cop humor, everyone took seats. By shear chance, Romano and Santini were sitting beside each other and facing the coat room. Santini was pleased because he had his eye on the girl inside.

An hour later, as coffee and desert was offered, Mike happen to glance across the table and saw two attractive women stop at the coat room. They had a quick chat with the attendant, then proceed to the ladies room.

They had caught his attention, especially the little red head dressed all in white. As he watched her walk away, Mike heard angels humming a tune inside his head.

Guy broke into his rapture with, "Hey Mike, what do you think of those two? Nice, huh?"

"Yeah, especially the little one in white, the red head in white. She's five feet of angelic dynamite. I think I'll stay as long as she does and take her home."

Guy laughed aloud, "Are you kidding? We all joke about you going gay since your divorce. When we hang out as a group, you stay a while and never react to the cop groupies. I've never even seen you with a broad outside of our women, except for Sophie from warrants and that's only business."

When the women returned and walked past them, the tune in Mike's head began again but with the steady the beat of celestial wings. He thought, *Saint Michael, is it time?"*

Mike then answered Guy's question.

"No, I didn't cross over to the other side and I'm not dead yet, I still have time. The time is now."

"Bullshit."

"Tell you what Guy, we'll run a tab at the bar and the loser pays the bill. What da ya say? "

"Done," was Santini's cheery response. "You'll never do it. You don't stand a chance in Hell, but good luck anyway."

***

The attendees began to vacate the tables. Most of the cops left the premises while some went to hang out in the bar area. Mike and Guy left the confines of the dining area and moved into the eclectic throng of Friday night patrons and remaining cops.

Sergeant Billings was sitting at the bar, chatting up the taller of the two women that had caught Mike's eye. Ignoring them, he ordered a Dewars on the rocks, then moved towards the piano where several people were congregated, including the little redhead.

Before his final approach, Mike stood back for a minute and focused on her. As he stared, the other half dozen people around the piano seems to fade away. She was beautiful and the only person within the group that remained in focus The others had become nothing more than ghostly apparitions.

Being a cop, he instinctively analyzed what he saw; she was pretty, about his own age, petite yet beautifully proportioned and maybe only about five feet tall in bare feet. He was transfixed and involuntarily held his breath.

When he remembered to breathe again, Romano continued his observations; white slacks, white tailored blouse adorned with eyelet trimming, her almost shoulder length red hair was loosely pulled back, complementing the overall picture. On her feet, she wore red high heeled backless shoes. *What a vision.*

His heart throb appeared friendly. He decided that she was obviously acquainted with the piano man and all those standing around him indicating to Mike that she may be a regular in the place.

His mind raced, *Wow, Saint Michael, did you send me this sexy angel here on Earth? You've always been good to me and kept me safe, but I never expected this, thanks. Yeah, I'll take the hint and go meet her.*

Drink in hand, Mike slowly threaded his way through the crowd until he was directly behind his quarry. She never turned around. After a few minutes, Mike managed to enter the varied conversations within the group. Irritated by the interloper, the redhead turned to see who it was and found herself staring at his neck.

She quickly raised her gaze and looked him in the eye with increased annoyance, "Just who the hell think you are and why are you here?"

"Hi, first questions first. I'm Mike and I'm here with some friends. Right now I'm just hanging out for a while. Care for a drink?"

"No thank you. I have one and please back up and give me some room, you're invading my space."

"Sorry, but it's crowded here. We'll have to share."

In complete silence as if dismissing him, she turned away.

Mike liked her and her spunk. He was hooked. Something clicked inside of him and he went into his bulldog mode. He had taken a small bite and liked the flavor. He decided that the wait would be worth it.

Minutes seemed like hours. Finally, he noticed that the glass in front of her was empty. *Yeah Saint Michael, I got it.* He made his move.

"Hey, I told you my name and you never told me yours. My glass is empty and yours is too, can I get you a drink?"

"Persistent, aren't you? You must have been some kind of bulldog in a prior life. If you insist, you can get me a club soda."

"Funny that you should refer to me like that. My partner says that my persistence is one of my better qualities and he even calls me Bulldog. I'll get your drink, save my spot, will you? "

Pushing up to the bar next to Guy, Mike ordered another White Label on ice and a club soda.

Guy stated, "Trying hard are you? There's still hope for you yet, but club soda? Guess it's gonna be a hard sell. I wish you luck."

Romano wound his way back to the piano group and again positioned himself behind 'his redhead' before speaking. "Here's your drink Miss, now can I have your name?"

She turned, looked up at him, smiled like an angel and answered, "Thank you, it's Lillian, but I like Fonzi."

"Fonzi, huh, but I'll call you Lillian, it just sounds better. Kinda soft and sweet like you."

She gave him a tolerant smile and turned back to her friends.

Romano continued to be gently relentless in his pursuit. Minutes became hours, and Lillian, began to soften her resistance. They moved away from the piano because the group had thinned out. The piano player had taken a break and the jukebox was on. They hovered next to the jukebox.

Some patrons were dancing to its tunes and their gyrations caused Lillian to slam into Mike. She almost lost her balance as she bounced off his firearm that was hidden by his jacket. Startled, Lillian tried to jump away, but Mike held her elbow to gently steady her and then very slowly loosened his grip but never quite released her.

Lillian, feeling silly asked, "What's that under your jacket that feels big and hard? Just who and what are you?"

Mike thought, *Odd, she's not intimidated at all; there's a slight touch of a devil in this little angel.* With a smile and a chuckle he answered, "I'm a cop. That's my gun."

Half serious, Lillian came back with, "Naw, no way. With my luck, you 're a gangster."

"No, I'm really a cop. When you came in, you passed a big dinner group. That was for one of our guy's retirement. We all work narcotics."

With a coy smile, Lillian commanded, "I don't believe it. Cops have ID, show it to me." Guiding her close to the jukebox, Mike withdrew his Identification.

"Ohhhhh", she squealed, grabbing his wrist. "Come there's someone I want you to meet". She almost dragged him through the crowd to the bar.

"Hey, Linda, there's someone I want you to meet." The girl she came in with turned around, "This is Mike, he's a cop. Do you want to feel something big and hard?"

Linda got wide eyed, "No thanks, it's more than I need to know."

"His gun dopey, he carries a gun, it's under his jacket and I just bumped into it. I told you he's a cop and that's what I meant silly. Mike, meet Linda, my sister. Linda, meet Mike, my new friend."

Pleasantries were exchanged after which Linda stated, "Fonzi and Mike, there's someone I want you to meet too."

Standing directly next to her, was a rather big brown skinned man. As the man turned to face them, Mike thought, *this is funny; I'm going to be introduced to Jim Billings.*

Proudly, Linda stated, "See, I also met someone tonight. This is Jim, he's a cop too. Jim, meet m y sister Lillian and her new friend Mike."

Jim and Mike broke into laughter as Mike said, "Hello Jim, haven't spoken to you in a couple of hours."

Jim quickly responded, "That's Sergeant Jim to you Mike."

Lillian broke out with, "That was very funny guys. He's your Sergeant?"

"Yeah and sometimes we even work together," Mike replied.

Linda broke in with, "See, you 're not the only one who met someone new today." Then like a little girl in a school yard, added, "I met Jim and my guy is better because he's your new friend's boss."

Billings answered that statement with, "Mike is occasionally on loan to me, so I really, I'm not his boss. I just outrank him."

As the night moved along, Lillian and Mike found that they enjoyed each other's company and Lillian had abandoned her club soda and switched to White Russians. She was having fun.

Romano was beginning to think about the earlier boast he made to Guy Santini. That's when Providence gave assistance.

The little group didn't know that they were being observed. The piano man, who's break was over, was about to return to his instrument but first approached Lillian, and broke in with, "Fonzi." Lillian quickly turned her head in his direction.

Hearing her 'preferred name' instantly informed Romano that they knew each other well, possibly beyond the confines of Dennis'.

Looking slightly startled and embarrassed, Lillian, began to quickly, fire off introductions, "Oh, hi. Jim, Mike, this is George." Then she gently waved her arm in Romano's direction and continued, "George, this is Mike and he's here with friends. Of course you remember, my sister Linda and that's Jim, Mike's boss. They're cops together."

The two men shook hands with George. Then he directed his full attention to Lillian. "Fonzi, I only interrupted you to remind you that I'm leaving early tomorrow morning to pick up my son from his college in Boston, so I can't hang out tonight after work, sorry."

Still shaken, Lillian answered, "Oh, sure. This week end, I remember, no problem, its fine."

Romano though, *that was rather gallant.*

George spoke directly to him, "Well, nice meeting you Mike. Gotta get back to work now." He put his hand gently on Lillian's shoulder and said, "Have fun. I'll talk to you soon," as he walked away.

To the unseen voice in his head, Mike, thought, *Stop drumming those wings, I know, I know. It's gonna be alright.* Then, aloud he spoke to Lillian, "Wow, that was nice of George. He saw you talking with someone and then backing away, like that. Are you two an item?"

Romano, wanting to mask the surprised feeling of jealously that he was feeling at the moment and before getting an answer, he turned to the bartender and quickly ordered a round of drinks for the foursome.

As he returned his attention to Lillian, she spoke softly, "No, I remember that he really had to go pick up his son this weekend. He told me last week. Yes we do date a few times a month. He's a really nice guy."

Mike wasn't used to the emotions that he felt. Quickly wanting to mask anything that his expression might reveal, he turned to humor, complete with an exaggerated smile and asked, "Nicer than me?"

The little red head smiled sweetly, "Well, I don't know you well enough to make any judgment."

Recovering his composure and trying to peak her interest, he countered with, "Don 't worry, you will."

"Boy, I was right about you. You were so pushy at the piano and broke into the conversation with my friends, you're like a bulldog, you never let go. I guess that makes you a good cop, right? "

While chuckling he responded, "That's the name my partner Alex gave me. He's away now but you'll meet him soon."

"There you go again, being persistent and pushy. Are all cops like you?"

"Only the good ones."

"I thought all cops are good guys."

"Most of us are, but when I said good ones and that term pertains to how good he or she might be at their job. The really good cops never give up."

"Oh, I see. You must be real special then," was her mocking response.

Mike couldn't help himself and answered, "Oh I am. You'll see."

"You're doing it again," Lillian answered with a giggle.

The crowd had continued to thin out. By midnight, only maybe a dozen or so people remained. To Mike's joy, George had said his goodbyes and left. Only two other cops remained besides Mike and Jim; Santini and one of his team members.

The few patrons that remained were playing the juke box for all it was worth, and occasionally a couple or two would dance to a selection, even Mike and Lillian.

Lillian was to be a fairly accomplished dancer and giggled at Mike's attempts to keep up, remarking, "My God, you do the same step to everything, but you are as usual, persistent."

It was almost 2 a.m. when a small Latino man walked up to Linda and began chatting with her and Jim.

Later, Mike learned that his name was Leon and he was a chef at an upscale French Style Restaurant, The Brasserie. It was located on the street level of The Pan Am Building and it closed at midnight. Leon's duties were done. There were other people to tidy up the kitchen, so he came to Dennis' to spend some time before driving home.

He had been friends with Linda for several years and was hoping to find her there. Within several minutes, the happy little group was chatting away as if they all knew each other for years.

Jim broke the mood when he reminded Mike, "Listen my friend, we have to work tomorrow, oh, it is tomorrow, and be in the office at 8:00 a . m. Some genius downtown wants an area covered, I couldn't tell him we had a party planned, so I'm going to leave now. You should too."

"Not quite ready yet, but I'll see you later."

Jim offered Linda a ride home even though she lived in New Jersey. He felt it was the least he could do because she was well on her way to high intoxication. She declined explaining that Leon lived near her in Jersey and he would take her home if necessary.

Leon had quite a crush on Linda and quickly announced that he was available. "Anything she needs. I am always at her disposal."

Lillian leaned over and whispered in Mike's ear, "He secretly loves her but never told her."

Guy and his teammate also decided that it was time to go. Moving close to Mike, he whispered, "It still isn't closing time, so good luck. I'll be rooting for you. When I see you let me know what your bill was. Of course, only if you win."

Mike was totally enamored with Lillian and was surprised when he heard the bartender announce, "Last call it's 4 a . m . Order if you gotta and settle up."

Only the two sisters, Leon and Mike remained. Linda had accepted Leon 's offer to transport her home, especially because he never drank alcohol.

Earlier, it was established that Mike would drive Lillian to her house in Queens. He assured her that she was safe with him because she knew where he worked.

By 4:15 a.m., they were walking to his car in the police parking area of the First Precinct. Once at his car, Mike playfully opened the car door, bowed deeply and held Lillian's hand as she climbed in. She looked directly into his eyes and smiled, causing his heart to skip a beat. Mike Romano knew that he was making headway.

*

CHAPTER TWENTY SEVEN

Mike Romano could not believe his good fortune. He was, sitting in his car, about ready to drive home a woman he had just met. She was possibly the woman of his dreams. He started the engine and flicked on the lights. Mike turned to face her, about to ask for her address, but could only sit motionless and silent, just staring at her.

The glow of the dashboard lights, cast an almost iridescent glow on her face, as if emanating from within. Her white clothing completed the rapturous vision, causing his mind to race in keeping pace with his heart.

It was at that moment that he silently made a life changing decision. *This spicy angel; this little gift is not getting away. I don't know how or why she's here but I believe that we are destined to be together.* He was enjoying the moment.

Lillian brought him back to the real world. "Well, put the car in gear and tell me your whole name and lets' get going. Jim is expecting you at work in the morning. Oh, it is morning. He's actually expecting you later."

"Oh yeah, Romano. Michael Romano at your service. Yours?"

"Vallachi, Lillian Vallachi, now head for Queens, Howard Beach, if you will driver, please," she ordered in a playful tone.

Romano swung his car uptown and headed for the Brooklyn Bridge. As he descended on the Brooklyn side, Lillian gasped, "Oh my God, I left my bag behind the bar and I cashed my check after work." She took two breaths and added, "All my money is in it."

Mike trying to be her knight in shining armor responded, "Don't worry your pretty head about it. We'll just go back and get it."

With the combined emotions of disbelief, despair and hope, Lillian asked, "How can we? We're already in Brooklyn? It'll take too much time and everything."

Mike answered, "No, it won't. We'll be there in less than five minutes." Gently increasing his speed, he negotiated a street level U-turn, swinging back onto the Manhattan approach to the bridge. When the car straightened, he then reached under the dashboard with his left hand, triggering flashing head lights and a blaring siren.

Lillian squealed like a schoolgirl. " Oh, just like in the movies, lights and sirens. I thought this is your car not the city's."

"It is. I'll tell you about it after we get your bag. Right now, hold on and use the seatbelt."

The engine roared and Lillian was unexpectedly mashed against the seatback as Mike took off with tires squealing almost as loud as she did.

Mike raced shot over the bridge, winding towards Dennis' as if his life depended on it. As the grey Chevy approached the corner of Moore and Hudson streets, the blare of other sirens joined his in a shrill chorus of sounds, reminiscent of a scene from an action movie.

Bouncing up onto the sidewalk directly in front of the entrance, Mike silenced his siren and struck his high beams. On his left, a marked Port Authority Police car materialized and stopped alongside. With dome lights still flashing, the doors swung open. Launching themselves onto the street were two uniformed men, the driver and a sergeant.

Mike didn't get a chance to think before, on his right, another police car and a yellow taxicab nosed unto the curb and poured out their occupants. Everyone except Romano had their weapons ready and pointing at the bar.

The uniformed sergeant, assuming Mike was a cop asked, "We got your back Officer. What do you have? We're here to help."

Embarrassed, Mike quickly answered, "It's not an emergency Sarge. Sorry to alarm everyone but we had to get here in a hurry. My lady just remembered that forgot her pocketbook inside. She left it behind the bar and had cashed her paycheck before coming here tonight. We left when closed, not more than fifteen minutes ago. Realizing what happened, we rushed back ASAP to get it. Thanks for responding."

As the cops calmed down, the Sergeant, with a mischievous grin said, "Well, you just go in and get it for her while we wait. That's the least we can do for such an enterprising fellow officer."

Still anxious, Mike and Lillian hurried up to the front door and found it locked, but there were lights on inside. Banging on the door produced negative results.

The sergeant flopped down in his car, hit the siren a couple of times then picked up the dash microphone. Keying the car's loudspeaker he announced, "This is the police, open up inside or we'll drive through the door."

Mike thought it was a rather bold and highly illegal statement, but the sergeant was having fun with the situation.

Within seconds, the shocked face of the night cleanup man popped into view just inside the inner doors. The confused man dropped his mop and held his arms out to signal desperation and shook his head.

The sergeant again ordered him to open the door. The cleaning man, in broken English with a thick Latino accent, answered that it was impossible because his boss always locks him in for protection while he's working. Someone opens up in the morning and then he goes home.

The sergeant thought the story absurd and repeated his threat with negative results. Turning toward Lillian, the he asked, "Can you get him to look behind the bar for your bag, we might get lucky. There's windows up there. Maybe, if he can get up there, he can drop your bag out. If not, we'll break the door. Don't worry."

As Lillian got close to the door, the little man recognized her at once, waved vigorously. "Hola, Senora, what is the problem?", he shouted.

Mike's heart skipped a beat as jealously reared its head, again reminding him that she knew the piano man well.

Lillian now realized that during her frequent visits, she had often seen the man, but thought that he was a kitchen worker or busboy. She didn't know that he also worked overnight.

After some trouble finding the proper words to express her needs, along with very animated hand gestures, he seemed to understand what she was trying to tell him. Vigorously nodding his head in acknowledgement, he ran behind the bar and returned with her handbag.

Holding it like a trophy, he again told everyone that he couldn't help because the door was locked. With typical working class Latino gallantry he added, "On my honor, Senora, I will keep it safe until you come back in the morning."

Lillian was visibly upset, and kept shaking her head while trying to express to him that she wanted him to throw it out the upstairs window. She was getting nowhere when Mike stepped in.

"Before the Sarge breaks the door and we all get jammed up, I'll try my limited Spanish on him."

"Give it hell son, and good luck or we will break the down the door for your little redhead. She looks like a fine Irish girl. Far be it from me not to assist a fair bonnie lass like her."

Mike thought, *Aha, Sarge is an Irish romantic. Now I understand.*

Romano's brain struggled, finally remembering the proper words for up, high and window. He managed to string them together well enough to express what he wanted done and got a very animated acknowledgement from the night worker. He quickly held Lillian's bag aloft for a second, then disappeared from view.

Several anxious seconds passed before the sound of a window opening was heard from just above the entrance. "Senora, mira alto," was shouted as the cleaning man waved Lillian's handbag.

Once she acknowledged it, he proudly waited for somebody to get below the window but as Mike and Lillian quickly advanced, he excitedly dropped it. Mike lunged and caught the handbag. Instantly he handed it to Lillian, who shouted thank you several times to the man in the window.

Lillian excitedly checked the contents. Finding everything intact, she announced, "It's all here, everything, thank you." Then she waved to the cleaner who had remained in the window, watching the night's activity.

For him, the excitement surely broke the monotony of his lonely overnight task.

First she thanked Mike and all the cops for their willingness to help. Then she rewarded Romano with a hug and a kiss.

The Sergeant commented, "You're a lucky man. That's some fine looking lady you have there and I don't blame you for rushing to her rescue."

As they pulled away and resumed the trip to Queens, Lillian's thoughts returned to her fascination with the siren in Mike's car.

Teasingly acting like a domineering, demanding woman, she asked, "Now, explain why you have that siren and those flashing lights in your car and if it's really your car and not the city's."

"Yes, it really is my car. Several months ago someone attempted to steal it. They never got it but messed up the whole dashboard and ignition system. After that was repaired, I brought the car to a friend of mine who was my neighbor in my prior life. He owns and alarm shop and he installed the alarm."

"Sounds plausible. Why the extra switch?"

"Being a good friend and fond of gadgets, he asked if I wanted a switch that I could activate it while I was driving. I was going through my divorce at the time and was feeling a little depressed and in need of a lift. I said yes."

"Oh, you're divorced?

Mike continued without comment. "Normally, the alarm sets when the doors are locked and disarms when opened with the key. It'll wail if the door, hood or trunk is opened without using a key."

"How do you test it to see if it still works?"

"Well, every few weeks, I roll down a window, lock the car with the key then reach in, manually unlock it and pull the door open to test it. The only way to shut it off is to use the key again, either in the door or ignition; so far so good."

"Impressive. You're certainly very different Mike Romano, I'll say that for you."

Mike was lost in thought; *she's warming up to me. Gotta spend some time with her. I'm gonna try to kiss her and see what happens. I've got nothing to lose.*

Tanking his time driving back over the bridge, he planned his next move. Mike knew that he had to hit the local streets to access the ramp to the Brooklyn Queens Expressway and head towards the JFK area of Queens.

They had traveled less than three blocks Mike was forced to stop at a red traffic light. He was determined to make some kind of overture towards his goal.

Romano did something quite outside the realm of his normal behavior. He leaned over, reached for Lillian with his right hand, put it gently under her chin and in one swift motion guided her face to his, gently planting a warm lingering kiss on her lips, with no resistance from her.

When he leaned back and looked at her, she was smiling like a school girl waiting for another one. Being a giving type of guy, he was willing accommodated her silent request.

It was a good thing that there wasn't any traffic at that time of the morning, because in between several other those kisses and lingering looks, the light had turned to green and back to red again. When noticed, they laughed in unison.

"Hey, listen Lillian, I need to spend more time with you. If you're not too tired, as we pass Sheepshead Bay, I know a 24/7 diner, how about we stop, get something to eat and have some serious conversation?"

"I'd enjoy that, but it's almost 5:30, don't you have to go to work in the morning, uh, soon?"

"Yes, but I can call for an emergency day if need be. You know, as far as I'm concerned, being with you constitutes and emergency."

"Sure thing, then I can learn something about you while I try not to tell you too much about myself."

He looked at her, unsure if she was serious, then relaxed when she added, "You cops want to know everything. I'll tell you, but don't frisk me, I'm ticklish."

Needless to say, he certainly wanted to. Playfully, he reached for her just as the light changed again.

Lillian quipped, "There goes the green light again. Put the car in motion, not your hands."

Mike was fascinated by her and wanted to learn everything he could about this woman, so he reluctantly backed away saying, "Yes, Miss Fonzi."

He headed to the highway, mumbling as he drove, "Lillian, your name's Lillian. Fonzi is a male character on television and you're a real person."

They arrived at the diner by 5:50 and found a quiet booth tucked away from the early morning patrons; mostly fishermen, who were grabbing quick bite before boarding one of the many party boats among the fishing fleet that the Bay is famous for.

When the waitress asked for their orders, Mike opted for two eggs over easy, home fries, bacon and rye toast. Lillian ordered the same except, she wanted white toast, and two coffees, one for each of them.

While they waited for their order, they probed each other for personal details. Lillian finally asked about the demise of Mike's former marriage.

Before he could answer, the waitress delivered their coffees. When they were alone again, Mike told an abridged version of returning home from work one night and finding Betty in a compromising situation with another man, what happened next and the current status or lack of his relationship with his two children.

"That must have been difficult for you. As you told the story, your eyes told me that you were reliving every word as you spoke." She reached across the table and took his hand, "I'm sorry for you."

"Thank you," was all he could say as he looked deep into her eyes and saw that she genuinely meant what she said. *Wow, she's compassionate and as beautiful on the inside as she is on the outside.*

After a pregnant pause, Mike continued, "Enough about me. Please tell me something about you; I assume that you 're single. Live alone? "

"Divorced, fourteen years ago, live with three adult kids, two boys and a girl. I have no desire for a steady man in my life right now."

"What about George?"

"Not really a steady guy because I can't seem to find one that I'm completely comfortable with making me a very guarded person. I don't let anyone inside the little protective wall that I've built around myself. Sometimes I date, even had a few long relationships, but have never committed to anyone. After a while I usually end the relationship. Self-perseveration I guess."

"Wow that covered everything. It must have been hard for you raising children alone."

"Yeah, it was, but I managed and my kids are pretty much self-sufficient now, except we all share one roof. After all that's what family is about, loving and sharing."

Their food arrived, giving them some breathing room. The conversation changed, fluttering around like a butterfly in a flower garden, never getting serious again. They were just enjoying each other.

They left the diner at 7:30 a.m.. The sun had climbed out of the waters of Jamaica Bay and was ascending into the morning sky as Mike began to pilot his Chevy along the Belt Parkway towards Queens.

Lillian asked, "Hey, do you really think that you're up to going to work and chasing bad guys today. What's Jim going to say when you show up late? "

"I'm planning on going home, sleeping all day and going out on a proper date with you tonight."

"How are you going to do that?"

"I think Jim already anticipates that I'll be calling in for an emergency day. There's a gas station on the center island near the Brooklyn/Queens border. They have a bank of pay phones. I'll call in from there."

"What's an emergency day mean? Why don't they call it a day off day? Sounds like the name means a day for emergencies only." Lillian smiled at the silliness of own statement.

The mythical Greek God, Morpheus, was stalking him. In an effort shake off the relentless pursuit, Mike first imagined spending the day with her before he answered.

It helped. "Police Department rules require a prior written notice for a day off and they prefer two days. But, in the real world, people have emergencies or circumstances in their lives that occur because they're human. As a result, The Job allows for 'emergency days'. It's just bureaucratic double talk, to allow you to use vacation days or accrued overtime, known as lost time."

"What's lost time?"

" Some cops take their overtime in time instead of cash."

"Why would a cop take overtime in time rather than cash? I thought the goal is to make money."

"Those who take hours instead of cash say it's because the Government can't tax time. So they always take overtime as time and use it without burning vacation days. Some of those cops have a side business or another job and it allows them time off for those interests."

Mike glanced sideways to gage Lillian's reaction because she remained quiet during his answer. Then, out of the blue, with a fake frown on her face she asked, "Just what makes you think that I want to see you again? You're nice, but I just met you. I have a dog at home and I don't need another one, especially a bulldog." As the last word exited her lips, a giggle fell out too.

Mike was thoroughly enjoying the tone of the current conversation. In his mind, Lillian wanted to learn about cops and the Department because she was contemplating dating him. Several second later he finally responded.

"Well, meeting you was totally unexpected, and I believe it was the result of karma, destiny, or whatever. It happened and I want to spend more time with you. The guys at work make fun of me because I don't chase women, like most cops do. Well, now I want you and you date the piano player, so I have an emergency."

Mike waited for a response to his explanation. There was none, so he covered with, "Oh, there's the gas station on the left, up ahead."

Pulling his car close to one of the several pay phones, he stopped and exited his car. Lillian remained silent as he walked to a phone. She watched, deep in thought as he dialed.

"Hello Sarge, it's me, Mike Romano. I need an E-Day please."

Jim responded with, "Man, I could have bet my life on this phone call. Are you still with her? "

"Yes. I'm taking her home."

"Some of the guys are already here and started making bets that you would ask for a day. It showed all over you last night. You found yourself some kind of woman. I guess it paid to wait for someone special. Where are you? "

Not wanting to push his luck and have Jim tell him it was okay if he had to come in late, he answered, "I have no idea, someplace on a highway with lots of grass."

"Well, be careful Mr. Lucky. You have the day." Jim clicked off.

Mike returned to his car and found Lillian smiling at him. He motioned for her to roll down the window. She did and he leaned down, gently pulled her face to his, kissing her mouth ever so tenderly. Without uttering a word, he walked around to the driver's side and climbed in. Lillian didn't move as he restarted the car, she was still facing the opened window.

As nonchalant as possible, he announced, "Well, I got the day, so it's all ours. Got any ideas? "

Slowly, Lillian turned to face him, leaned over and gingerly returned his unexpected kiss. "Yes, as a matter of fact I do. When you drop me off, I'm going to bed for a few hours' sleep. I have a busy afternoon."

"Oh. Well what about tonight? Can we spend some alone time together?

"His mind was racing. *This woman has just got to be mine. She's dating someone and if I don't keep the pressure on I might not move ahead and into the relationship that I want. Am I nuts?*

The look in her eye was impish, "Look, get me home. Drop me off and if you can find my house again, pick me up tonight at about 7:00 p.m. Good enough for you? "

"Done", Mike replied as he put the car into gear and sped onto the parkway. "Howard Beach, here we come." They both chuckled.

Minutes later, Mike announced, "Cross Bay Blvd. exit up ahead. Right or left? "

"Right and then swing into the left lane. I'll direct you."

Several twists and turns later, Mike pulled up in front of Lillian's house. He opened his door and was about to get out when Lillian held up her hand. "No need. I'm a big girl and should be able to open my own door. See you at seven, if you remember how to get here. Bye."

Romano watched her walk away towards her home. He enjoyed her movements as she climbed the four steps to the entrance. Then she turned around and smiled before entering and closed the door. Mike was left staring at the ornate panels of the dark wood portal to his new treasure.

Mike's mind raced. *My God, she's beautiful and in those heels, wow, just enough sway. She moves like a well-oiled timepiece, WOW.*

See you later for sure and then I'll get your phone number too. Somehow, soon, if I have a say, you'll say good bye to that piano player forever.

Before he pulled away, Mike reached into his glove box and withdrew a cigar. He removed the cellophane wrapper carefully and slowly lit it taking long pull while savoring the flavor and then blew smoke rings. Two draws later, he glanced back at her house and drove off.

He entered the Belt Parkway heading towards the Verrazano Bridge and Staten Island. While driving home, Romano celebrated his new lady gift by puffing on his smoke, singing and humming. He was trying to remember the words to an old WWII song, Lilly Marlene.

As he continued driving, Mike labored trying to remember the exact wording; *your sweet face haunts my dreams.* He tried in earnest, not quite remembering much of it. *Lilly of the lamplight, she's my own Lilly Marlene. The glow of my dashboard lights were my lamppost.*

Mike's thoughts fluttered around like a feather in a gentle breeze. *Thank you Saint Michael and you too God.* All he kept thinking was *Lillian, now my Lillian,* throughout the entire drive back to his apartment. Mike couldn't remember feeling so happy in quite some time.

***

Later that same day, after sleeping for seven hours, Mike crawled out of his bed. Padding sloth like into the kitchen in bare feet, he set up his coffee pot. Mike, even in his rather lazy state, decided that he was hungry and pulled a cold slice of pizza from the fridge. After sprinkling the top with a copious amount of ground red pepper as a quick pick me up. Then he moved to his lounger and fell into and thoughtfully chomped on the chilly repast while Mr. Coffee did his thing.

After three cups of the dark elixir, straight up as always, he put on some old clothes and drove to a local service station that had a coin operated, do it yourself, car wash station. After diligently vacuuming the interior and double washing of the exterior, he went back home feeling that his chariot was now presentable enough for his date, later that evening with his red haired sassy angel, his naughty and nice gift from his Celestial Benefactor.

After a fitful short nap, Romano buzzed around his apartment performing busywork and smoking cigars in an effort to keep occupied. He was getting impatient as time passed ever so slowly in his anticipation of the pending return encounter with Lillian.

Mike after his date would be on a two day swing, scheduled to return to work on the 31st, Halloween. Lillian had touched something inside him that he didn't fully understand and he planned to spend as much time with her as possible, even calling in for another E-Day if things went well.

Mike allotted himself a full hour to drive to Howard Beach, estimating it would take close to 45 minutes, giving him a cushion of 15 minutes. His plan was to knock on her front door as close to 7:00 p.m. as possible and if he was early, he would sit in his car a few blocks away and wait.

After three quick raps on the door at exactly 7:00 p.m.. It swung open revealing a smiling Lillian.

"Well, punctual, I see, that's a very commendable trait."

All he could say was, "Hi", and stared at her gentle smile feeling like a school boy on his first date. Embarrassed at his lack of a better response, he added, "Nice to be here." *Damn, I feel like a mumbling jerk,* as he shuffled his feet.

"Please, come in while I find my wandering handbag."

Humor about last night's incident. She's beautiful and funny.

Mike stepped inside the entry porch. He wanted to kiss her, but she turned and walked further into the house. Gently he closed the door without taking his eyes off her. His nerves tingled, but as cops are prone to do, he mentally recorded what he saw. Soft curving hips in blue jeans and heels, never completing the inventory before she disappeared out of his line of sight.

Alone with his thoughts, it was the longest three minutes he ever spent, before Mike heard his new lady love coming down from the second floor accompanied by a another person.

As they came into view, behind Lillian was a pretty young girl who appeared to be about eighteen or nineteen years old. Lillian motioned for him to move forward, into the living room, "Michael, this is my daughter, Lucy, her two brothers aren't home."

Turning to her daughter, she continued, "Lucy, this is Mike Romano, the cop I told you about. "

The young woman exhibited an extremely sweet smile as she responded, "Nice to meet you. Mom said some very nice things about you. Have fun tonight." She then turned to kiss her mother and whispered in her ear before leaving them alone.

Mike had a chance to really look at Lillian while she introduced her daughter. He liked what he saw even more than the fleeting glimpse of her when she walked away after inviting him in.

Her red hair was attractively arranged, complete with a jeweled clasp holding every hair in its proper place. The figure flattering jeans and high heels that he first noticed were complimented by a yellow sleeveless knit top. It took his breath away by graciously displaying the fact that she wore no bra and had a figure that was firm enough to do it with class, completing his fantasy.

Indeed she had the figure of a woman half her age. *My Lilly Marlene is a timeless beauty and a little bit of a vixen too,* he thought, as his head swirled with intoxication of the visual stimulation.

In her left hand, looped through the strap of her handbag, Lillian also carried a light sweater. Mike was hoping that she would never put it on that night. However, she did so every time they entered a building that entire evening and removed it when they were leaving. He became even more fascinated with her because of the naughty and nice facet of her personality. It was as if she only allowed him to enjoy the view.

For a split second, it appeared to Mike that he was caught gawking. Embarrassed, he quickly said, "Your daughter seems like a very sweet girl. Maybe she can meet my daughter someday."

Lillian, seeing the look of appreciation on his face responded with, "Thank you. "

Then with an impish smile on her face, she took his arm and added, impishly, "I'm ready for whatever you have planned, let's go Mr. Romano."

CHAPTER TWENTY EIGHT

As far as Mike was concerned, their first date went extremely well. First, a superb meal at Fabrizio's, an Italian restaurant in Little Italy that served fine food. Mike often told friends that their fare ran neck and neck with his Grandmother's cooking.

After their meal, the couple visited two clubs. The first was chosen by Mike, a jazz place in The Village. The second stop, at Lillian's suggestion, was a very eclectic three story place in the Chelsea District that was quite different and appropriately called Chelsea's. He had never seen anything like it.

The interior was long and narrow with an arched doorway on the far side that led upstairs.

Upon entering the street level, people were greeted on both side with old glass showcases. One side had wine only dry bar, a cash register and two bartenders. Both rows of cases were filled with antique dolls and other funky small items for sale. The couple opted to forgo the wine. Mike thought the decor was unique and took his time looking at the collection as they made their way to the loft entrance.

Each of the other levels hosted a different theme; rock and roll on the second floor, jam packed with gyrating humanity and on three, classic jazz, complete with a grainy throated songstress on the piano. The newly dating couple, bypassed the rock and roll area and went directly to the jazz bar. The jazz floor was smaller than the other two areas and crowded as a New York subway train at rush hour. Mike thought the area had a cozy and intimate feel to it that added a unique ambiance to their date.

Mike and Lillian spent their entire time at Chelsea's on that level listening to Jazz and splitting their time between the bar and standing at the piano. They talked for hours and shared many thoughts and feelings. For Romano, always a guarded cop, the relaxed, intimate conversation was highly unusual. He explained that sharing his thoughts with her made him nervous, but it felt right.

Lillian had similar feelings. She expressed that she couldn't understand why she felt comfortable when she began sharing her previously secret information with him back at the diner.

When he asked her to try, Lillian could only repeat what she had previously just said. She went on to note that before George, she had a previous ten year relationship with a wealthy business man, he never quite penetrated her wall. Then she added, "In retrospect, it's probably because I didn't want him to. Deep down inside, I must have known that he wasn't the right man for me."

In an effort to understand their feelings, they both agreed that it was probably atmosphere of the club. Mike attempted to explain why they were so relaxed.

"Lillian, it's as if we're the only two people here. I feel safe, wrapped in a cocoon, complete with music in the background.

Lillian heartily agreed and laughed. "Nice thought but I think our euphoric feelings must be the result of the numerous drinks that we've had."

Mike preferred to chalk it all up to Kismet, an Arabic term for the Will of God.

Lillian responded, "Now, for some unexplained reason, with you, I no longer feel it's necessary to hide behind my wall. Maybe you're right Michael and it is kismet."

Then she kissed him gently.

Elated, Mike thought, *yes. There is hope. This little red haired angel is gonna be mine.*

They were totally caught up in each other and continued sharing most of their personal secrets. Reality caught up with them at 4:00 a.m.

The bartender announced "Last call, we close in half an hour. Sorry folks."

Not wanting to leave, they nursed what drinks they had, finally leaving twenty minutes later.

Walking three blocks to Mike's car, they hung on to each other like high school lovers, without even speaking, but simultaneously erupted numerous times with childlike giggles. Each time, they stopped time for a quick kiss and a hug.

As the car's engine roared to life, so did Mike's. He turned to face Lillian. Mixing fact with fiction, offered a proposal.

"I feel foolish, but I'm bushed and think I need to rest awhile. Being this far downtown, my place is about fifteen minutes away. Care to stop off for a quick nap and some coffee before I take you home? It's safer than driving to Howard Beach and I want to spend more time with you."

Lillian smiled coyly and answered, "Sure, that makes sense to me and I could certainly use some coffee, but there are diners you know."

"Yeah, but my coffee's better and the atmosphere is more relaxed. Okay? "

"Fine, but I have a busy day with family later in the day and can't be home too late."

Butterflies danced in his gut. As he drove to his apartment, Mike began humming his now favorite tune.

"Mike, what's the name of that song?"

Romano smile as he answered, "It's about you. You're, my Lilly Marlene."

Her response was a question, "Who? Me? "

Mike was more than happy to explain. "The original song, was written in German, as a love song during World War II."

"It's about a soldier standing outside his barracks on guard duty under a lamppost. Soon a girl walks past. He's bored and begins a conversation. The girl's name is Lilly Marlene."

"The soldier felt that fate made her walk past as he stood alone under the warm glow of the lamp. He falls in love. Anyway, he goes off to war and every time he sees a lamppost or thinks of her, he remembers their two shadows. They were so close that they appeared as one person. Throughout the entire song, he's constantly yearning to be with her again."

"How sweet."

"I'm told that somewhere in Germany, there's a lamppost with a statue of the girl leaning against it, as a monument to the song. I don't know if the story is real, or if they ever got together. It's kind of sad if they didn't."

Lillian sat quietly, studying his face during his explanation of the song's origin and saw tenderness. She thought, *Oh my, Michael Romano a, tough Narco cop, is a romantic with the soul of a poet. He's tough as a bulldog but with a marshmallow center.*

Mike continued, "I was surprised after meeting you last night, your name being Lillian and all, so, you have become my Lilly Marlene. So, Fonzi, whatever that is, is out and Lilly is in and I'm not going anywhere. In my version, boy gets girl, a happy ending."

"That's a beautiful story and I'm flattered but a niece and nephew gave me the nickname Fonzi and I began to like it."

Mike asked, "Why Fonzi, isn't that the name of a TV character from the 50's sitcom?"

"Yes it is. There's also a girl in the series who likes to wear pink and that's how it all started. We had a big family get together and I wore an entirely pink outfit, pink being my favorite color. The kids began calling me Pinky after the girl in the show."

"Cute, but that isn't Fonzi."

"As the day progressed, I told them that Pinky sounded too girly and soft for me. I'm a single mother, so they started calling me Fonzi after the macho motorcycle guy in the show. Fonzi is tough on the outside but has a heart, just like me and I identified with it. I liked it and it stuck. "

Mike smiled as he responded, "You exhibit a hard exterior, your wall, if you will, but it's not you. It's definitely not necessary with me, so I'll call you Lilly, if that's okay with you? "

Lillian, didn't yet understand why she was so comfortable with Mike, but answered, "Its fine Mike, after that beautiful story, I would like it."

It was almost twenty minutes before Mike pulled up in front of his apartment, the ground level basement of a private house.

Once inside the entrance Mike stepped aside, bowed and said, "After you miss, make yourself right at home while I start some coffee."

The floor was fully covered with a tastefully patterned dark muted red, short pile carpet. Just inside the doorway was a long hallway. Midway down, on the left was a bathroom. Further on, it opened into a large open room with sofas on the right and left walls.

To the right, almost like a separate room, was a large kitchen. The floor was covered with non-descript tiles. What made the area unique were the three walls lined with cabinets above continuous counter tops. There was also a typical work area complete with a stove and fridge.

Separating the living area from the kitchen was a square dining table and four chairs and Mike's large television that sat on a rolling stand just before the tiled floor. Mike's lounge chair was directly in front of the TV with a small table next to it; on top was an empty glass.

At a right angle to the larger sofa was a sliding door closet. The only other pieces of furniture in his apartment were a desk and chair sitting between a set of sliding glass doors that led to a back yard. The doors were covered by a set of opaque drapes. On the desk were Mike's telephone and a small lamp.

Lilly was surprised as to the neatness of the place, "Wow, Mr. Romano, you keep a clean home and look at the size of that kitchen. There are three walls of cabinets. Whatever do you keep in them? You can't have so that many pots, pans and dishes, or do you entertain often?

As he readied the coffee pot, he responded with a chuckle, "Clothes, all my clothing is in there except for a few hanging items in the closet next to the big sofa."

Smiling, he pulled open several cabinet doors revealing, "Shirts, underwear, socks, pants and lots of other stuff." With some bravado he asked, "So wadda you think? "

"Nice, no wasted space and no drawers to pull out. I see several ashtrays. You obviously enjoy cigars, where do you keep them? "

"They're in the fridge, along with my Dewar's White Label. The scotch is always cold and the cigars, fresh. While the coffee pot does its thing, have a seat. Would you like a drink? I have Kahlua and milk, we can fake a White Russian. Sorry, I have no vodka."

"Sure, thank you and don't think you're going to get me drunk and have your way with me."

Lilly slowly looked around and walked over to the smaller sofa.

The thought never entered my mind. Wanna bet?, he told himself before answering, "Of course not and I'll join you with a scotch on the rocks."

Grabbing two glasses from the cabinet over the sink, he prepared the drinks then joined her on the sofa. Without saying a word, they tapped their glasses together, sipped their drinks and then gently put them down on the coffee table in front of them. Then, still in complete silence they embraced with a soul searching lingering kiss.

Finally apart, Lilly asked, "Mike, how come there's no table in front of the other sofa?"

Feigning embarrassment, Mike responded, "Too much to move, that's a large sofa bed, it's where I sleep."

Lilly reached for her glass before answering, "Oh, I see."

Romano's heart raced, as once again, inside his head he heard the rhythmic sound of wings. He listened to a disembodied voice softly telling him not to pass up an opportunity before he answered.

"Lillian, I can open it and we can stretch out to watch television or not. Okay?"

Coyly, Lilly answered, "Okay, but don't burn the coffee and don't forget to take off your big and hard." We don't want it to go off unexpectedly, do we?", she giggled.

Mike's heart was now racing. *Coffee isn't gonna happen now,* he thought. He stopped in the kitchen and unplugged the coffee pot, then moved the television and found a late night movie.

After opening the sofa bed, he crossed the room, picked up both glasses and holding them in one hand, gently guided Lillian to the bed. He put a glass on each armrest and while still standing, without a word, held her close. The embrace spoke volumes.

Lilly squiggled away. "Yes, me too, Mike, I'll be right back," she said before picking up her shoulder bag and headed to the bathroom. He heard the door gently close and the sound of running water.

Mike reacted with primordial instinct. Quickly, he disrobed. With his heart pounding in anticipation, he threw his clothes, out of sight, to the floor on the far side of the bed. He then climbed naked into the bed and pulled the sheet over himself. Mike was excitedly hopeful, as he listened to the sound of running water. To steel himself against a possible miscalculation, he gulped a mouthful of Scotch before putting it down on the floor next to him.

Mike Romano's heart skipped a beat as Lilly emerged barefooted , with her hair loose, and wrapped in his large white bath towel. She moved as graceful as a cat and seemed to float towards him, he was awestruck. Speechless, he glanced upward towards the heavens and thought, *Thank you for this gift.*

Lilly stood next to the bed, dropped the towel and climbed in next to him.

Several hours later, the couple awoke, curled in each other's arms. To Mike, their lovemaking was intense yet gentle. There had been an ethereal quality about it. He could not remember experiencing anything like it, not even during his early days with Betty.

After propping himself to an almost upright position, he gazed down at the reclining form next to him and watched as Lilly's eyes closed blissfully again. He never felt more alive and the decision that he made just a day before was reinforced, he would never let her go. Mike had given his heart and soul to Lilly. He prayed that the emotion would be reciprocal.

Slowly, he eased himself from the bed and went to the kitchen. He located a pair of briefs from one of the cabinets, pulled them on then started fresh coffee. Mike glanced back to his bed, smiled and headed to the bathroom.

Reluctantly, not wanting to wash off the real or imagined aroma of Lilly from his body, he quickly showered. Mike then returned to the living   area after drying off and putting his briefs back on.

Lilly appeared to still be sleeping. Quietly, he grabbed a cup of black coffee and sat on the smaller sofa. Watching her breathe from across the room he relived the past several hours in a kaleidoscope of mental imagery. He knew that he had fallen in love with his own Lilly Marlene, his own spicy angel.

Finally, Lilly stretched and sat up, causing the bed sheet to gather at her waist. She then turned her whole body around to grasp the two bed pillows, exposing her flanks and derriere. After fluffing the pillows, propped them behind herself, she leaned back against them and faced Mike wearing only a broad smile.

Mike drew a deep breath at the sight of her and thought, *She can sure tease. If this keeps up, I'll have a heart attack.*

 "Good morning, my red haired angel. You have the figure of a twenty year old and the glow of the morning sun. I'll bet you make other women jealous."

Smiling broadly, Lilly responded. "Why, thank you Michael. What a nice thing to say. Would you please bring me some coffee with milk and sugar? Thank you."

He was up in a flash, hitting his shin on the coffee table as he rose, wincing in pain.

"You 're cute too, but not very graceful. Did that hurt?"

Playfully limping away, he answered, "Not at all, I'm still intoxicated with you and didn't feel a thing. Be right there, Miss Lilly Marlene."

As he handed her a cup of coffee, Mike gently kissed her on the lips. Then quickly grabbing her cup to steady it and prevent a spill, he planted a quick kiss on each breast.

Lilly giggled, "My, oh my, seconds already?"

"No, not necessarily, I just want to say, Good Morning, to all of you, however the rest of you will have to wait."

Mike climbed on the bed next to her and said, "You know, even though tomorrow's Halloween, Oct 31st, and it's my next scheduled work day and I'm seriously considering calling in for another E-Day. You said that you have family stuff later today, all day. Are you free tomorrow? I'd like to see you again real soon."

Lilly's reaction to the question, scooting under the sheet and tucking it under her arms to hide her body, bothered Mike. Her defensive actions told him that he would be disappointed with her answer and he was.

Lilly sounded contrite as she answered him.

"Sorry Mike, remember George, the piano player you met. Well, we set up a date before I met you. We planned to go to the Annual Halloween Parade in the Village on Sunday night."

Mike felt ill.

"I always try to keep my word whenever possible and I've known him for some time now. As you know, we were sort of dating, though nothing exclusive. I don't know what came over me when I met you, but I would like to go to the parade. He and I have always had a good time together and as you have gathered, he's a gentleman."

Mike couldn't breathe.

Seeing the hurt look in his eyes bothered her. "I hope you understand. Of course we can see each other again, whenever you want to, but not tomorrow."

It took a few seconds for him to gather his thoughts and breathe. When Mike finally spoke, he was intense.

"Lillian, I don't know what's come over me either, but I don't want to share you. You've gotten inside of me and filled an empty space. You complete me. Call it infatuation, love or whatever, but that's the way I feel. I know that we just met and I may sound stupid but, I think I'm in love with you. I can't explain it and I want you for myself."

Lillian remained quiet and pensive. Looking directly into Mike's eyes she spoke.

"Mike, I told you last night that I feel as though I can take my wall down with you and I can't explain why either. Maybe we have something special between us. I don't know, so I'll tell you what, if you feel so strongly about an 'Us', then tell me not to see George ever again after tomorrow and I'll think hard about it all day and see if I feel the same way about you. I'll give you an answer the following day, Deal?"

Very quietly, Mike said, "Ok, I don't want you to see him again or anyone else for that matter, because my feelings for you are that strong, sort of overpowering."

After he got the words out, the thought of Lilly seeing George again, made Mike feel as if he was going to be sick. He excused himself and went noisily rifling through the kitchen cabinets, looking for clothes to get dressed.

Lillian felt his pain as she watched him. At that point, she wasn't feeling too well either. She grabbed the large discarded towel, wrapped it around herself, quickly rose from the bed, and hastily headed for the bathroom.

There was little conversation before they left the apartment. It was hard to determine who was under more stress. In an unspoken effort to say, "It's gonna be okay", Mike and Lillian exchanged both their home and office phone numbers. Each vowed to call the other the first chance they got following that ill-timed parade.

The ride to Howard Beach was nearly conversation free. Each of them had withdrawn into their own head and their wheels of thought were working overtime.

After a quick consolatory kiss, Lilly gracefully exited the car and walked directly to her front door. Mike couldn't take his eyes off her. He thought, *she moves effortlessly as flowing water.*

Lilly put her hand on the door latch, hesitated for a few seconds, then turned back to look at Mike. She flashed a quick smile then turned away and disappeared inside. As the door closed behind her, Mike's heart ached and his stomach knotted as he fought a growing feeling of disappointment and possibility of a love lost.

CHAPTER TWENTY NINE

Mike was quiet as he entered his team office half an hour before the start of his tour. All he could think of was, Lillian, his Lillian, going out again with George the piano player while he had to work. *Will she tell him that he, Mike Romano, had won her heart? Would she tell George that it was nice for a while, but was over between them and she had moved on?*

With his mind fully absorbed on the possibility of losing Lillian, Mike didn't notice that Jim Billings and Marvin Landers walk in together. He was slightly startled when Marvin spoke.

"As you may have noticed, we have two teams working tonight. It being Halloween, the annual freak parade is on beginning at 1700 hours and we will be working it to completion. There are to be no marijuana or possession collars. The only action you will take is making arrests for sales only, not possession. The powers that be want us there to prevent a drug supermarket atmosphere. Gus, Alice and Phil will be our UC's out there tonight. It will be crowded and noisy, so stay close to them." He turned to Billings, "Jim?"

"Nothing to add to what Sergeant Landers already said except, be careful out there tonight. These parades get a little crazy at times. Remember our first priority is to go home at end of tour. Mike, will you ride with me please when we leave? Okay, everybody get your gear and get moving. We gather at Park Avenue South and 16th Street. Two teams from upstairs will cover the north end of the parade."

Motioning to Romano, Jim said, "Mike, a minute please."

"Sure Sarge, soon as I gather my stuff. Okay?"

"Now please," was the unexpected response.

Jim began on a light note, "Well, tell me about the little redhead. How did everything go? You called in before tour the morning you met her. I thought it was going good. Right now you look like you lost your best friend. We need you alert. Are you okay?"

"It went well Sarge, at first, extremely well but now, there are complications."

Billings raised his eyebrows, "Oh?"

"That piano player at the bar, well, she's been dating him for some time and is seeing him tonight. That could be a problem, so I'm not in a very joyous mood. Some work activity will help; maybe even a collar or two. I'll be fine."

"Well, I'm sure it will work out for you."

"Thanks. Can I go?"

"Not yet. I want to ask you something important. I want you to think about coming over to my team on a full time basis. I know you and Alex Veranos are partners. Talk it over with him when he returns and let me know. I need a man like you, give it some serious thought. If I could, I would take both of you."

"Wow, Sarge. I don't have an answer now but, I will think about it."

"Good. Now back to your redhead, I got three calls from her sister, Linda. She may have still been intoxicated because all she did was talk trash and aggravate me. All I'll say is; you got the better of the two. I'm happy for you, good luck and do whatever you can to hold on to her, she seems to be a keeper. Are we good?

"Yeah Sarge, we're good."

"Great, let's go to work."

After parking and securing their autos at the 16th Street assembly point, both teams spread out among the crowd. Two local uniformed officers were assigned to monitor the parked cars as part of their assignment for the night. Usually, the presence of narcotics cops was low key, and would not be announced. However, because of the parade, the brains in The Puzzle palace reasoned that parking all the cars in one place would hopefully alert the " 'ner do wells" that undercover officers were in the mix. The goal was to hold their illicit activities to a minimum.

* * *

Even though Mike was pleased about by the offer to join Billing's team, he was having guilt feelings about walking away from Alex. His partner had often expressed feelings of comfort and safety that he felt working with Mike. Alex even appreciated his tenacity and had given him the Bulldog nickname. *Hell, he even fought the Taz when he wanted to pull me off the 147th Street case.*

Mike felt an obligation to Alex and wondered if he should break up their partnership. Deciding to delay his decision, Mike thought, *At least I can try to throw myself into my work tonight and try not to think about personal stuff.*

It didn't work. Distraught and hurting over what Lilly might tell him the following day, Mike spent much of the night alone, wandering through the crowds looking for Lillian with negative results. When team members asked what he was doing, he uncharacteristically lied and answered that he was watching a potential target.

The parade and the crowd began to wind down by 11:30 p.m. The entire MSN crew was back in the office less than an hour later. The team only netted three collars for the night. Mike wasn't needed to assist and quickly signed out.

The drive home was agony for him. His only thoughts were about the possibility of losing his Lilly Marlene. He even tried to enjoy a cigar during the ride. It tasted bitter and he tossed it out the window.

Unable to relax, Romano put four ice cubes into a water tumbler followed by his cure all, Dewars White Label. He filled the glass to the brim needing the double dose, then climbed into his lounge chair. After taking several long swallows, he put the glass down on the side table, within easy reach and stared at the ceiling.

Romano was startled into consciousness by the shrill ringing of the telephone. He sprung from the chair as the mechanism snapped into place and stumbled, in an effort to quickly get to the phone. He struck the table and knocked over his glass. His first thought was, *Shit! I just wasted all that good stuff,* and was surprised when he saw nothing had spilled. The glass was empty. Without realizing it, he had finished every last drop and didn't remember doing so.

He finally reached his desk. Before picking up the receiver Mike shook his head in an effort to realign his brain cells. Lifting the receiver, he was startled when he heard a cheery and familiar voice say, "Hello Michael, I told him, what's next?"

Mike Romano, the usually quick witted and vocal cop, was struck dumb. As the fog lifted he said, "Huh, Lilly? Is that you?"

"Yes, Mike, last night, I told George that I would no longer be dating him…….. Please say something."

"Huh, sorry." His smart ass gene kicked in as he continued, "Just peeling myself off the ceiling. I wish you were here right now. Lilly, you have made me a happy man and you'll never be sorry."

His mind raced, "When can I see you? Are you at work now or what?" he asked as he looked at his wristwatch, it was 9:53 a.m.

"Yes, I am and well, I usually get home about 6:30. Can you meet me at my house tonight? I'd like to have some quiet conversation later."

"Sure. We're supposed to work tonight, but I'll call in for the day. No problem."

The tone of her voice as she answered, told Mike that she was pleased yet concerned.

"Mike, you don't have to do that. It's fine, there will be plenty of time. There's no one else any more. Don't jeopardize your job."

"Lillian, it's not a problem and for you, anything. See you later. Besides, it's not an E-Day, it's a C-Day."

"Okay Mike, if you're sure you won't get in trouble, but what's a C-Day?"

Almost giddy, as if intoxicated, he answered, "Something new, a Celebration day, it'll be fine. It's no problem."

After a few several silly back and forth comments they hung up.

Seconds after putting the phone down he called his office and asked for Sergeant Billings. Told that he wasn't in yet, he then asked if Lieutenant Tazzara was available.

"Hello, Romano, I hear through the grapevine that you have a new lady, the chick you met at Colombo's retirement dinner. Sorry I missed it. Good for you."

"Yeah, Loo, I have a date with her and need the night off. See you tomorrow? Are we good?"

"Sure Mike and good luck."

Besides his work, Mike Romano, had a reason to feel alive again and spent the rest of the day feeling as if he was in high school and about to date the prettiest girl in class.

Mike arrived at Lillian's house by 6:15 p.m. and parked near the corner. From his vantage point, was able to see the train arrive and remained in his car, waiting until he finally saw her.

Mike saw her turn the corner. As Lilly got closer, his mind's eye began to change his surroundings. Even though the evening sky had begun to darken, for Mike Romano, the sun was shining, the sky was blue and the birds were singing. He couldn't be happier. Bounding out of his car, he thrust a bouquet of roses at her and embraced his lady. They were now a couple.

Lilly spoke first, "Michael, please let's go inside, the neighbors may be watching and I feel that you're about to lose control of yourself. Besides the walk to the front door will do us both some good. You'll calm down and I won't drop the roses."

Embarrassed for a second, he began to release his smothering embrace and said, "Oh, yeah, I forgot. You 're a private person. No sense in telling the neighbors that you have a new boyfriend, not yet anyway."

Releasing her, but still holding onto her right hand, Mike took a step backwards. He raised his free arm and threw his head back in an expression of joy.

Thinking that he was about to howl or something, Lillian said, "No, please don't."

Grinning but in a normal volume, he announced, "Everyone in the world, know that Mike Romano and Lillian Valachi belong to each other."

Laughing, Lilly stated, "You're crazy Mr. Romano, get inside." Guiding him up the front steps, adding, "I hope my kids aren't home to see this." They weren't.

While Lillian was upstairs, Mike had time to get friendly with the family dog, Gidget. She was a rescued "sooner dog". The sooner you figure out the mixture, the sooner you know. In his estimation, she was probably about fifty to sixty pounds and appeared to be a Pointer/Shepard mix a because of her color and pointed ears. Gidget was predominately white with some tan markings. Her fur was of medium length. She was a fine looking animal who, when she walked, pranced like a Lipizzaner Stallion.

Lilly changed out office clothes, and put her roses into a vase, leaving them on the breakfast counter in the kitchen. She then wrote a note to her kids, "Went out with the cop, be back later. I'll call you, Love Mom." She put the note next to the vase containing the flowers.

Just before leaving the house, Lilly, seeing the bond developing begin between Mike and her dog called, "Gidget, come officially meet Mike. Mike hold out your hand."

The dog pranced over to them rapidly wagging her tail. Lillian continued, "Sit, give paw."

After taking the dog's paw, she put it in Mike's outstretched hand and continued, "Gidget, meet Mike, Mike meet Gidget."

Looking directly at Mike, the animal woofed a greeting as if she understood. The dog's lips curled back along her snout, as if snarling but without making a sound.

"Holy crap, Lilly, the dog is smiling at me," he said.

"That means, she likes you. Let's go before you fall in love with her too and I'll have a rival."

They dined at Fruitti di Mare, an Italian seafood restaurant, in Sheepshead Bay. Later they sat at a small corner table in its bar area for several hours talking, as new lovers do, totally engrossed in each other. Time flew by and midnight approached before Lilly remembered to call home. Her daughter, Lucy answered, saying that her brothers were asleep. Lilly said that she expected to be home within two hours.

After delving deeper into each other's past, likes and dislikes, the new happy couple agreed that fate or destiny had indeed brought them together at that particular time in their lives.

Digging further back to their teenage years, they were both surprised to learn that they were neighbors back in the Fifties. They had lived across the street and a few doors down from each other, yet they couldn't recall ever crossing paths before their fateful meeting only a few days earlier.

After sharing a kiss at that discovery, they giggled like children and again agreed that their meeting must have been written in the book of destiny with a touch of kismet.

It was 1:30 a.m. when Mike walked Lilly to her front door and kissed her goodnight. He declared that one day, probably sooner than later, he would marry her. It was a tossup as to which one of them was more shocked at positive determination and lifelong devotion that those words implied. Reluctantly, he turned to leave promising to call her later and drove off feeling like a teenager experiencing love for the very first time.

CHAPTER THIRTY

When Mike retuned to work, he had only three tours left in that set to do before he would have a three day swing. After signing in, he went directly to Jim Billings' office.

"Hey Sarge, I'm back and ready to go. Before you ask, things are terrific. My E-Day worked out well. Thanks."

"Happy to hear it Mike, you look happy and contented. Your redhead sure is a pretty girl. Enough of that. Now there's work to do, we're going out in an hour."

"I'm ready," Mike answered with a big grin on his face. He was still thinking of Lillian.

"We're working Clinton Street today. One PP, has been getting lots of complaints about the area between Delancey and Pitt Streets. They set us up working with a building owner near the far corner. We were given a key to the roof. It's a little taller than the rest of the buildings, making it a good OP. You'll be our eyes on the roof by manning the OP and directing the ground troops. Get your gear and get ready. Oh, only use point to point channel 6."

"Sure thing Sarge, ready in five minutes."

"One more thing Mike, take a notebook to the roof. We need to get multiple buys on the block and at least one collar for every buy, so accuracy is important. I want you to give good scripts, and also locate the stash if possible. If a buyer, a hand to hand or a steerer starts to move off the block, keep track of him or her.

Keep us informed of their movements and we'll take them before they disappear. Got it?"

"No problem at all, Boss."

"Good, we'll be using UC's from four teams. They'll all use the same signal if a buy is made. They'll scratch their neck or pull their ear on the right side when they have one. Don't forget. Go, see you in five."

Mike looked at his wrist watch,1 0:15. *Just enough time to call Lilly and tell her that I'll see her at her place later and that I'll try to call at least once more today too. No overtime collars for me today.*

Bulldog made his call, then met with the entire team as everyone assembled in the garage. It took Billings only five minutes to formulate a game plan, set who was where, tell his people what he expected and designate their respective assignments. He then explained a sequence for the UC's to work the block

Mike rode with Jim to the set. He was dropped off at the OP location and then climbed the tenement stairway to the roof. Once outside, he found the most advantageous spot, combining the best vantage point with the least chance of being spotted. He then crouched down below the roof parapet and checked his equipment; two pairs of binoculars, a notebook, two pens, radio and a spare battery.

As he settled in, Mike was surprised, that even though it was only mid-morning, on a Lower East side tenement block without any businesses, there was an abundance of foot traffic. His experience alerted him to the probability of drug traffic because he could see pockets of people milling about. Seconds later, a single person would break away, walk up to a lone pedestrian, walk with them a short distance, then break away again as they passed one of the groups. The pedestrian would linger a moment with the group, then move on. *Here we go,* he thought, as he scanned the area.

Mike chuckled to himself as he remembered the last time he was alone on a rooftop. It was a windy, rainy day several months in the past when No Balls Marvin ordered him to a housing project rooftop on Cherry Street.

There he was perched 14 stories above the street, overlooking a ball field and park on the river front. His binoculars were useless because the rain distorted the lenses. It was miserable and cold. The wind cutting him like a knife. He spent two soggy hours up there trying to spot drug sales, because an extremely overzealous Police Commissioner called in from his car as he drove to work.

The PC had seen lots of people on the field and surmised that it could only be drug sales because of the weather. He believed that nobody in their right mind would be there considering the conditions.

Mike was not happy when he was told that "the drug dealers and their customers" were nothing more than a company of recruits from the Police Academy on a training exercise. He loudly cussed the PC as everybody laughed, especially Marvin.

He thought, *anyway, today is a warm and sunny day.* The radio crackled and Jim announced, "OP, be on alert, first UC is on the set."

Keying his portable, Mike answered, "Ten-four Sarge. OP is ready to rock and roll."

Two hours later, the teams amassed nine arrests, five plastic bags full of vials containing apparent crack, thirty loose glassines of powder, several dozen assorted pills and over six hundred dollars. After assisting the 'catchers' with post arrest searches, Mike took a meal hour at the luncheonette near the office for a burger and fries. When he returned he spent a few minutes with Sergeant Billings talking about the day's activities before going to catch up on his paperwork.

Later, as soon as he could, Mike signed out of the office. He jumped into his car and bee lined for Howard Beach. Mike was sitting on the front steps waiting for his lady love when she arrived home. The "newbies"(as couples go) went out to a restaurant for dinner and some quiet talk. Then, for desert, some good old fashioned necking in the car. They repeated that for two more nights before the week end arrived.

Lilly spent that entire weekend with Mike, staying at his apartment. The first night there, an incoming call interrupted one of their "conversation sessions."

It was Alex, "Ola Mikey, hope I'm not calling at a bad time"

Before he answered, Mike thought *No, of course you're not. I'm just getting a little loving that's all.* He contemplated hanging up. "No, not doing anything important. What's up? "

Alex continued with a slight urgency in his voice, "I called to tell you that Mom and I are back from New Mexico. How's chances for you to come out to the house tomorrow evening and visit. I'm leaving the job and there are some things I need to talk to you about."

The statement almost floored Romano. "What the hell are you talking about. Are you two alright? Is anything wrong?" Looking at Lilly and shrugging his shoulders, he continued, "Do you need me now? Are you sure you're good? "

"Tomorrow is good, we're fine. I bought property that has a store front and a residence in the back. I want to start a business. The climate is better for my mom and I have enough time to vest out, so, I'm going. You're my friend. Actually I look at you like the brother I never had and I want to tell you about it in person before we go back to work. Can you make it? "

Mike was relieved at Alex's answers. He could remain there with Lilly. "Yeah, I think so, hold on."

Covering the phone he said, "Lilly, my partner wants to see me tomorrow evening. I'll only go if you come with me. I'd like you to meet him anyway. Okay? "

"Sure, tell him yes and hurry back here."

Before he answered his partner, Mike drank in the vision of his Lilly Marlene like a thirsty camel that had just trekked across an arid desert and came upon on a spring fed pool of crystal clear water. She was naked on the bed smiling at him and giggled as she pointed at his male package.

Looking down, he saw that it had lost its enthusiasm during his telephone conversation. Mike shrugged and chuckled, then his eyes returned to Lilly.

Her disheveled hair framed her beautiful face. Her alabaster, curvaceous body glowed from within. He was transfixed by the vision before him.

"Hey, brother, are you there? Can you make it? "

Al's voice brought him back from nirvana. "Yeah, sure. I met someone and she's here with me now and will be coming with me. I want you to meet her, because eventually, we're gonna get married."

He looked back at Lilly who just stared blankly at him. Mike wanted to tell her, *Holy crap, I said it again. Well, now I'm committed and a bulldog never gives up.*

Alex erupted with a short guffaw before answering, "Hey, I go away for a couple of weeks and you get into trouble even after I warned you to be careful. Wow, she must be something special. Good for you. You deserve a good woman and sure I'd love to meet her."

Mike, responded with, "We'll be there. How's six? "

"See you then Mikey, by the way, what's her name?"

"Lillian and she is special, as special as an earth bound angel. See you."

"Wow, you got it bad, Mikey. See you tomorrow." The line went dead and Mike returned to Lilly and resumed their 'conversation'.

***

The following evening Mike introduced Lilly to Alex and his mother. Anita was a pixyish little woman, and in true old world style, insisted that they must sit down and share a meal.

Half an hour later, Lilly and Anita were chatting away in the kitchen while Anita prepared a meal for them. Sitting at the dining room table, the two men enjoyed listening to the women.

Anita, was chatting away with her heavily accented English. Lillian exhibited a genuine interest in everything the tiny woman had to say. Their interaction left Alex time to explain to Mike what he was planning for the next few weeks.

In his usual soft, understated style he began, "Mikey, you 're like a brother. As part of my family, I wanted to tell you my plans in person, eye to eye, away from all the shitheads at work. For several years, I've been saving money to buy property in New Mexico."

"New Mexico. Why so far away?"

"I spent some time there in the military, and enjoyed it. I promise myself that I would settle there one day, now 's the one day."

"What are you gonna do? You need an income?"

"I decided to open a small business in the City of Las Cruses. The city has the University of New Mexico with thousands of students. My plan is to open a small business selling them cheap transportation, mopeds and scooters. They're less expensive than cars and kids are always short of money."

Mike was surprised and could only comment, "I'm stunned that you want to leave the job. What about benefits and retirement money? Is a new business gonna give you enough to live on? You have to buy inventory. How are you gonna live? Then there's your mom. You have to take good care of her."

"I already told you that I found the perfect property and we'll live in the back. There's two bedrooms and everything. The business will pay the mortgage. I already set up a consignment deal with two companies. Also, Mom will have terrific state sponsored health coverage because of her age and doesn't have to pay for anything. In five years after my pension kicks in, I'll have coverage from the job. Right now I have some health benefits from my time in the military."

Mike remained silent with his mouth open as if he wanted to say something. Alex saw the look of puzzlement on Mike's face as he continued. "So here's what's going on. I'm renting a truck to move all our things. I need you to drive my station wagon out for me. I'm towing my old jeep and I can't pull two cars."

Alex was on a roll and continued without waiting for any comments from his friend.

"I know you'll take care of my station wagon if you agree to bring it. Can you do it? It saves from leaving Mom alone and flying back to pick it up myself. I really don't have anyone else that I trust. I'll pick up all the expenses including motels and you can bring your new lady along too. What a nice trip you'll have. You can take your time and have fun along the way. Stop often and enjoy the trip out. No rush.

"Wow, Alex, I'm flattered that you would ask me and yes, I'll do it, even if Lilly can 't or won 't go with me."

"Mike, I asked you because you're a straight, standup guy and won't hurt my car knowing that I'll need it out there. Enough said; I'll give you a date soon as I have one. We're due to close on this house within a week or two. Let's have some Coquito that I made earlier today and toast new beginnings. Does Lilly drink?"

"Sure. What's Coquito?"

"It's a Puerto Rican drink made with coconut milk, regular milk, rum and mild spices. We drink it on holidays and other happy occasions. Today qualifies as a celebration."

Later as they said goodnight in the driveway, Alex quietly put his arm around Mike and said, "Brother, Lilly is to be cherished. My mother loves her and you seem to stand a bit taller too. She's a crispy million dollar bill. Don't ever drop her because someone will grab her up before she even hits the ground. You're indeed a rich man."

Mike was surprised and grateful at the analogy. He put his arm around Lilly and drew her close.

"Don't worry, I'll spend the rest of my life making sure that this bill never leaves my hands."

They all chuckled as Alex said, "See you at work day after tomorrow Mikey."

With a Sir Walter Raleigh type bow, he said, "It was our pleasure, Momma and I, to meet you Lilly."

As the happy couple closed the car doors to leave, the last thing Alex said was, "Always make each other happy."

On the drive back to Mike's apartment, the couple excitedly discussed the planned cross country trip. Lilly, excited at the thought of the adventure, told Mike that she would definitely take the time off from work.

"Michael, I've always wanted to drive cross country. I'm sure this trip will be memorable."

"Lilly, just being with you gives me all the memories I'll ever need."

They chatted like kids all the way to his place. Lillian commented that the thought of a cross country road trip made her feel like a kid running away from home with her boyfriend. She thought it had a romantic feel to it.

All Mike could think of was being totally alone with her for at least five consecutive days and nights. During the entire drive, he hummed the tune to Lilly Marlene, all the while resisting an impulse to clap his hands in joy like a little kid anticipating the approach of Christmas.

*

CHAPTER THIRTY ONE

On the first day of Alex's last two sets of tours with the NYPD. Mike and Alex met at the sign in desk. Both men were early as usual. There was ample time before Marvin would call a team meeting and they agreed to walk to the luncheonette to grab a bite and chat. While the walked, Alex spoke.

"Mikey, including today, I have exactly two weeks before I'm separated from the job. As soon as Mom and I got back, I filed my papers. I'm gonna miss it all, especially you. I'm sorry."

Two days earlier, when Alex had told Mike that he was leaving, the thought of his partner not being around didn't really sink in. Now, with an actual date, Romano felt as if his world had taken a turn for the worse. He was about to lose his best friend in the world but he thankfully had Lilly.

"Alex, how come you didn't tell me you were leaving days ago if you knew your date of separation? Why today, at work? Is it because you're going to slack off and just do paperwork? "

Alex responded with his calm way, "First and second questions; I got confirmation of closing on my New Mexico property just last night and I have to be there. I anticipated the date when I filed my papers. The job said they would hold them if my closing was delayed. The answer to the question answer, is, Hell no, I'm going out with a bang."

"I'm happy to hear that. What do you have in mind? Are you planning something special? "

317

"You know how many times we had our UC's try buy from the crew of that dirt bag, Carlos Ramirez. His local supplier is that little bodega on the corner of Pike Henry Streets. "

"Yeah, what about him?"

"Then add in the fact that, even with all our street harassment, we can never get any of his boys to roll over on him or never got a buy inside the bodega so we could get a warrant for the place."

"Yeah, of course I do."

"Well, we're gonna pop him now. Carlos lives in the housing project two blocks away from there."

" Great. How are we gonna get him?"

"I have a neighbor down the block from me, a Housing Authority Police Officer. He just got an arrest warrant for a roommate of Ramirez. The guy's wanted for assault with a gun, seems he pistol whipped a guy."

"How are we involved?" Mike asked.

We were exchanging stories and when I told him that we've been hot on Carlos, he invited us to be present for the bust. We can't go inside but he would like us to be outside, down in the street, and act as if we were just passing by and lucky to be there."

"But, if they're doing an arrest warrant what are we gonna do in the street?"

"He's worried about crap coming out of the windows. We just happen to be passing and see it falling. By luck, grab the contraband and hold it for them. It's all coincidental of course. We may even get a chance to question Carlos. Sound like a plan?"

Mike heard wings thrumming in his head and shouted, "Sure, I'm in, when do we do it?"

"Day after tomorrow."

"I love it, Marvin's gonna shit when he finds out!"

"They're planning to hit the place at 1800 hours. Their information claims that Carlos is usually at home for supper. It's some kind of tradition. He considers it lucky."

"Alex, we can't tell Marvin or The Taz; they'll never go for it."

"Leave it to me my boy, I'll get us there. First, when we go out that day, we make sure that Marvin's Kids collar up and we get to spend the rest of our tour doing kites. That gets us out. It should work."

Mike was pleased that his bulldog tenacity had finally infected his partner and said so.

"Woof, Woof, two bulldogs will be there."

On Wednesday at 1500 hours Marvin's kids brought in two collars each. Alex quickly announced that if not needed, he and his partner were going out to check some kites until end of tour. Marvin, always nervous around Alex, quickly gave the okay and out they went.

The partners drove around checking various kite locations. They made sure that they were on foot outside the target building at exactly 1800 hours. As they approached they found two plainclothes housing cops also milling about.

As they were introducing themselves, the HPD radios crackled, "We're in, watch the windows damn it. Watch the windows." At that point various things rained down on the four cops.

The scene was chaotic and reminiscent of the old Max Sennet, Keystone Cops movie with the four cops scooting around, trying to prevent glassine envelopes from falling into the hands of passersby. The wind making it worse by whimsically scattering them like confetti at a parade forcing the cops to perform helter skelter dance lunging and jumping to grab them. Among the fluttering glassines were rubber stamps, ink pads and bundles of unknown glassine packed powder bound by rubber bands. All light stuff.......at first.

Instinctively the four cops began looking up in an effort of self-preservation, when heavy stuff began coming down and hitting the ground with muted thuds. The heavy objects were two handguns and several cylindrical shaped packages wrapped in brown oily paper that resembled old Cosmoline paper that was used to ward off moisture from stored or shipped firearms. The cylinders were much heavier than the recovered handguns. Several split open on impact revealing thick pancakes of compressed brown vegetable matter. If any one of those objects had hit one of the cops from ten stories up, it would have meant a trip to the ER, maybe even the morgue.

When the deluge stopped, the four cops finished gathering everything they could find and went up to the apartment. Alex and Mike were elated at the prospect of seeing Carlos there, however, Carlos was not home.

The subject listed in the warrant and two of Carlos' lower echelon workers were in the apartment and summarily arrested. They were charged with possession of guns and possession of narcotics with intent to sell.

Alex thanked his friend for allowing them to be present. The two MSN partners returned to their office and signed out.

The following day, the partners were informed that when analyzed, the compressed brown pancakes from they later tested positive for heroin.

Alex remarked, "Damn I should have known. The last time I saw crap like that was in Nam and it was coming through Cambodia. I should have known, but now Carlos will get his."

Two days later Alex and Mike learned that the end result of those arrests didn't have the Hollywood ending everyone had hoped for. All the evidence was tossed out at the first evidentiary hearing even though the arresting officers brought a floor plan of the subject building.

They were informed that the defense attorney had successfully argued, "Maybe the cops down in the street picked the wrong window and the contraband came from a different window. After all nothing illegal was found in the apartment, just some videos and there's no laws against having them."

Mike thought, *As good as our criminal justice is, sometimes it sucks.*

However, if one is tenacious, patient and lucky, justice is sometimes properly meted out. Sometimes the forces of the universe come into play. Unknown to Mike, one of the videos taken from the apartment, showed Carlos standing near an airplane with some Asians.

The following week, a DEA team bought a kilo of heroin from a woman in a neighboring apartment. She gave away her right to a speedy trial and pled guilty at arraignment for an open ended sentence of twelve to twenty five years in a Federal Prison instead of risking a trial that might have resulted in a term of twenty five to life.

Eight days and several collars after the window incident, Alex informed Mike that he was leaving the following day after they swung out. The two men almost lost it as Alex said, "Mike, I love you, you're my brother. Here are the wagon keys. Please wait a week then you and your lady bring my wagon to Las Cruses."

Mike once again would be without a working partner.

***

Romano came to dislike Sergeant Landers even more after working with Sergeant Billings. With Alex all but gone, he realized that before it got ugly, it was in his best interest to get away from Marvin, so he appealed to The Taz.

"Lieutenant, when Alex was away, I worked with Sergeant Billings' team. It was much more comfortable for me that being with Marvin's guys. On a personal level, I stayed because Al was my partner. We have something special."

"Get to the point Mike. What do you want? To move over?"

"Yes Boss. We really don't get along. It's that our personalities don't mix well."

"Romano, I know you, there must be some other underlying reason for your request, besides a personality clash. Before I decide to say yes to your request, give it up."

Mike paused and in his mind, reviewed the incident that was the straw that broke his personal camel's back. *It happened after a short struggle on a stairway during an arrest. The guy fought a little, I dropped him down on the steps and was putting on the cuffs. While I was cuffing the guy, spineless Sergeant No Balls beat him with his four cell aluminum K- Lite. Later that day, I had words with that pea balled wonder and ended up threatening him. Before I really beat the ass of Sergeant Wimpy Landers, I gotta get away.*

He didn't want to give up the real reason and open a can of worms. Romano broke one of his cardinal rules, he lied by tainting the truth.

"Well, Loo, he's always hiding behind one of his kids if there's a potential for danger or violence whenever we go to make a collar, for instance, if the guy resists. As you now, I personally don't care for people who act like pussies. They jeopardize everyone around them. Now that Alex is gone, I want off his team and would like to move to Billings."

"Well, Bulldog, before you take a bite out of your supervisor, I better move you. As of this minute, you are officially moved to Sergeant Billings' team."

Mike, took his Lieutenant's hand, "Loo, I can't thank you enough."

"Oh, and by the way, thanks, for the heads up, I'll watch him. I don't want anyone in my module that's a cringing, peas for balls, coward."

After a fantastic two days off spent entirely with Lillian, Mike returned to work and was informed by Billings that the DEA wanted to meet with him regarding Carlos Ramirez at noon that very same day in the offices of Connie Whitehead.

"I don't know what she wants, but she's a heavy weight. Get over there forthwith."

"Thanks Sarge, I know who she is. We've met before."

Immediately, Mike gathered the plethora of notes and other information he and Alex had saved. He signed out a vehicle and proceeded downtown.

As Mike entered her office, Whitehead rose and shook his hand, "Congratulations, Detective Romano, please sit down. We have a few minutes before we meet the others."

Mike thought it would be impolite to correct Whitehead, but he did so anyway.

"Sorry ma'am, but its Officer Romano. You may recall that I'm a White Shield investigator."

She smiled graciously, waving her hand at the empty chair in front of her desk. "Oh, I gather that you haven't been informed yet. You have been promoted and you should officially hear about it by the end of the day."

Embarrassed and more than surprised, Mike said, "It comes as a total surprise and thank you. How can I help? "

His mind was running, *Wow. It's finally happened. Wait till Lilly hears about this. A celebration is in order; too bad Alex is already gone. I wonder if Jim knows yet. Wimpy Marvin is gonna shit when he finds out.*

Whitehead's voice brought him back, "Detective, you're here because we've heard that you're the local authority on Carlos Ramirez."

"Ma'am?"

"We know that you and your recently retired partner, Alex Veranos, have diligently pursued him for some time. I'm sure that you'll be happy to know that we've indicted him on conspiracy to distribute narcotics, based on a recovered video from the housing project apartment where he lived."

His celestial voices told him that there was more to come and there was. He felt as if electricity ran through his body and Whitehead continued.

"We are also pursuing additional subjects based on information developed from the warrant you and your partner served some time ago."

Bingo, Mike thought as he hung on every word.

"We compared airplane tail numbers from two videos in our possession. The video from your warrant and a video recovered from the Ramirez apartment. They are the same."

"Unbelievable."

"We also believe that both videos were made in Cabo Rio, Puerto Rico, probably on the same runway. You may also be pleased to know that, as a result of material recovered from your warrant, to wit, a phone number. Now we are looking to bring charges against an elected official's chauffer, for conspiracy. We hope that he can be turned and his cooperation will help us work our way up the line to catch bigger fish."

"That's nice to hear Ms. Whitehead. What do you need from me?" *Wait until I tell Taz about the chauffer. He won't be so pissed off now.*

"Mr. Ramirez has frequently mentioned your name during questioning by our investigators. He has a rather vivid imagination in that he has also accused us of working for you and your partner to put him in jail."

Mike chuckled and commented , "Really ? He must be sampling his own product."

She smiled. "That's funny, believing that we're working for you. I cannot even conceive how he would even put that thought together."

Maybe it's because we always tried to get him dirty on our Federal Day."

"You may or may not know that a woman was recently arrested by DEA officers for selling a Kilo of heroin to an undercover agent. That woman happens to be his mother."

"Yes ma'am. I heard about it."

"Well, we want the Asians and as many others as possible that are involved in this importing and distribution operation. We need leverage and we have his mother. Because of his fixation on you, I and my associates feel that you might be the key to his cooperation. That's what we need from you. What do you think?"

Mike thought, *so they're squeezing Carlos and I'm the juice squeezer. Let's do it.*

"Sure ma'am, ready to help. We understand that he worships his mother. If it comes to me making him a deal, do I have your permission to make the offer? "

"We tried that and he remained uncooperative, but you can try again because he only wants to speak with you. No deals on your own. Clear everything with my office first."

"Yes ma'am."

After a few hours with pressure from Mike and DEA investigators, a deal was made to guarantee that his mother would only serve the low end time of her sentence.

She would also be transferred to a minimum security facility in Virginia.

Mike never found out why Carlos would only deal with him, but it worked. Perhaps it was because Alex and Mike never abused or degraded him during their attempts of trying to arrest him. Maybe in his mind, with some sort of unconventional logic, it was professional courtesy. Ramirez agreed to cooperate, even to wear a wire if necessary.

Whitehead thanked Romano for his help and promised to keep him informed as to the progress of their investigation.

When Mike returned to MSN, he went directly to Tazzara's office. The Taz wasn't there, but on his desk was a copy of the latest personnel orders listing promotions. Mike almost jumped with joy when he saw his name listed and the words, "Promoted to the rank of Detective, Michael Romano, Manhattan South Narcotics".

He knew his promotion was real because he saw it in writing. Quickly he grabbed the sheet and made several photocopies. The orders stated that the promotion ceremony was two days away in the auditorium of One Police Plaza.

His next stop was Sergeant Jim Billings. "Hey Sarge, the Federal Prosecutor told me I got 'The Shield' and I just saw the orders on Tazzara's desk. Did you know?"

"Yeah, Mike, the lieutenant told me right after you left. Congratulations, you've earned it." He gave Mike a congratulatory hand shake, "Get your uniform pressed the ceremony is day after tomorrow. Go directly there, sign in from the field and don't be late. Michael, you sure are moving along, first a new lady and then The Shield. Lilly will be proud."

"Excuse me. Speaking of Lilly, I have a phone call and some announcements to make. Not necessarily in that order."

Mike then went directly into the team room, and found Landers and his "Kids" there. With sarcastic joy he announced, "Guys, I got the Golden Fleece. 'The Shield', and the Promotion Ceremony is two days away."

Landers said nothing and quietly left the room. The rest of the occupants offered congratulations, with various degrees of emotion, including a tinge of envy. Mike's next move was phone Lilly at work.

Breathlessly, like a kid who just got a new puppy, he shared his joy. "Lilly, I gotta tell you, I just got promoted. I got the Gold Shield. You're dating a New York Detective."

Lilly squealed an unintelligible joyous sound. She obviously was sharing his joy.

Mike continued, "Promotion ceremony is day after tomorrow and you have to be there. Yes?"

Lilly thought to amplify his good fortune by saying, "Detective, please slow down, will you?"

"Lilly, you called me Detective. Do you know how good that sounds?"

"I'm truly happy for you. I know how hard you worked to get there and of course, I'll be at the ceremony. It's not going to be a problem. I'll take an extended lunch hour or the day off, whatever is necessary." In an effort to be humorous she added, "Maybe I'll even take an E-day."

Mike Romano stood before the desk set up in front of the Auditorium in One PP at exactly 9:00 a.m. the morning of the ceremony. He turned in his White Shield and signed for his Detective Shield. After pinning it to his uniform, he scanned the crowd for Lilly. He was unable to see her and entered the auditorium found, his assigned seat and settled in.

The ceremony began promptly, at 1000 hours. Resisting an impulse to stand, Mike twisted around several times in an attempt to spot Lillian with negative results. Mildly disappointed, but not doubting for a second that she was somewhere in the crowd, he waited for his turn on the stage. After waiting for what seemed like an eternity, he was called to the stage and officially received his certificate of promotion from the Commissioner.

As he left the podium area, Mike again in scanned the audience and spotted Lillian. She, uncharacteristically, was standing and enthusiastically applauding.

He never felt as proud and then remembered something Alex once told him," *Being a man is not only a matter of age. A man really becomes a man when his woman makes him feel like one."* At that moment, he felt as if he grew three inches taller and was as invincible as the fictional "Superman".

Later, in the lobby, Lillian jumped up and down several times, hanging her arms around his neck, kissing him and cooing, "You're my personal detective. I'll never be afraid of anything again. There are no more walls."

They embraced unashamed.

After their little love fest, Mike spent several minutes happily introducing her to some friends. Sophie showed up carrying a camera.

"Mr. Romano, opps, Detective. Is this the little lady that I've heard about? The woman who stole your heart?"

"Yes, she is. Lilly, this is Sophie Kaminski, She handles all the warrants for the city. Sophie, this is Lillian Valachi, the girl that I'm gonna marry someday."

Oh my God, I said it again. She must think I'm crazy.

"Pleased to meet the woman that took this bulldog a peg or two. Good luck with him and don't bore him. He'll fall asleep."

"My pleasure. Mike will fill me in on that one later."

"How about a photo? Will you two please stand over there for a second?"

After the photo and some further intros, Mike and Lilly were about to leave. He asked, "Do you have to go back to work Lilly? "

Seductively, she asked, "Why Detective, just what do you have in mind? "

"I thought that we could have a fancy lunch somewhere, then go back to my place and celebrate but not necessarily in that order. I have to go home and change clothes anyway and I'm so shaky, I might need some help with it. Just say yes and I'll call in for the rest of the day off."

"Well Mr. Smarty, I anticipated some kind of celebration and before I left the office, I told my boss that my work for today was completed and that I would not be back. What do you think of that? "

Mike gave her a kiss and happily, Mike answered, "Don't move, I have to find a phone."

Back in his apartment, later that evening, Mike repeatedly tried to prove to Lilly that indeed, he was Superman, but always fell just a little short, weak and exhausted, as if exposed to Kryptonite. Bulldog that he was, he kept trying.

***

Back at work and wanting to be certain that nothing would interfere with his vacation trip to New Mexico, Mike would only assist the other team members with arrests, making none of his own. Sometimes he acted as a spotter or ghost. Sergeant Jim Billings understood and allowed him to choose assignments until he returned from his vacation.

Finally, the morning of their trip west arrived. Lilly had spent the night at Mike's place. Several days earlier, Alex had parked his station wagon in the garage under the station house before he left New York and gave Mike a set of keys.

Rising early, the couple drove into Manhattan, to switch cars. They pulled into a space on the far end of a common parking area between the Fire Station and the 4th Precinct. The two commands and their parking lot encompassed the entire block.

After turning off his car engine, and asking Lilly to standby, Mike jumped out, cut through the station house lobby to avoid going around to the garage ramp on the far side building. Almost flying down to the garage, he jogged to Alex's station wagon and launched into the driver's seat.

In less than a minute, he pulled in next to Lilly, jumped out and had opened the tailgate of the wagon. It took additional several minutes for the couple to pull their luggage from Mike's car and comfortably pack it into Al's station wagon. They wanted to keep everything behind the rear seat. Within five minutes of arriving at the station house, they locked the Chevy, shared a kiss and drove off. They were as excited as two kids on their first trip to Disneyland.

Five blissful days later, after reveling in their own private world for almost a week, the couple arrived at Alex's new place in Las Cruses.

After hugs and kisses all around, Alex remarked, "Well Mikey, I see you hung on to that million dollar bill."

"With both hands Al, with both hands."

Turning to Lilly, he said, "I'm happy for you both. Lilly, if he mistreats you in any way or you tire of him, please call me, I'm at your service."

"Thank you. I'll call if necessary," Lilly answered as she ran off to the kitchen in response to a shout from Anita.

Mike announced, "Lilly isn't the only good news Al, I moved away from Marvin to Jim Billings' team and...". When he finished he reached into his pocket, withdrew his hand and shouted, 'I got the shield,' proudly displaying it.

"Hold on, Mikey. Momita, Please bring the Coquito, we have another celebration."

***

Because Alex was busy with his business and was unable to give his friends much time, he gave the old Jeep to Mike for their personal use while visiting.

"The old girl is a good four wheeler for exploring the desert and rough areas around here. It's yours for as long as you stay, enjoy. There's a Coleman lantern, two warm jackets and some blankets in the back, in case you get lost. It's very dark and cold here at night."

After another delicious meal prepared by Anita, Mike and Lilly put their luggage into the jeep and checked in at a Super 8 motel just on the outskirts of town. In the days that followed, they enjoyed the use of the Jeep. They toured the area like tourists. Almost every evening, they visited with Alex and Anita.

The wheel capacity of the Jeep was especially useful when visiting the other worldly landscape of White Sands National Park and hunting for opals in the foothills of the Organ Mountains.

White Sands is the world's largest gypsum deposit. It is 275 square miles of white crystalline sand like granules, giving the area its name. The couple enjoyed exploring the 115 square miles of public area, sliding down the dunes and attempting to catch one of the quick, almost invisible lizards that abound there.

Romano had never seen anything like the vast white landscape before. Later whenever he described the park he would often that viewing the relative silence of the 360 degree panorama of nothing but glistening white dunes with an occasional hint of vegetation, was like being on another world.

The couple spent an entire day in the park. The only signs of life that they saw besides the tiny lizards were an occasional rabbit and a few birds. They felt like a couple of extraterrestrial explorers. Only the sound of the breeze could be heard enhancing the off world effect except when military flights or test missiles screeched overhead, then Mike likened the experience to being players in a science fiction movie.

The opal fields of the Organ Mountains were completely different. The foothills were full of snakes, large boulders and loose rocks.

The Jeep with its high ground clearance came in handy to negotiate the rough terrain especially for Mike.

Whenever they got out of the vehicle, Mike enjoyed the view each he had to boost Lilly into the passenger seat. It made his day and Lilly giggled each time. It was a hands on assist.

While hunting for opals in the foothills, Mike amazed at an honor system of lock boxes attached to posts scattered about the area. On them was a request for prospectors to drop in a donation when finding an opal to help maintain the area as a park. Being a cynical New York cop, Mike found it hard to believe that not a single box among the many they saw was damaged and every lock was intact.

Early the following day, the vacationing couple crossed the border into Ciudad Juarez, Mexico. It was a first time experience for each of them. They spent several hours looking for a pair of western boots for each of them and absorbing the flavor of the city. After eating in a touristy restaurant, they returned to their motel without purchasing anything.

After White Sands, their favorite attraction was the famous Carlsbad Caverns. The caverns are a system of 188 limestone caves. The United States Park Service only authorizes three caves as part of the public tour. Other sections may be accessed by permit for spelunkers and scientists.

Lilly was awed by The Big Room because of its size; 4,000 feet long and 275 feet high. "Michael, this place could hold my entire neighborhood. It's truly magnificent."

During their three hour walk through the system, they even ate in an underground café.

While touring the park, Mike and Lilly learned that the Caverns are home to one million Mexican Free Tail Bats and they would be viewed every evening they blotted out the setting sun as they exited. Later, as evening approached, the newbies found a place to sit around the tiered entrance to the "Bat Cave" and waited for the show.

As the sun dropped closer to horizon, a whirring sound could be heard within the cave entrance. Seconds later hundreds of thousands of the tiny creatures began swirling out of the opening. As the swarm grew in size, it funneled a foul stench of guano behind it and literally almost blocked the setting sun from view.

The less than floral odor that followed their flight did nothing to dissuade the hundreds of tourists from remaining until the creatures were out of sight. Mike and Lilly even returned for a second visit and there still wasn't a mosquito in sight.

***

As the couple discussed their trip, Lilly decided that watching the state's bird, the Roadrunner, gave her the most pleasure except for their nights alone. She liked to watch them move. Every time she saw one scamper along, she would remark in childlike fascination, "Gee, Mike, they look just like the cartoon and are almost as fast he is."

During their stay in Las Cruses, the couple ate breakfast every day at the same local restaurant. On one particular morning, after sleeping late, they walked in about noon and sat down at an empty table. The only waitress hurried over and said, "Please move to any other table you like, this one's reserved for the narcotic cops and they always sit here at lunchtime."

Mike thought it was strange that the whole town might know who the local Narcs were and where they ate. That kind of information could get a cop killed back in New York City.

Later that day when he related the incident to his old partner, Alex explained that there wasn't too much for those cops to do in Las Cruses, so it didn't matter.

He added that the city obtained Federal money for a narcotics team so they created one.

Mike still thought it was odd that the team was so well known.

Alex further explained that to justify their existence and continue the flow of Federal dollars, the sheriff's office and the team developed a system. Every few weeks, they would arrest a local Indian for possession of peyote. Later, the courts would just slap their wrists. It was something about religious freedom.

It was just short of two weeks since the couple left New York and their vacation days were running short. They booked a flight back home out of the closest airport, El Paso, Texas. The flight was scheduled to land at Newark Airport. From there they planned to take a taxi to pick up their car and still have a couple of days to relax before their regular routine began again.

The night before they were scheduled to leave, Mike packed the Jeep just before they went to sleep. The plan was to pick up Alex in the morning and he would bring them to the airport.

Early that morning, Mike went down to put Lilly's last item, an overnight bag, into the Jeep. He was shocked to find the vehicle unlocked. A quick inventory revealed two jackets and two blankets gone and nothing else missing. Their camera and two cartons of Lilly's cigarettes were still there on the front seat floor.

Arriving at Alex's for the ride to El Paso, Mike explained what had happened and apologized profusely for losing the items.

Alex calmly said, "It happens all the time. 'Los Mojados', wet people, migrant workers must have passed through and saw the blankets and jackets. They're not bad people. They only take what they need. All your stuff was still there right? They're not really thieves, just poor and needy. For me, it's no problem. I feel sorry for them and have other jackets and blankets. You're going home and don't need them anymore."

Mike replied, "Wow this is not at all like New York."

"That's nothing. Sometimes the migrants even break into a person's home while the owners are away, eat their food while they stay overnight or a couple of days. As payment, there's usually something like a thank you note and the home is cleaned top to bottom; sometimes the garden is even attended to as if they were hired to do it."

"Holy crap. That's unbelievable."

"To my knowledge, nothing has is ever been reported missing with the exception of blankets or warm clothing like what was taken from the Jeep.

Usually, there's little or no damage at point of entry. It's amazing."

Mike and Lilly chuckled. Mike said, "Nice town, everyone knows the Narcs and the thieves only take stuff to keep them warm. No wonder you like it here."

"Yeah, I hope it stays like this forever but you know progress and human nature will screw it up."

After hugs and kisses for Anita, Alex got them to the airport two hours before their flight. Naturally the goodbyes were bitter sweet; however Alex extracted a promise from them to return some day.

Mike in turn, made Alex promise to attend their wedding if it came first. Mike and Lilly then walked into the terminal. Everyone was happy.

CHAPTER THIRTY TWO

Several months had passed since their trip to New Mexico. and one snowy, blustery day in March, with the snow up to his hips, Mike gathered his possessions and moved in with his lady love.

Lilly had discussed it with her children and it seemed like it was the natural thing to do. He was instantly accepted, and for Mike it was as if he had been given a new family to replace the one he lost as a result of his ex-wife's infidelity.

After spending much of his free work time with Guy Santini and laughing about finally spending money, Mike had what he wanted.

It was a fine sunny day in April when Mike showed up in Lilly's office carrying a single flower. It was an Iris, the color of her birthstone, an amethyst and Lilly's favorite color next to pink. He handed her the Iris said, "Lilly, you have made me complete. Will you marry me?"

Before she could even answer, when her office heard the proposal, gave the expected chorus of ohs and ahssss. Her best office friend Daisy knew, that in the center of the flower was a diamond engagement ring.

Lilly, still shocked at the proposal, never noticed it, prompting Daisy to say, "Smell the flower girl, smell the flower."

She finally did, and found the ring. With her body shaking like a leaf the wind, she shouted, "Yes!"

Lilly pulled the ring from the flower completely destroying it in the process. Her hand shook so much that Mike had to make two attempts to thread it onto her finger amid shouts of encouragement from her office mates.

It was now official. They were an engaged couple and would be married in three months' time, on June 28th of that year.

***

Since being transferred to Jim Billings' team, Mike had become an even more aggressive investigator then he had been under Landers. Billings respected Mike and his abilities, giving him more leeway and even allowed him to develop his own unofficial informant.

It all started one afternoon, as Romano was about to walk into the Fourth. He was approached by a small disheveled man who stopped him and asked for a couple of bucks for a sandwich.

There was something in the tone of his voice that struck Mike's heart. Mike always had an inner need to help people but he didn't want to give money to someone who might spend it alcohol or drugs. Instead, Mike offered to buy him a meal at the local luncheonette. At first, the man refused the meal. He explained that he may have a twisted sense of pride but he wanted to hand over money for his meal himself, even if he had to beg for money.

Mike, thought it was an odd request.

"You'll earn it. I'm writing a book, so you can earn the meal by telling me about yourself. I may be able to use the information in my story. Consider me your employer. We'll talk while we eat."

After introducing himself as Ernie Lowery, Mike learned more. Lowery was a homeless Viet Nam vet. Ernie explained that he kept a post office box to receive his monthly disability checks and was living on the piers that dotted the lower east side waterfront, doing day work when he could find it and moving whenever necessary.

When Mike asked if Ernie had family that could help him out, he explained that when leaving the military, he came home hooked on hard drugs and his family disowned him.

Ernie then proudly declared that he had finally kicked his addiction about four years earlier, but the rift between him and his family in Idaho was too wide to be repaired. Ernie continued to explain that when he realized what his addiction had cost him, he became strongly anti-drug.

After seeing Mike working in the area, he had decided that Mike wasn't heartless like many of the other cops. On that particular afternoon he decided to approach Romano and offer to give up information about drug activity that he sometimes was witness while living on the piers. After their meal, Mike gave him twenty bucks of his own money and the office telephone number. Their relationship had begun.

Occasionally, Ernie would call Mike at the office and try to give information of goings on a pier and giving the pier number. Mike would politely meet with Ernie and hear his information, then give him a twenty dollar bill. The information was always of low quality resulting in a few arrests for possession or discovery of a shooting gallery. Nothing was ever of any real value, except once.

Ernie occasionally earned money by asking for day work among the piers that made up the Fulton Fish Market area. As a result of one of those work days, Ernie excitedly brought Mike a story that could have been scripted for television.

"Yeah, Romano, I was working at this place, Pier 11, Gamma Fish Company, off and on for months now. They sometimes let me work for a few hours. Anyway, yesterday I dropped a box of fish and most of it spilled on the ground. The lead dago, sorry, huh, guy, no offense meant.

The lead man, almost shit himself. He began cursing in two languages, when I bent down to pick them up."

"Well, you dropped his fish and turned them to trash. Just what did you expect?"

"Yeah, and I thought that he was upset because the fish got dirty and had to be thrown away, you know they couldn't be sold. Hey, what do you think I saw next to make him carry on like that? "

Feeling bad for the lost soul, Mike humored the little guy, "Ernie, I really have no idea. What happened?"

"That guy almost had a heart attack. He grabbed me my by the shirt and was yelling in Italian again. I was scared shitless and thought that I was gonna get whacked."

"Did he rough you up?"

"Naw, he just jammed a fifty in my hand and sent me home telling me to forget whatever I thought I saw. Now, I'm telling you about it."

"What did you see?"

"Well, the heads of the fish weren't attached. They were kinda held in place by the ice around them. The first layer of fish had the heads attached. The loose heads were the ones in the next layer and on down to the bottom ones."

Mike was all ears now.

Ernie was getting excited. "Anyway, when the fish fell out and the heads fell off from some of them, some kind of plastic bags fell out. They were kinda dirty from the fish and ice, bit I think that they were filled with white stuff, powder. It had to be drugs or he wouldn't have gone off like he did."

"Holy shit! What happened?" Mike thought, *there goes Saint Michael's wings beating again, so I gotta check this out.*

"It sounds good Ernie, let's go see my lieutenant and try to get you a reward. The city pays for the information if it results in arrests or large drug recovery."

"Yeah, nice and I can sure use the money."

" In order to get paid for this information, you have to be registered with the PD as a confidential informant. Is that okay with you?"

"Sure"

Mike put Ernie into a chair outside the precinct's complaint room. "Sorry, I can't take you upstairs to the office, undercover cops and all that. Let me see if the lieutenant thinks this can work out, if he thinks we can do it, he'll come down here."

"Okay. Since getting clean, I have this hard on for drugs and dealers. They cost me everything and I hate them fuckers."

"Be back soon. Don't leave."

Louie Tazzara was not impressed with the tale that Ernie told. "How many times did this guy ever give you any good information? "

Romano had a feeling that the info was good. He tried to avoid actually answering the question. "He's given me tips at least five or six times Boss."

"Don't get cute with me and try to live up to you nickname Mister Bulldog. I'll ask you again. How many times did he give you good information. I didn't ask how many times he fed you crap."

Mike was caught, "Huh, never Boss. The only info he ever gives results in arrests for possession, nothing else, but I know that this one's good. You should have seen his eyes when he told me the story." "That's all this guy has?"

"Yes Loo. There isn't any more. I feel sorry for him."

The lieutenant got right to the point, "Michael, in order to be registered, an informant has to have a track record. This guy never gave you a live tip. How do you think our office will look if we tried to sign him up? It's a no go Michael. Thank him for his time and slip him a couple of bucks."

"But Boss. You know how I sometimes get strong feeling about things and become instant. You know like the phone number in the safe and the green Jaguar. They worked out, didn't they. This is one of those times too."

Reaching into his pocket, The Taz pulled out a ten dollar bill and handed it to Mike.

"Mike you're a pain in the ass. Add this to whatever you feel like giving him and send him on his way. We have real things to check out like kites and ongoing cases. We don't have time for fairy tales. Sorry."

Mike knew better than to argue. He was dismissed and quietly left the office.

Gently, and trying not to offend Ernie he twisted the truth. "My boss explained the whole signup procedure to me Ernie. He would bring you downtown if you had a track record of prior good information. Unfortunately, some of the other tips you gave me were handled by other undercover officers from another unit. By the time we moved on them, the bad guys were already busted. Sorry, we can't satisfy the past record requirement but keep your eyes open and don't get hurt."

Ernie looked disappointed but remained silent.

Mike added another ten to Taz's and gave both of them Ernie. He then sent him on his way. "Thanks again for trying Ernie. Maybe there's another way we can use the info and get the guys. I'll let you know."

Mike returned to the office and sat alone thinking of another way to accomplish his goal. He wished that Alex was there. He could think of nothing. Then his bulldog gene kicked in. After some serious soul searching, capped with a twisted sense of justification, he decided to reach out to his old friend, Rocco Banducci.

After several failed attempts to reach the 'made man' by telephone, Rocco finally picked up, "Yes?"

"Hello. It's Mike, how are you doing? Hope all is well in your house."

"Michael, my friend. Where the hell have you been? It's almost a year since we last spoke. I've heard the good news. You're a Detective now, working Narcotics and boy, is your ex-wife pissed."

"I'll bet she is. Good for her."

"All she talks about is the fact that she filed for an increase in child payments because of your promotion and your slick attorney stopped her in her tracks. He's a sharp old guy and by the way, how's your love life? "

With that question, Rocco just touched on his new favorite subject.

"Terrific. I met a woman by pure chance. We fell in love and now we all live together in her house. I have a new family and we're gonna get married soon!"

Rocco chuckled, "I heard my friend, and after all, you live in Howard Beach. I was just checking out the rumor, that's all."

Mike knew just what Rocco was implying. It was common knowledge that the current mafia don, Sam Costello, "Il Capo Di Tutti Capi", the Boss of Bosses, in the New York families, lived there too. Rocco was usually well informed. He also remembered how paranoid Rocco was on the phone.

"Yeah, we should talk about old times and my ex-family and kids. When can we share a meal and a beer?"

Always cautious, Rocco jovially answered, "It would be great fun watching your face as we discuss your ex-wife. Tomorrow evening at around six, at the old place?"

"Sure. That's fine."

You do remember our favorite place for food, don't you?"

His friend was referring to their past meetings at the Privateer Diner on Astoria Boulevard, in Jackson Heights Queens. Rocco was always comfortable there.

"Six it is. See you then and thanks."

Later that evening he told Lilly he had scheduled a dinner meeting with his old friend Rocco the following day and would not be home until sometime after nine.

Lilly had heard about Rocco and knew who he was. She wasn't like his ex-wife and didn't push for details except to ask, "Work related? "

Mike softly answered, "Yes, just checking some information I received about a location."

Lilly trusted Mike's instincts. "Be careful and don't get hurt. It would be nice if, some day, I get to meet this Rocco guy. "

"Yeah, it would and he'll love you." Smiling he opened his arms and gently commanded, "Come here, Lilly Marlene, let's talk."

***

Romano pulled into the spacious rear parking area of the diner several minutes before six, parked his Chevy and walked around to the front door. Mike knew that they would again sit in the rear dining room and went directly in. He found Rocco already seated at a booth in the far corner of the room. Banducci smiled and held up a drink as a salutatory toast when he spotted Michael.

As Romano slid into the booth, Rocco put his glass down, reached over the table and shook Mike's hand. "Please get something; it'll keep our hands busy while we talk. Now, to what do I owe this pleasure? "

Before answering the question, Mike waved for the waitress. "Dewars on ice with a splash of water and another of whatever my friend is having. Thank you."

She smiled and left.

"Rocco, we've been friends for a long time now, sometimes sharing confidences and information, always careful to never crossing the line between our different worlds. You know that I'm a narcotics investigator now and I know that you hate drug traders because of a personal loss."

Rocco winced at the reminder, but remained silent, giving a quick nod of acknowledgement.

"I fell across some information I'd like to tell you about. I don 't the names of the players are if you might know them, but I want to share this with you. Maybe you have some idea on how to I could handle it.

"What is it? "

"Yesterday, I went to give my lieutenant the same information you're about to hear. I also brought along my half assed informant. The boss turned me away."

The waitress was back. "Okay, Michael. You have my ear but first let's order some food."

Rocco, seeing his friend's nervousness, tried to relax Mike him by talking about his ex-wife and kids while they waited for their orders. Rocco, a family man, commented that it was a shame Mike didn't have an ongoing relationship with his children and that he should work on it.

Finally, their meals were placed on the table. Mike knew that they would be left alone for at least ten minutes. He explained about Ernie and the fish, including the name of the company involved and the reason his boss turned Ernie away.

Rocco listened without comment the asked, "Just what do you want from me, Mike? "

"I know this could be touchy, but do you have any thoughts on how I can handle it? I don't want the action to keep going without trying to remedy the situation. You know how I am. It makes me feel inadequate inside and I have an inner need to do something and would like your input. Any ideas?"

"Michael, we go back a long way and you have given me good counsel that personally helped me. Let me think a minute. Order us a drink will you?"

Rocco was quiet for several minutes. Then he leaned across the table and answered Mike in his usual short, cryptic style.

"Well, I'm not a saint and have done things that I'm not proud of, but I do hate drug dealers, especially if I find them within my circle of associates. They all know my feelings about that kind of thing. Give me some time and I'll get back to you."

"Great. How much time do you think?"

"You'll know when I have an answer. Now, let's just relax and enjoy each other's company. It's been a while."

After the meal, they each ordered double espressos spiked with Sambuca. Rocco picked up the tab.

As they rose from the table, Rocco shook Mike's hand. "Stay straight and righteous, don't ever change my friend. You'll hear from me soon and say hello to your girl Lillian for me."

Before Mike could ask how Rocco knew her name, he was gone.

Three weeks later, Mike learned via the Six O'clock news that there was a fire down at the Fulton Fisk Market. The Gamma Fish Company was completely destroyed.

Once again he almost crossed an invisible line and was slightly ashamed to feel good about it.

CHAPTER THIRTY THREE

Lillian worked as Director of Membership for a Wall Street area for a firm whose members were solely composed of stock analysts and brokers. Her employer occupied the entire floor of a loft building directly across from the famed Trinity Church, in lower Manhattan; the resting place of Alexander Hamilton, Robert Fulton and other persons of historical note that includes signers of the Declaration of Independence and the U. S. Constitution.

Within her office complex was an extremely large banquet room used for seminars and presentations. There was a full restaurant kitchen and staff that served a daily lunches and sometimes dinners during the work week. Mike and Lillian had planned to have their marriage ceremony and reception there.

On June 28th, at exactly 5:00 p.m., a few short months after Mike proposed, Supreme Court Judge, Ruth Kerokowitz, a cute, short spicy officiated. Mike had met the judge when she presided over one of his more serious cases and they became fast friends. Lilly loved her.

Because they both had been married before, the Romanos carefully chose Smokey Robinson's rendition of "Save the Best for Last" as their wedding song. The irony of the piece was joyously cheered and enjoyed by everyone present.

Their celebration was attended by the happy couple's parents and family members from both sides, including their respective children, completing their extended family. Also in attendance, as expected, were most of the members of Manhattan South Narcotics, except Marvin Landers, who declined an invitation. As he promised, Alex Veranos flew in just for their wedding, spending most of his evening with Sophia Kaminski. Mike never knew that they were such good friends.

The surprise of the evening, known only to the newlyweds, was the arrival of someone who stopped by for a quick congratulatory visit. The party was in full swing.

One of the food servers walked quietly up to Mike and said, "Mr. Romano, there's a gentleman waiting in the elevator lobby who says his name is Rocco. He has asked me to find you and Mrs. Romano and requests that I bring you both to him. What should I tell him?"

Mike was more than surprised; he was delighted, "Yes, please tell him we'll be right there. Thank you."

After locating his stunning new bride, the couple walked hand in hand out to the lobby and met a smiling and dapper, Rocco Banducci.

Before they even got close to him, Lilly jokingly whispered, "So that's Rocco. Be good to me Romano. He's a tall, good looking man with money."

Rocco spoke first, "Michael, congratulations." Reaching for Lilly's hand he continued, "Rocco Banducci. You must be the brand new Mrs. Romano. I'm very honored and extremely pleased to meet you. Michael is one of my favorite people, like family. He's a good man and always genuine. But, you already know that because you married him."

"Lilly, please, Mr. Banducci."

"Rocco please, or I'll call you Mrs. Romano", he replied. Chuckling as he spoke.

To Mike he quipped, "You did good Michael, she's lovely."

"Thank you Rocco. I think so too."

After some quick small talk, Rocco looked Mike straight in the eye and asked, "Is everything good at work?"

Mike knew the implication and answered, "Yes, fine and once again, thank you."

"No, on the contrary, thank you. Now if you'll both excuse me, I have to be somewhere and must leave. Be good to each other."

The two men shook hands and then in old world fashion, Rocco gave Mike an Italian man hug and slipped an envelope into his jacket pocket, "Una regalo di nozze." (a wedding gift)

He then turned his attention to Lilly giving her a gentle hug, kissed her and said something she did not quite understand, "You have become part of Michael, and therefore you are part of me." Then he quickly spun around and left.

Lilly's only comment was, "He's quite a charmer. Let's go back inside; we can't let our guests have all the fun."

Five hours later the couple checked in at the World Trade Center Marriot Hotel to celebrate their first night as a married couple. The next morning, they left for a two week road trip through the New England States. They spent their time enjoying the scenery, the small towns eating lobster and antique hunting. For Lilly, eating lobster twice daily made the trip.

Their two weeks away passed too quickly. When the couple reluctantly returned to their daily routines, it was as husband and wife. Lillian especially enjoyed it when Mike would call her office. If one of the girls picked it up, they would shout, "Lillian your husssssband is on the phone and asked for his Lilly! Just what the hell is he talking about?" giggles usually followed.

Months passed and Romano continued to enjoy his stint in narcotics, but began to tire of the long hours and as a result, put in two requests for transfer (UF57), with negative results.

Daily he fought the mixed emotions of just toughing it out or push harder to obtain a transfer; that's when fate once again stepped in.

An old patrol friend from Staten Island phoned the office and asked for Mike, "Hey, Mike, it's Henry Pilon. I'm in the process of interviewing for a slot in narcotics. Do you think that there's some way to get in the same office as you? Can you help? I'm almost finished with all the investigation and medical stuff, only the personal interview is left. Can you help me?"

Consistent with his 'help everyone,' personality, especially fellow cops,' Romano instantly said, "I'll try but no promises." After some small talk, their conversation ended.

Mike had met many of the power people during his tenure in the Narcotics Division and visited one of them two days after Pilon's call.

Two weeks later, a very happy Henry Pilon almost flew into the team room and repeatedly thanked Mike for his help. However, Henry was assigned as a UC to one of Lieutenant Aloe's teams and would be working from the floor above.

"Good luck Hank and I'm pleased that I was able help, enjoy it. It's great here. I'll see you around the office and maybe someday, we may even get to do a case together."

While on a swing several weeks later, Mike received word that Henry had been killed in the line of duty. He was found shot by an unknown perpetrator while making a drug buy in one of the tenement buildings of "Alphabet City." There were no leads.

Mike agonized about it for several days, blaming himself and vowed never to help another cop secure an assignment. The incident reinforced his resolve to get out of narcotics ASAP.

Mike hadn't attended a cop's funeral since a close friend was killed just after they shared breakfast years before. He attended Henry's and it shook him to his core.

Only a day after attending the funeral, Mike, still upset over Pilon, decided to reach out for the old Staten Island Commander that befriended him during the Capelli case, Robert Stranire. At that time he held the rank of an Assistant Chief. He was now elevated to Chief of Patrol of the entire Department. Mike phoned his office on the 14th floor of One PP.

After speaking to an aide, Mike finally reached Chief Stranire. "Mike Romano, one of my finest cops and a fellow Italian too. Did you see me? I was there at your promotion. Congratulations by the way. Is there something I can do for you?"

"Boss, I'm sorry to bother you, but I'd like to come and see you if it's alright, I need to discuss something."

"What is it? Can you say it on the phone?"

"Sure, I'd like out of narcotics."

"See you in my office at 10:00 a.m. tomorrow and bring coffee. Make it espresso and no pastry."

"Done and thank you," responded Mike to a dead line.

The following morning Mike stood in the red brick plaza the red bricked shared by The Manhattan Municipal Building, The Church of Saint Andrew and One Police Plaza. There was always a plethora of pushcart vendors scattered within it. Mike stopped at a cart that specialized in Italian pastries and coffee. He ordered only two double espressos before entering the Puzzle Palace.

Once upstairs and behind the glass doors that led to the Chief of Patrol's office complex, Mike was directed to room 1424.

As he looked for the correct room, he recognized the voice of Chief Stranire. "Romano get in here on the double and lend a hand."

Mike hesitated in disbelief as he entered the room.

There was the Chief of Patrol, one of the highest ranking members of the World's most famous New York City Police Department, grunting and red faced and in shirt sleeves, as he alone, pushed a large oak desk across the floor. "Don't just stand there son, lend a hand," he bellowed.

Mike snapped to with, "Sir," putting the bag containing their coffees down on the floor, and ran over, giving the desk a mighty shove. After a couple of manipulations, the desk was positioned and Stranire voiced approval, than sat on top of it.

"Grab that bag Mike, have a squat and tell me the reason for your request."

As they drank their now tepid coffees, Mike explained his desire to leave Narcotics, touching on the long hours and his new home life, but emphasizing his regrettable feelings about the Henry Pilon incident.

Mike made sure to add that he had first tried to follow normal procedures by submitting two "Request for Transfer" forms but he was never answered. It was his belief that they must be somewhere in a pile of dormant paperwork or completely lost.

Stranire listened with the attention of a doting father as Mike explained everything. "Wait here. I'll be right back."

By habit, Mike glanced at his watch; it was 10:23 a.m. Unable to get comfortable sitting on the desktop, he paced the floor for twenty minutes.

Later when the Chief finally came back, he was in full uniform, looking all bright and fresh. "I have a meeting at City Hall. Sorry to run kiddo, but go see Lieutenant Murphy in room 1427A, he's waiting for you. Good luck and congratulations on your marriage by the way."

Does everyone who even knows me keep tabs on my personal status. "Thank you Chief and good luck with your meeting."

Three minutes later, Mike stood before Lieutenant Murphy who tapped a pile of papers in a basket on his desk and said, "Your papers are right on top, you'll hear soon."

"Thank you, Sir. Sorry to be a bother."

"Good luck Detective", followed by a gesture that said, *"I have no time, you can go now."*

Mike went back to his office. When he told Jim Billings that he would soon be leaving his team and the office.

"When I signed off on these 57's, I just knew that you would go quickly. Bulldog is a very appropriate name for you. You should officially change it. You'll be missed."

At home that evening, alone in their bedroom, Mike told Lilly about the meeting . She listened without commenting. Lilly was secretly happy that her husband was finally leaving narcotics, it was too dangerous.

"I'm sure you'll be happy with the results, just wait and see. Now please close the door, I want to have a conversation with you."

Three days later Detective Michael Romano received his copy of the Personnel Orders directing him to report to the 64th Squad in Bensonhurst, Brooklyn in two days. As he read it he thought, *boy are they gonna love the Bulldog.*

Later that night, after a celebration diner at an extremely expensive Italian restaurant, The Romanos skipped desert and spent most of the night deep "in conversation."

Joe DeCicco is a retired New York City Detective and licensed private investigator. Originally he attended college to practice electrical engineering.

Life circumstances decreed that he join the New York City Police Department.

Joe's writings rely on his life personal experiences in a well-defined attempt to show that, "The Job", is not a vocation but an avocation that spans all the nuances of the human spirit.

His works show the complex personalities of those who choose to be the daily guardians of our society.

Joe has been a featured guest on American Heroes Talk Radio, San Dimas, California and Blue Line Radio, Wilmington North Carolina.

Joe DeCicco now resides in the coastal area of Wilmington North Carolina with his wife Judy and is a licensed private investigator.

www.ingramcontent.com/pod-product-compliance
Lightning Source LLC
Chambersburg PA
CBHW031144270326
41931CB00006B/140